Blur

Warp Speed: America in the Age of Mixed Media

The Elements of Journalism: What Newspeople Should Know and the Public Should Expect

Blur

*How to Know What's True in the
Age of Information Overload*

BILL KOVACH AND
TOM ROSENSTIEL

BLOOMSBURY

New York • Berlin • London

Published by Bloomsbury USA, New York

All papers used by Bloomsbury USA are natural, recyclable products made from
wood grown in well-managed forests. The manufacturing processes conform to the
environmental regulations of the country of origin.

LIBRARY OF CONGRESS CATALOGING-IN-PUBLICATION DATA
Kovach, Bill.
Blur : how to know what's true in the age of information overload
/ Bill Kovach and Tom Rosenstiel.—1st U.S. ed.
p.   cm.
Includes bibliographical references.
ISBN 978-1-59691-565-7
1. Journalism—History—21st century. 2. News audiences—
History—21st century. 3. Journalism—Technological innovations.
4. Attribution of news. I. Rosenstiel, Tom. II. Title.
PN4815.2K68 2010
070.9'09051—dc22
2010019766

First U.S. edition 2010

3 5 7 9 10 8 6 4 2

Typeset by Westchester Book Group
Printed in the United States of America by Quad/Graphics, Fairfield, Pennsylvania

For Lynne—*BK*
For my mother and father, again and forever—*TR*

CONTENTS

CHAPTER 1

How to Know What to Believe Anymore

Melanie Moyer first senses something is wrong when she arrives to pick up her father at the hospital.

At the nurses' desk, she overhears a doctor telling people he has already sent his wife and children north to New England. "If we start taking in all kinds of people, I don't want to have to worry about my family at home," he says.[1]

Taking in all kinds of people from what, she wonders?

"I got into the car and turned on the radio and started hearing that there was an 'incident' at the plant," a nuclear power facility nearby, she recalls later.

Across town, Maureen Doherty first sees something on the TV news. "I remember thinking I was going to die," she says later.[2]

As word spreads, workers at the plant begin contacting family and friends to warn them that something very serious is wrong. Many, like the doctor Moyer overhears, advise their families and friends to assume the worst and react accordingly.

These people, in turn, begin e-mailing others about their plans to flee. Grainy cell phone images and video of emergency vehicles, worried officials, and panicked plant employees begin to appear on local TV and then on cable news. Experts, uninvolved but supposedly knowledgeable, are invited on the air to speculate on the possibility of a nuclear meltdown.

Video clips from the movie *The China Syndrome* are played and go viral on YouTube.

The message, offered sometimes in apocalyptic terms and other times more cautiously, is that there's a problem in the reactor core, which threatens to spew radioactive particles into the atmosphere, turning a local electricity plant into an international nuclear nightmare. The entire mid-Atlantic region of the United States is at risk. Roughly a third of the U.S. population could be contaminated.

The blogosophere moves even faster than TV news and YouTube. Within moments, established bloggers begin to expound on the safety of nuclear power. Soon new blogs, including some by former plant employees, are launched and linked to by others. Within hours, competing blogs appear, some defending the role of nuclear power, and some of these include inside information. The plant's owner also creates a blog. Then three sites appear that present themselves as independent information providers but in reality are controlled by political groups, including one by the nuclear power industry, and are designed to counteract the critics. Their backers spend hundreds of thousands of dollars in keyword fees to make sure that in any Google or Yahoo search, these are the sites Americans would likely see.

The news on more-conventional news Web sites is fragmentary and often contradictory. The mix of messages is hard to sort through and depends on which site one visits and when.

On drive-time radio that afternoon, the nuclear event, still only a possible disaster, becomes a political wedge issue about power, the environment, and federal policy in the war of words among talk radio hosts on the left and the right. The same stylized talking points play out again on cable talk shows in prime time later that night. The message on cable news is particularly confusing. One channel seems to tilt toward the idea that the government is covering up the seriousness of the incident. A rival channel, in a manner equally hard to pin down but just as unmistakable, seems to infer that there is no incident at all and that the whole thing may be a rumor designed to destroy the U.S. nuclear power industry all over again, just as it was finally getting back on its feet after a generation of misguided and exaggerated claims about safety. A third cable channel seems to veer in both directions, inviting familiar political advocates along with various hazily identified experts to debate the meaning of the event that is unfolding.

As for print editions of newspapers (whose staffs are down by roughly 30 percent from ten years earlier) and for network news (where cuts in news gathering have been even steeper), they offer careful reportage but seem slow and out of step—appearing late in the day or the next morning.

The people around the nuclear site itself operate in still another world, buffeted by rumors electronic and in person that create randomly fragmented communities of information. One neighbor is convinced that a nuclear catastrophe is at hand, another that a minor incident has occurred. Others anxiously trying to weigh contradictory messages consider leaving the area but worry that could become deadlier than the nuclear threat if choked roads turn mass evacuation into mass hysteria.

Welcome to the Three Mile Island nuclear accident imagined in the age of the Internet.

This is not how the story played out. The reactor core of the nuclear power plant near Hershey, Pennsylvania, did overheat in 1979, but the incident occurred in a very different information world.

Melanie Moyer is real, and she did first hear about the accident at the hospital and then rushed to listen to her car radio. So is Maureen Doherty, who first learned about it on the local TV news. As they and people everywhere waited and watched, almost everything they learned about the incident was filtered through a mainstream news media at arguably the height of its prestige, trust, and influence in American history. On television, a handful of anchormen, whose networks did not expect their newscasts or their news divisions to make a profit, told the country what they knew without trying to dramatize for ratings. Newspapers, most of them flush with cash after vanquishing their rivals and becoming a monopoly in their markets, sent their reporters to nail down a single accurate account for that day's edition. It was an industry that all but controlled the news, took that responsibility seriously, and by and large did not recognize its own shortcomings. As such, it tended to speak to the public with a tone of authoritative reassurance. It did not, generally, shout or even raise its voice to attract attention.

Though it did not know it, Three Mile Island would become one of the last great domestic emergencies the media covered before the age of cable news, the concept of the "message of the day," the reinvention of the word "spin," and the notion that "mainstream media" could be a slur. And what occurred showed how the gatekeepers of public knowledge could verify the news before publication or broadcast and help calm a panicky nation with facts.

The crisis began at about four A.M. on Wednesday, March 28, 1979. A valve in the plant's cooling system got stuck in the open position, letting water that would have cooled the reactor leak out. Without the coolant, the reactor core began to overheat and the nuclear fuel pellets began to melt. At nine fifteen A.M., the White House was notified. At eleven A.M., plant officials ordered all nonessential personnel off the plant's premises. With that, word of "an event" at the plant began to filter out through the surrounding community. Workers called family and friends and neighbors with the news, which sputtered through the grapevine, often growing ominously with retelling. By midday, helicopters hired by the plant's owner, General Public Utilities Nuclear, and others from the U.S. Department of Energy could be seen circling above the plant, sampling the radioactivity in the atmosphere.

The worst, witnesses recalled, was grappling with the unknown. The fear generated by rumors and confusion was more intense for those nearby than for those further away. "The situation changed hourly," Maureen Doherty said. "I lived three miles away, in Hershey, PA. Evacuation routes were slid under the door to my apartment." But that information helped little. As it turned out, she said, "There was no gas available at the gas stations. The highways were jammed with people trying to escape."

Unable to flee, Doherty began to rationalize: "I was very afraid, but resigned to the situation. Dying of radiation poisoning was not how I wanted to die, but I felt that it was already too late; we had already been exposed. I remember putting white sheets over the windows—I'm not sure why."[3]

That night, the nation's most watched newsman began his broadcast in a tone that was serious but not panicked. "It was the first step in a nuclear nightmare. As far as we know at this hour, no worse than that," CBS anchor Walter Cronkite said in opening his evening newscast. "But a government official said that a breakdown in an atomic power plant in Pennsylvania today is probably the worst nuclear accident to date."

The news reports also recalled the harrowing scenes of the hit movie *The China Syndrome*, starring Jane Fonda, Jack Lemmon, and Michael Douglas, which had opened nationwide to huge audiences only eleven days before. People knew from the movie the possible result of a nuclear plant meltdown: Molten reactor core products could burn through containment and into the Susquehanna River, creating a steam cloud that would produce radioactive fallout over the entire region. Eerily, the movie even had a scene in which gauges in the control room showed water levels in the reactor core rising to high levels. The scene exactly paralleled the event being described in the news.

With all those scenarios in mind, for the next two days a carefully restrained mainstream news media nonetheless conveyed a sense that the situation was an accident but not yet a disaster. The reactor had not melted down. The area had not been evacuated. "We'll stay here," Sue Showalker, the mother of two children and pregnant with a third, told reporters. "They won't let us rot under the sun."[4]

Then on the morning of Friday, March 30, plant operators released a significant dose of radiation from an auxiliary building. The maneuver was a gamble. It relieved pressure, which would maintain the flow of coolant to the core. But it was also possible that the hydrogen released could burn or even explode and rupture the pressure vessel. If that occurred, it would mean a full-fledged radiation disaster. The governor of Pennsylvania, Richard L. Thornburgh, in his first year in office, consulted with the Nuclear Regulatory Commission about evacuating the population near the plant. He decided to evacuate those most vulnerable to radiation and publicly advised pregnant women and preschool-age children within a five-mile radius of the plant to leave the area.

On the ground, rumors swirled. One night, around nine P.M., all the lights in town went out. "We later found out that a car struck a utility pole, but no one knew that then," an eyewitness told the *Washington Post*. "Within minutes, most of my neighbors had loaded their cars with prepacked suitcases, and were leaving. The sense of fear and uncertainty that night was incredible."

The press, however, remained cautious. "Networks held meetings to choose among words like accident, incident or disaster," a reconstruction of the media's behavior reported. "ABC decided never to use an adjective that had not been used by authorities. Americans everywhere had a solid dose of information about nuclear energy and radiation. Useful features included glossaries of nuclear terminology, medical stories on the impact of radiation on humans, advisories for pregnant women, reports on nearby reactors, analyses of low-level radiation studies and even a report on how to decontaminate a reactor ('very carefully' advised the *New York Daily News*)."[5]

Finally, on Sunday, April 1, experts determined that the hydrogen bubble inside the plant could not burn or explode after all. There was no oxygen in the pressure vessel to make it flammable or explosive. The utility company had also managed to reduce the bubble's size. To register a sense that experts now considered the crisis averted, President Jimmy Carter visited the plant and, accompanied by TV cameras and reporters, casually walked through the control room where the incident had begun.

After four fear-ridden days, during which most of the media stayed on the story around the clock, radio and television stations stopped their continuous news updates and resumed regular programming, a signal, unmistakable to Americans, that life had returned to some sense of normal. Newspaper headlines now deemed events in distant places more important. People around Three Mile Island began picking up the threads of their lives.

A generation later, how would the Three Mile Island incident play out? Is the scenario we imagine far-fetched? No matter what one thinks of the changes technology is bringing, it is certainly hard to imagine such a relatively orderly or homogenous process of information dissemination. It is easier, rather, to see something more chaotic. The question is how each of us, as consumers and citizens, will make sense of information about the next crisis. And how will we understand even the day-to-day events that play out more incrementally? How will we decide what information to believe and what sources to trust? And what, increasingly, will be the role of the old press? In other words, what is the future of truth and how as citizens are we to discern it?

That is what this book is about.

Some people observing the media landscape today have wondered whether truth even matters anymore. Perhaps, they speculate, in the new information age reality is simply a matter of belief, not anything objective or verified; now there is red truth and blue truth, red media and blue media. Perhaps gatekeepers such as Walter Cronkite have been replaced by cheerleaders such as Bill O'Reilly and Keith Olbermann; rather than trying to find out what is going on, they have already decided. Perhaps, in a sense, we have already moved from the age of information to the age of affirmation.

What is really occurring is different. Most of us have not retreated to ideological corners for our information. Not yet. At least so far, as we end the first decade of the new century, the old brands of journalism, and the old journalistic norms they represent, dominate the new information ecosystem. The problem these institutions face is that the Internet has decoupled advertising from news. Advertisers, including individuals connecting with one another through Web sites like Craigslist, no longer need the news to reach consumers. Old journalism's problems have much more to do with a loss of revenue due to technology than a loss of audience.

The most fundamental change is that more of the responsibility for knowing what is true and what is not now rests with each of us as individuals. The notion that a network of social gatekeepers will tell us that things have been established or proven is breaking down. Citizens have more voice, but those who would manipulate the public for political gain or profit—be it corporations or the government—have more direct access to the public as well.

Utopians have heralded this as the end of journalism and the information monopoly of elites and see a citizen media culture that instantly self-corrects—a kind of pure information democracy. Critics see a world without editors, of unfettered spin, where the loudest or most agreeable voice wins and where truth is the first casualty.

We think both of these views are overwrought. The reality of the change is not the end of one media and the rise of a new "we media" culture but a blending that is tending toward a new way of knowing.

This new way of knowing is no longer a lecture by professional authorities but rather a dialogue, with all the strengths and weaknesses that implies. It is a partnership between all of us as consumers of news and information and the former gatekeepers we once relied on to verify and vet information for us.

This is an enormous change. In many ways, it even redefines what we mean by the idea of citizenship. The old idea, operating for the past three hundred years, was that people engaged periodically. They might vote in elections, attend the occasional town meeting, or work through other mediating institutions to pick leaders or monitor government. That old idea is giving way to something new. Rather than relying on the press, Congress, esteemed commissions, or other social authorities to filter information for them, citizens increasingly will filter information for themselves from a competing array of sources. Though we may little understand how, we are all assuming more control over what we know about the world beyond our direct experience. We are becoming our own editors, our own gatekeepers, our own aggregators.

The problem is that much of what this implies about our responsibilities as citizens is unresolved. What is the role of the new citizen—a realistic role, not a utopian one? What responsibilities does it convey? What are the skills we need to be our own editors? What is required of us in the new way of knowing?

There is no code written down. There are no mathematical equations for good citizenship. Whatever the skills required, they have been left largely and curiously untaught, even unexamined. As a society, we preach the virtues of an informed public. The corporations that profit from the business of media claim to champion its cause. The government and many of our best thinkers justly applaud technology for giving us more tools to engage. But generally our culture does little to teach what those skills might be. Our educational system by and large has not imagined them. Many of our journalism schools would be hard pressed to catalog, even for their own students, how to test the veracity of the news they produce. Those skills, however, can be identified. If we look at those who have been in the business of empiricism—people in journalism, law, intelligence, science, medicine, and elsewhere—we will see a set of common concepts and skills that have developed over generations. There is a discernible discipline of mind. Those skills and that discipline amount to what could be called a tradecraft of active skepticism. This book is an attempt to distill that tradecraft. It draws on the skills that were once the province of experts in discerning the truth about public life and outlines a method that citizens can use themselves—a new role for consumers in the do-it-yourself information world. Those skills center on knowing how to evaluate information from the press and other sources so that people can become participants in the new age of information rather than its victims.

It is important to know first that this kind of disruptive technological change has happened before. We can identify a half dozen similarly major advances in technology that have transformed communication and human learning. Each occurrence has, in sometimes larger or smaller ways, redefined the role of citizenship. And each occurrence has seen certain patterns repeat themselves, patterns that we can see today, including disrupting social orders, creating new authorities, and reviving simmering tensions in the two major approaches to learning about the outside world.

Today, as it occurs anew, it is critical to know how to cope with what might otherwise be a sense of chaos or, worse, the feeling that the truth is becoming irrelevant, a casualty to prejudice and to the might of those whose rhetoric is loudest or simplest, or whose marketing and spin are cleverest. There are, we submit, six steps in what can be called the "way of skeptical knowing," the discipline and skills required of a discriminating citizen. The first step is identifying what kind of content one is encountering. There are several distinct models of producing journalism in the contemporary culture—with different and in some ways competing sets of mores. Many of the new forms of dissemination, from social networking to blogs to citizen journalism, may involve any one of them. As consumers, we must first recognize what we are looking at.

The second step is identifying whether a news account is complete. Next comes the question of how to assess sources, something even many journalists have approached too hazily. Discerning consumers have often perceived this and have questioned how journalists work. Lawyers, doctors, police, social scientists, and those who work in other realms of empirical knowledge often have more refined ideas about sourcing, which some of the best journalists have adopted.

The fourth step in evaluating the news involves assessing evidence. This book will explain the difference between observing and understanding and the difference between inference (forming a hypothesis about what something means) and evidence (proving or establishing that this inference is true). Next we will explore how the more recent news models tend to use or interact with evidence, and how that is often a key way of establishing what kind of journalism you are encountering.

The last step in the process of evaluating the news involves exploring whether we are getting what we need from the news more generally. There are several tests and telltale signs that journalists themselves have used or identified to question the news they encounter. These bits of hidden tradecraft can be a key to discovering and creating great work.

Finally we also must ask what should become of journalists and the press. The dominant metaphor used to describe journalism in the twentieth century, that of the press as gatekeeper, no longer works when the press is only one of many conduits between newsmakers and the public. A new descriptive metaphor is required. What is it? What is role of journalism in the twenty-first century? And how do the new journalist and the new citizen work together? We will outline what we call the "next journalism." We will describe what we think citizens require of journalists. We will offer ideas about how newsrooms must change to provide it. And we will describe a newer, broader definition of journalism's function in a community that suggests a window into new business models and a path to a commercial reinvention of journalism.

The outline we offer here of how citizens can function as their own more demanding and discriminating editors is not a strict formula. It is intended, rather, to describe ideas, to open a way of thinking about information. We hope it may start people on a path to being more conscious of their consumption and evaluation of news, whether they are journalists or not—in much the same way that studying algebra or chemistry or English in school helps us navigate the activities of our lives, even if we do not become mathematicians or chemists or English professors. People who are more conscious of how the news is put together will find themselves talking back to the television set, stopping and rereading paragraphs of text, or commenting on the quality and content of news accounts to friends. To these seemingly odd behaviors, we say bravo.

The issues are vital. The future of knowledge is the overriding question in our new century, as we struggle again between modernism and medievalism, between information and belief, between empiricism and faith. These forces in the end must coexist.

They have in the past. Haltingly, often against the interests of a powerful status quo, the march of the human family through history has been toward a more accurate understanding of the world. Sometimes, with two steps forward and one step back, risking imprisonment, even death, with wars fought over the progress, we have learned that the earth moves around the sun, the secrets of the atom, and that people can rule themselves rather than believing their rulers talk to god.

Key to this march have been professionals who work at the boundaries of knowledge, who consider themselves part of a trained cohort, schooled in certain methods and techniques and dedicated in their particular disciplines to learning what is true. In medicine, it is the doctors who fight disease. In knowing the stars, it is the astrophysicists who study how our universe came to be. In biology, it is the geneticists who study the building blocks of life. They study, err, share, and debate, striving for an objective search, which they call the scientific method. As theories become accepted realities, their knowledge is embraced by a more general population.

It has been an accumulation of ever-increasing knowledge of the world around us. Each generation builds on the information amassed by the preceding one, instituting new explosions of knowledge. The process is now becoming overwhelming. At the beginning of this century, it was forecast that more new information would be created in three years than had been created in the previous three hundred thousand years.[6]

The question of the new century is how will that process work? How will we as citizens learn what is true? How will we find out what information we can trust in an age in which we are all our own experts and power has been ceded to everyone?

CHAPTER 2

We Have Been Here Before

The numbers are shocking. In the initial ten years of the twenty-first century, newspapers saw nearly half of their ad revenue disappear. Roughly a third of all newsroom jobs vanished. The audience and revenue for network news were less than half what they had been twenty years earlier. More than two billion dollars in news gathering annually disappeared.

Yet for all that the information revolution may seem startling and disruptive, it is not unprecedented. We have been here before. Through the history of human civilization, there have been eight epochal transformations in communication that, in their way, were no less profound and transformative than what we are experiencing now: from cave drawings to oral language, the written word to the printing press, the telegraph to the radio, broadcast television to cable, and now the Internet.

And with each information revolution, certain key patterns have repeated themselves and certain tensions have remained. Each new method of communication made the exchange of information easier, more textured, and more meaningful. Communication of shared knowledge and shared curiosity brought people together in larger and larger communities based on common ways of knowing. Each advance in form and efficiency also had a democratizing influence: As more people became more knowledgeable, they also became better able to question their world and the behavior of the people and institutions that directed their lives. And those new levels of awareness resulted in shifts in power arrangements, toppling or changing old authorities and creating new ones. We moved from shamans to tribal leaders, from tribal leaders to kings and city-states, from city-states to nations. Each change, in turn, forced existing power elites to try to exploit communication in order to reorganize and direct the energy democratization released at the grassroots level.

And as it reorganized social order, each change in popular communications was accompanied by a renewal of the tension between two strands of knowledge or ways of trying to understand existence: the tension between knowledge based on observation and experience and knowledge grounded on faith and belief—the tension between fact and faith.

All these patterns—the forming of larger new communities (community and democratization), the toppling of old authorities and the creation of new ones (reorganization), and the increasing gulf between empiricism and faith (tension)—are evident in the technological revolution of the twenty-first century. Even the bloggers, cable demagogues, citizen Web sites, and populist political movements of our new century all have parallels in earlier moments of technological and socioeconomic change. Our challenge as citizens today is to understand and learn, as more power cedes to each of us, how to use the power and not be thwarted by it.

The Written Word

The first record of communication, in which humans tried to reach out to people beyond face-to-face communication, are cave drawings, dated to about 15,000 B.C. The earliest-known cases—in Altamira, Spain, and Lascaux, France—share two striking characteristics: Both feature pictures of hunting and, more tentatively, illustrations of star clusters that suggest some kind of spiritual communication, a searching for answers about the place of humans in the universe. They express, in other words, two kinds of knowledge: that which is temporal and empirical and that which is based on belief about what cannot be proven.

Oral language is thought to have begun around 6000 B.C., and anthropologists have traced the third breakthrough in communication, the written word, to 5000 B.C. Written language took its first form in the development of numerical symbols, which could be used to measure, record, and distribute the wealth individuals accumulated. That was soon followed by the codification of spoken words into written symbols. Written communication differed from oral in important ways. Unlike oral knowledge, which might be forgotten or altered with each retelling, what was written was preserved. The symbols were fixed, and their permanence made them more reliable and more precise. The communication became deeper, more complex, and more empirical. The written word was also mobile. What was recorded could be carried from place to place and stored to be referred to months or years later. One could experience the precise thoughts and observations of an unknown and unseen person.

These qualities of permanence, complexity, and mobility effected profound change. They helped move the human race from a hunter-gatherer culture of primitive tribes to a civilization of organized communities based on agrarian life. The codification of records and deeds enabled the domestication of plants and animals and the settlement of larger populations in communities that could communicate across large distances. In the earliest-known written stories, the tales of Gilgamesh, the king of Uruk, there is evidence of all these patterns. The stories tell in great detail of the building of walls, the organization of community, the discussion of politics, and the contemplation of man's place in the universe—the same subjects found in the cave drawings made ten thousand years earlier.

The tensions between the two ways of understanding the world—fact and faith—became even greater as written communication reached a new level of sophistication in ancient Greece. In his dialogues, Socrates advanced a disciplined method of empirical questioning of the world. In the Socratic method, each person uses personal observations and reason to challenge the assertions or beliefs of another. Then together, in dialogue, people employ reason and experience to compare assertions with observed reality to form knowledge. It was the most formalized approach yet recorded to what we might call, in modern terms, empiricism and consensus.

Socrates' student Plato further extended his teacher's dialogues, but Plato distrusted sense experience alone. In the "Allegory of the Cave," he argues that what we perceive as the real world is simply a shadow, an illusion, of ideal reality. These shadows can help us understand the world, Plato suggests, but such knowledge is insufficient as a basis for a moral life. And if forced to choose, Plato argues, moral truth is more important than empirical.

Plato's approach of employing faith and reason together profoundly influenced future conflicts between the two ways of knowing. It inspired Saint Augustine, for instance, who developed a history of knowledge that helped clear the way for church and state to work together for centuries. Yet the tensions that dominated the Middle Ages, and saw violent expression in the Inquisition, didn't ease significantly until the next great shift in communication a thousand years later.

The Printing Press

If art was the first great development in communication, language the second, and writing the third, the next epochal transformation was touched off in fifteenth-century Europe when a craftsman named Johannes Gutenberg perfected a machine for moveable type. Gutenberg's printing press made it possible to quickly produce mass quantities of books and pamphlets. At the time he developed his press, around 1450, it took a monk roughly a year to hand copy a single Bible. In its first full year of production, Gutenberg's press printed 180 Bibles. The printing press left in its wake the transformation of Europe, the Renaissance, and the Reformation. Before the printing press, Oxford University owned 122 books, each equivalent in value to a farm or vineyard.[1] By 1501, fifty years after its invention, at least 10 million copies of an estimated 27,000 to 35,000 books had been printed in Europe.[2] New universities independent of religious orders opened, and the reading public slowly expanded.

The explosion in writing and reading led to a boost in empirical thought. Scholars began to see the physical world as more important than medieval authorities had argued. The expansion of literacy led to the idea of testing generalizations by observation and of creating situations to be studied experimentally.[3] The *Oxford English Dictionary* records that the word "fact" first appeared in the English language in the sixteenth century—one hundred years after Gutenberg's printing press—and is defined as "something that has really occurred or is actually the case; hence a particular truth known by actual observation or authentic testimony, as opposed to what is merely inferred."

At the same time, Gutenberg's Bibles weakened the clerical monopoly on religious texts and meaning. Common people no longer had to rely on interpreters when they could read their own Bible and find their own road to salvation. A key principle in Martin Luther's Protestant Reformation was the idea that all Christians should become literate so they could read the Gospels daily by age ten. The pattern of community, democratization, and social reorganization forged by language and writing thus repeated itself.

And part of this was the birth of journalism. Within a century of Gutenberg's printing press, something called "news books," one-time reports of a current event, began to appear. The first newspapers soon followed in Germany, France, and England, starting around 1604. Despite censorship, suppression, and imprisonment of its practitioners, and often government control over its daily operations, the fledgling press grew. The shared information allowed people to question, challenge, and amend the information they received from established authorities. The crown, in effect, no longer had control over information or over people's thoughts about public affairs. Gradually but inexorably the notion grew that even the lowliest person in a community had the right to a personal opinion and that opinion should be heard in the councils of government. By the eighteenth century a bourgeoning political press, financed by opponents of the government, began to use new forms of language and even political metaphor to evade censorship and challenge the crown. The political press's audacity and newness created a sensation—much the way the brazen frankness of blogging, the popularity of YouTube, and the ease of Twitter have today. The social critic Samuel Johnson considered the work of these new political journalists better reading than any other publications of the time.

With journalism, too, something else happened. What had for centuries been known as common or vulgar opinion was transformed into a more venerated concept: public opinion. The idea, largely absent since Greece and Roman civilizations, reemerged in England in the writings of seventeenth-century philosopher John Locke, and soon the term itself was used in speeches in parliament and political essays. And with the spread of information came an even more powerful concept: the idea that people could be self-governing. Western civilization's greatest fruit, democracy, is itself a product of the evolution of communication.

The Telegraph and the Birth of News

The printing press gave rise in the seventeenth and eighteenth centuries to the newspaper as an organ of political opposition and debate, helping to forge the creation of political parties, but the nineteenth century brought the advent of another invention that created what we now think of as news. In 1844, John Morse used electric signals of dots and dashes to transmit language electronically over wires. Morse's telegraph made it possible for the first time for people to learn things almost instantly across very long distances. This technology created something that didn't exist before—news as a factual product independent of the observer writing it. Within two years, newspapers formed a nonprofit cooperative called the Associated Press to supply the news for them across the telegraph. The news stories from the AP had to be suitable for any newspaper to publish. Almost instantly a new language of communication was born. News writing took on a more neutral tone that wasn't tied to an author. It was also terse, since it was billed by the word when transmitted over telegraph wires. And it found a new form in the technique of organizing news accounts from the most important facts to the least important, the so-called inverted pyramid, with the thicker part at the top.[4] Previously, news narratives were more subjective and often told chronologically, with the most dramatic facts revealed toward the end. These older, more personal dispatches, frequently presented as letters from a particular person, resemble blog posts of today.

With more news to fill pages, growing audiences as populations gathered in cities, and the price of newsprint falling by half every ten years, the press became increasingly independent of any political party in the years following the Civil War. This independence gained further momentum from the commercial advertising that came with the growth of industrial America. With political independence, some newsrooms developed a progressive philosophy of reform, a philosophy recognized and seized on by rising reform politicians like Theodore Roosevelt. And in the early twentieth century, muckraking and financial independence elevated the professional aspirations of journalists.

Radio, Reassurance, and Disruption

The next great change in communications was not far away. While the invention of the telegraph in the 1840s gave people the ability to learn about faraway events within a few minutes or hours of their occurrence, the invention of the radio in the 1920s gave them the ability to hear some of those events for themselves. And with it came a repeat of the pattern of forming new communities, political reorganization, and continued tension between fact and faith. In a way local newspapers never could, radio began to knit together a nation whose population had become increasingly fragmented by the cascading change of the industrial revolution. Suddenly everyone was hearing the same national radio newscasts—a striking change from reading the local newspapers in the print-only age. Literacy, too, was no longer a requirement for learning the news. The new medium also altered print journalism dramatically. It was no longer enough to report the news. Newspapers now had to be more analytical, because people could get the facts from the radio before they would ever see the paper. Some newspapers responded by becoming more sensational and the "tabloid" era began, exploiting another technology, an enhanced ability to print photographs—and to alter them for dramatic effect.

Radio's impact on politics was no less significant. President Franklin Roosevelt recognized the intimacy of the new medium and its unifying and democratizing potential. In his radio speeches and "fireside chats," in which he talked to Americans as if he were with them in their living rooms, Roosevelt bypassed the press and spoke to people directly, explaining in reassuring and simple terms the complexity of the Great Depression and, later, the need for war.

The tensions between fact and faith also found expression via radio. At the same time Roosevelt used his broadcasts to help ease public fears about the Depression, reassurance of another kind came in the form of evangelical sermons by a new wave of radio ministers whose audience rivaled Roosevelt's in size. One of the most powerful of these ministers was Father Charles Edward Coughlin, a Catholic priest with a weekly radio audience estimated at thirty million. Not unlike the books offered by cable hosts today, the first edition of Coughlin's radio discourses, published in 1933, was a national bestseller, and he was considered by some to be the second-most-powerful man in the United States after the president.

Television, Newspapers, and the Nationalizing of Politics

Only twenty years after radio allowed people to hear the news themselves, an even more powerful new technology appeared. Television offered people the ability to see the news as well as hear it. Influenced by the toneless and authoritative style of radio news, television news developed an affect thoroughly different from the heavily mediated quality of the brief weekly newsreels people saw in movie theaters, which were characterized by stylized, almost cartoonish narration and little or no natural sound. What's more, the emerging TV network news divisions carried the sight and sound of events directly into people's homes every night. Even the names of the early TV news programs promoted the idea that people were seeing the news for themselves: *Person to Person*, *You Are There*, and *See It Now*.[5] The medium got its first boost in the 1950s by providing gavel-to-gavel television coverage of national political conventions. The public was riveted by the presidential selection process, and the conventions elevated a group of largely unknown network newsmen—Chet Huntley, David Brinkley, and Walter Cronkite—to "anchorman" status after they took on the supposedly unenviable job of narrating the coverage. The network evening news expanded from fifteen minutes to thirty minutes in September 1963. In less than a year, Americans reported that television had become the primary medium by which they got their news.

And again, familiar patterns repeated themselves—the creation of a larger, and more democratic community, political and social reorganization, and renewed tension. With newspapers, readers could pick and choose what articles they wanted to read, skipping stories that didn't interest them. Radio made the news more intimate and national. But television unified it. Americans largely gathered around two newscasts each night, NBC's and CBS's (ABC's was a distant third). Fully 70 percent of the televisions in use—sometimes viewed by more than a quarter of all Americans each night—were tuned to one of the three programs at the dinner hour. And unlike newspaper readers, television viewers could not pick and choose what they wanted to watch. They had to watch the programs as they were designed or turn them off. The effect was a growth in what social scientists call "incidental news acquisition"—when people learn about things they might not be interested in. And with a common enemy in the Soviet Union and a common news diet from the networks, social consensus rose. The political effect of Americans seeing the news for themselves, and to a significant degree seeing the same thing, was enormous.

Television in turn helped to nationalize politics to levels that had never been seen before. The daily reports from Washington, first from

NBC anchor David Brinkley and then a generation of network White House correspondents, fostered a growing fascination with political news. Newspapers increased their Washington bureaus, and a new aggressiveness and skepticism about government power converged with doubts about the Vietnam War. The ubiquity of the Washington view of political issues and activities had the effect of substantiating centralized authority. This was especially true of the authority of the president, the only public official elected nationwide, whose ability to perform on television became a powerful leadership tool. Where Americans once thought of their news in local terms, because it was brought to them by a local paper, radio, or television, they now began to focus on the institutions and political figures they had in common. With the civil rights movement, the images pouring daily into American homes of brutal public and police reactions to peaceful protesters in the South made it impossible for the political system to continue to ignore the challenge raised by black Americans' demand for equal rights. Television coverage of dramatic events, and the sense that the news was now less mediated, also gave ordinary citizens dramatic new power to effect political change. Televangelists, antiwar protesters, and members of the women's rights movement all were politically empowered by the new form of communication and began to change the nature of the political debate in the United States.

The reorganization also changed the communication order as well. The first print victims of the rise of television news were the afternoon papers, which generally were aimed at blue-collar readers who tended to go to work earlier and get their news at the end of the day. Television news came largely in the afternoon, and its quick accounting of the day's headlines was closer to the shorter, breezier style of papers aimed at these readers. Television's rise also made the surviving papers deeper and more analytical, targeting a more affluent and educated demographic. The morning paper and the Sunday paper entered a golden era. The push for elite demographics also gave more influence to advertisers. Morning papers that had begun to enjoy a monopoly status in their markets had more advertising than they had ever expected. The business was frankly easy, and lucrative. As a result, most newspapers were slow to react with creative thinking about their content until they were at risk of being relegated to a niche position by television, as radio had been. When newspapers did react, their confusion over the nature of the challenge was reflected in the fact that the two major innovations followed diametrically different paths. *USA Today*, started in 1981, adapted much of TV's appeal, providing more colorful pages of short, snappy "bright" writing and newspaper sidewalk vending boxes that looked like TV sets. Established national newspapers like the *New York Times*, on the other hand, offered a new deeply analytical format that combined hard factual reporting with analytical detail drawn from the reporter's own experience, observations, and conclusions. The *Los Angeles Times* effected an approach that was almost a paradox: the concept of a daily magazine in which the reporting and writing was so deep that it challenged the limits of a daily newspaper.

Cable and Continuous News

Just seventeen years after the networks launched the first thirty-minute evening newscasts came the next major shift in communications: the advent of cable television news. Long before Fox and MSNBC changed the norms of TV news, CNN, launched in 1980, shattered the relationship that had existed between the networks and their local affiliates. Before CNN, three networks tightly controlled what national and international news Americans could see—and the networks did not even share this footage with their own affiliated stations until after it had aired on network newscasts first. In 1986, the affiliate feed provided by the three networks (the amount of footage shared with local stations) was limited to thirty minutes a day.

Ted Turner's CNN network had a profound influence on the news by breaking that monopoly. To get more footage that could air on CNN, Turner began to offer local stations a bargain they had never enjoyed before. If they would share their local footage with CNN, he would share CNN footage with them. Turner's offer, combined with fledgling local news cooperatives, effectively ended the three commercial networks' stranglehold over national and international news. Network affiliates, caught in the middle, began pressuring the networks to provide them with more footage. By 1990, the networks each were offering affiliates up to eight hours of footage a day. The effect on network news audiences came quickly. Not only did people have other programs they could watch on cable. They also had access to national and international news headlines at four, five, and six P.M. newscasts, even if they didn't have cable or watch CNN.

Digital Technology and Consumer Choice

News was becoming something consumers could begin to access when they wanted, and they were become more accustomed to having choices. The evolution of cable news in a sense represented a precursor to the rise of the Internet.

The dominos began to fall more quickly thereafter. In 1994, Yahoo began, and Reuters made the decision to offer its news virtually for free. The next year, America Online was providing Internet access, near real-time audio was available, and 50 percent of America's schools were wired. In 1996, Microsoft and MSNBC launched MSNBC.com. By 2000, Internet pioneers like MSNBC editor in chief Merrill Brown were talking about a major shift in the patterns of news consumption online. Previously, with the exception of rare moments of breaking news on cable and some all-news radio, people acquired news primarily around the breakfast table or in the late afternoon to early evening, plus some local news on television late at night. No longer. Web sites began to chart news consumption throughout the day, with noticeable spikes around lunchtime, and late at night.

From 2000 to 2008, the increase in Internet use was dizzying:

- In 2000, only 46 percent of adults in the United States used the Internet. By 2008, 74 percent did so.
- In 2000, only 5 percent had high-speed Internet at home. By 2008, 58 percent did.
- In 2000, only 50 percent of Americans owned a cell phone. By 2008, 82 percent did.
- In 2000, no one in America was wirelessly connected to the Internet. By 2008, 62 percent of Americans were.

In a decade, we shifted to people having access to news and information virtually anywhere anytime. Some imagined that this would scatter the audience to a million new places for news, including blogs and articles by citizen journalists, and substantially away from traditional news values such as journalistic objectivity, the idea of the journalist as an independent broker who has verified the news that is published and who offers multiple points of view. The presumed end of the news oligarchy even found voice in some simple concepts such as the "long tail." This notion, popularized by *Wired* editor Chris Anderson, is that the market for information and goods on a wide array of niche topics from myriad distinct sources in various forms—Web sites, blogs, social networks, and mobile media—would eventually supplant the market and information previously delivered via mass media. Anderson argued that the mass media culture that emerged in the twentieth century was an anomaly specific to the newer but dominant forms of the time: television and radio. The Internet was allowing consumers to more easily gravitate toward news, information, goods, and services tailored to individual interests and one's (very exact) geography.[6]

Anderson's prediction, however, isn't really what has happened in journalism. When it comes to news, the reality, at least so far, appears more complex. Traditional online news sites got bigger, not smaller. For instance, in 2007 the top ten newspapers controlled 19 percent of newspaper circulation, but they received 29 percent of the audience for newspaper Web sites. In 2008, the top seven hundred news and information sites saw traffic grow by 7 percent. But the top fifty sites, almost all of them run by traditional newspapers or television stations, saw traffic grow 27 percent.[7] The front end of the tail is getting bigger online. So is the long end of the tail. It is the middle that's suffering.[8]

Why, then, are traditional news destinations still suffering?

The problem isn't fundamentally a loss of audience. When numbers from their new and old platforms are combined, many traditional media venues are seeing their audiences grow. The crisis facing the news industry created by technology has to do more with revenue. The technology has decoupled advertising from news. Many advertisers no longer need the news to reach their audience—be they big-box retailers with their own Web sites or individuals posting apartments for rent or bicycles for sale on Craigslist. At the same time, the Internet has turned out to be a poor delivery system for the kind of display advertising that financed news gathering in the twentieth century. News delivery for the past century benefited from a happy accident. A commercial system (advertising) subsidized a civic good (professional journalism). That system is now ending, at least as we know it. And it is not clear what, if anything, will replace it or at what scale.

But it is important, as we try to navigate our new world, not to be naive. We should take a breath and look back as well as look forward. Whatever the future news structure, the history of communications suggests that the old technologies will not disappear. But they will change, becoming smaller and playing a different role. Communication's history also suggests that new technologies do not change human nature. They simply allow us to express and satisfy our curiosity about the world beyond our own direct experience in different ways. Today, as bytes of information move through cyberspace in nanoseconds and as citizens in remote corners of the world are awash in the latest news, it can be difficult to contemplate how slowly information moved four hundred years ago. But there are clear echoes the history recalled here. The written word or printing press was in every way as profound a change as the Internet. The emerging newspapers of the seventeenth and eighteenth century were analogous to the embryonic blogs, social networking sites, video sharing platforms, and other online forums for citizen conversation of the twenty-first century. And the emerging newspaper industry of those earlier centuries had a political impact in democratizing Europe and North America—not unlike the impact of viral videos in propelling the career of Barack Obama in 2008 and in challenging his health care plans in 2009. In the simplest terms, newspapers made information that was once held by a few more transparent to many. The readership of the press in the 1730s was certainly not widespread, but nonetheless, information that was once essentially confined at court traveled in dramatic and profound ways. A century later the rise of a commercial press in the United States increased the spread of information and helped previously marginalized citizens become involved in public affairs and become a major factor in the challenge to the established order in American society and the crisis over slavery that ended with the Civil War. The emergence of political radio evangelists like Father Coughlin during the Depression and the New Deal era have their twenty-first-century analog in the rise of cable personalities like Glenn Beck.

And in those echoes the patterns also repeat. Each advance in communications technology has made it easier to learn about the world around us, to more easily become involved, to challenge and even dismantle old authorities who once controlled the flow of information, and to create new authorities. What we are seeing now is the end of old authorities, but be aware that they will be replaced by new ones. The ancient tensions, between the confusing and inductive empiricism of observation and science and the comforting and synthesizing power of faith and belief, have never been resolved but will find new expressions and disruptions as they seek a balance.

The net effect of these steps forward is more information in the hands of citizens. In the twenty-first century, access to information has reached a new high. The question we now face is how to proceed: How do we identify, with our new tools and options, what information is reliable?

CHAPTER 3

The Way of Skeptical Knowing:
The Tradecraft of Verification

Homer Bigart arrived in Vietnam in December 1961.

A veteran of combat coverage in World War II and the Korean War, Bigart brought with him not only deep experience but also an unusually probing method of reporting. That method had earned the *New York Times* reporter two Pulitzer Prizes and made him a legend among journalists.

Bigart's appearance in Saigon coincided with a major escalation of America's involvement in Vietnam. Politically, the U.S. government had begun to shower the Vietnamese countryside with elaborate aid programs designed to win over the hearts and minds of the population. Militarily, the United States had recently sent over a fleet of helicopters as part of a plan to do what the South Vietnamese soldiers apparently would not: press the war against the north in the countryside. As U.S. efforts expanded, the Kennedy administration and military leaders in the field were at pains to describe events in Vietnam in a way that would retain public support for the human and financial costs now certain to rise.

In the United States, newspaper editors were confronted with two versions of events. From officials in Washington and Saigon, they heard stories of the situation in South Vietnam improving. From some of their own correspondents in the field, they heard stories of corruption and defeat. Unsure how to reconcile the sometimes conflicting stories, the editors in many cases opted to feature the government's view in their reports. After all, government officials should know more than reporters. They were the authorities.

Bigart called such behavior—the practice of uncritically accepting the official version of things—"clerkism." Journalists should be more than stenographers, he thought. They have a responsibility to ferret out facts for themselves, to establish proof empirically, not accept other people's word secondhand. Over a lifetime in journalism, he had developed his passion for facts into a method of reporting that rose above either clerkism or guessing. During his relatively brief time in Vietnam, he had an impact on a new generation of reporters—including David Halberstam, Neil Shee-han, Malcolm Brown, and Peter Arnett—and on war reporting, giving the public greater knowledge of battlefield conditions than they had during any previous war. William Prochnau, a young combat correspondent, af-fecting Bigart's stammer, recalled him saying, " 'How ca-ca-ca-can a fact and a lie both be correct? Aren't we supposed to choose?' Then, after a pregnant pause, he would answer his own question: 'Yes.' "

Bigart's way of choosing which version to believe was to take nothing for granted and to take virtually no one's word for anything. He started with what was in effect a clean slate. He began his reporting as if he knew nothing. He assumed nothing, and he asked everyone to demonstrate or prove to him anything that they said or claimed. Halberstam, a young *Times* reporter who would soon arrive in Vietnam, called Bigart's method "portable ignorance." And it was aided by Bigart's Columbo-like manner and his stammer, which tended to make people underestimate him.

"He shows up knowing little and then finds out everything," Proch-nau said.[1]

Neil Sheehan, a young reporter for United Press International at the time, quickly learned about portable ignorance when he joined Bigart on a U.S.-led mission into the field in South Vietnam. For weeks U.S. mili-tary advisers had been boasting about the growing success they were having with South Vietnam's Army of the Republic of Vietnam (ARVN) units. A new "strategic hamlet" program designed to rid villages from Vietcong guerrilla control was working, the military advisers said. They claimed that village leaders were providing better intelligence in these hamlets and that they were aided by a new crop of combat helicopters. Pressured by Bigart, the military decided to take some reporters out to the countryside to show the program was working.

Most reporters simply readied for the trip. Not Bigart. "Before we went into the field, Homer would meticulously question the American advisers," Sheehan remembered. "He would ask, 'What do you expect to find? What units are in the area? In what force?' Endless questions."[2]

Others, including Sheehan, skipped all that. They were impatient to get out near the action—something the Pentagon had resisted allowing them to do until Bigart had pushed for it. What's more, many reporters would have thought that asking all those questions beforehand would have made them look slow or stupid to the very military officials with whom they were trying to maintain access. No doubt it tested the patience of those officers, but there was method to Bigart's queries. He was establishing criteria for knowing what to look for. That way, he could compare what was actually occurring in the field with official expectations. He would then have proof that either the policy was working or that it was a PR show. And after the trip to the field, dead tired from the stress of combat and slogging through paddies, Bigart was at it again, questioning officials: "What units did you find? Were you surprised? You said this unit would be here. Was it? How many were killed? How many bodies were found?" On and on, Bigart exquisitely dissected the expected engagement against the actual outcome.

The trip proved to be far less eventful than the military had told the reporters to anticipate. The helicopter raids had caught the Vietcong by surprise, but slow reactions by the South Vietnamese troops the Americans were assisting squandered much of that advantage.

"On the way back to Saigon after two grueling days in which limited action took place, but hours of dog-tiring exertion," Sheehan recalled, "I complained, 'Jesus Christ, Homer, we spent two days walking through the rice paddies and we don't even have a story.' Homer looked at me and said, 'You don't get it, kid. They can't do it. It doesn't work.'"

Back in Saigon, correspondents briefed by the U.S. military command filed utterly credulous stories about Vietcong soldiers surprised by newly invigorated ARVN troops using the latest combat helicopters and routed from their village hideout, with dozens of them killed.

An Associated Press dispatch appeared March 9 from Saigon:

> Vietnamese fighter-bombers today battered the Mekong River delta while ground forces pushed through swamps near the South China Sea hunting guerrillas . . .

Military sources said Vietnamese forces killed 33 guerrillas
and captured four in an operation Thursday supported by U.S.
Army helicopters in southernmost An Xuyen Province.

Bigart's account was different. He was able to build his report brick by
brick from events he had seen for himself and other facts provided to
him directly by officers whose lives depended on the reality of the battlefield. He not only provided a much more telling context than the stories
produced from Saigon. He was also able, in recounting both the helicopter raids' success and failures, to foreshadow the eventual failure of the
new tactic, which would come to dominate the U.S. military's approach
in Vietnam.

Bigart's article on the action read, in part:

But as usual the main enemy force got away. It slipped through
the trap even though the airborne attackers had achieved excel-
lent surprise in their vertical envelopment of the village. . . .

The [South Vietnamese] Government troops failed to exploit
the Viet Cong state of shock. They bunched up and dawdled in
drainage ditches and under the shade of coconut trees until an
American adviser cried out in exasperation, "Let's move the thing
forward."

By late afternoon it was apparent that the battle was over and
that most of the 200 Communists estimated to have been in the
village had got away.[3]

None of this was secondhand. Bigart had seen it all for himself, gotten
everything on the record, and shown unequivocally that the claims of
the press briefers back in Saigon were inflated and missed, or masked, the
larger point that the South Vietnamese army was incapable of capitaliz-
ing on American tactics and technology.

"That, to me, was Homer," Sheehan said. "Take nothing for granted."[4]

Bigart's eyewitness story is illuminating in another way as well, even a
half century later. The story is largely void of qualifying explanation
of how he knew what he knew and of aggrandizing descriptions of how he
himself went on the raid. The tone of the piece is startlingly plain. Bigart
serves as the reader's eyes and ears, and if he says it happened, it
happened—he had seen it himself.

Today, as more and more of our news comes second or thirdhand, as journalists increasingly are kept at a distance from original sources by communications "managers," and consumers become their own editors and sometimes their own journalists, how do we decide for ourselves whether something is true? What are the ways to distinguish between the empiricism of Homer Bigart and the clerkism of his trusting peers back in Saigon? How can we, as consumers, in short, adopt and develop our own portable ignorance?

One difficulty is that, for the most part, the skills that make up this kind of skeptical inquiry are not written down in a simple formula; they are not universal equations. By and large, most of these methods and techniques have been honed by professional journalists on the job by trial and error, often in private. The best journalists have borrowed techniques from good mentors they have met in the field, the way Sheehan learned from Bigart. And not everyone is good. The "working press" is made up of tough, disciplined empiricists, like Bigart, but also plenty of gullible clerks—and often those with friends in high places are rewarded more readily than the skeptics who wants proof.

To detect a good work of reporting, we as consumers now must learn some of the tradecraft of journalism for ourselves—the street knowledge of the savvy observer of public life, the methods journalists and political insiders use to tell when a story is faked, hyped, or spun. And we must know how to distinguish good tradecraft from bad, portable ignorance from clerkism, reporting from cant.

The best journalists, like Bigart, are independent of mind. They learn to overcome their own emotional leanings toward one faction or another. They learn to practice what we call the "way of skeptical knowing."

Consumers of information can adopt this journalistic tradecraft for themselves; they can learn to employ their own way of skeptical knowing. It requires discipline. It means adopting an empirical state of mind—and an open one. And it will, in its way, force people to move toward a certain kind of learning that is more difficult, more skeptical, and less comforting. But it also will help people to avoid the traps of delusion and safety and ultimately to avoid being continually surprised by developments that they should have easily seen coming if they'd known what to pay attention to.

Journalism, however, is not hard science. Decoding public events cannot be accomplished by mathematical equation. And, as we will discuss, we are often far less empirical in how we engage with news than we are in other realms of our lives. As we try to derive meaning from public events, we tend to blend our understanding of the facts with our subjective beliefs about what they imply. Do we think what the president said is good or bad? Does it seem like he is headed in a positive direction or a negative one? It is difficult to separate our values, inferences, fears, and prejudices about the world from our answers to such questions. But we can learn how to derive meaning in a more careful, skillful, and disciplined way. Our understanding of the news must be built on a foundation of facts—an accurate understanding of what has occurred. And this process of moving from understanding to assigning meaning is one that should be arrived at through a sequence. At the doctor's office, we talk first about symptoms, then move to diagnosis before discussing a prescription or course of treatment. Understanding our civic health deserves no less care—and can be approached with a similar commonsense clarity and skill.

By and large, however, until recently we haven't had to perform so much of the initial "symptom discussion," the basic sorting out of the facts of events, for ourselves. We relied on mediating authorities—the press—to do much of that for us. How well they did it is beside the point. Now, with so many competing news conduits and so many partial accounts, we must adopt some of these diagnostic skills for ourselves, so we can at least identify good journalism from bad. Many of us, though, can begin to do more: become our own editors, our own synthesizers.

These are the skills of the new citizenship that technology now demands.

The Way of Skeptical Knowing

Fundamentally, the way of skeptical knowing amounts to asking—and knowing how to answer—a series of systematic questions. These questions, and knowing how to resolve them, make up the discipline of verifying news. To some extent, though not always so consciously and rarely in such an itemized checklist, these are the questions that professionals ask not just in journalism but in all realms of empiricism. Others might word the questions differently, or break them up into a different number of questions. We have distilled our list for clarity and simplicity. We developed it from listening to journalists discuss their work, during our own years as reporters and editors and more recently in our work as press critics and researchers, and from systematically analyzing the content and nature of media. The process involves asking the following:

1. *What kind of content am I encountering?*
2. *Is the information complete; and if not, what is missing?*
3. *Who or what are the sources, and why should I believe them?*
4. *What evidence is presented, and how was it tested or vetted?*
5. *What might be an alternative explanation or understanding?*
6. *Am I learning what I need to?*

Much of the rest of this book will explore in detail how to answer these questions for different kinds of news and information and talk about examples of good work and those we find wanting.

Inevitably, these questions overlap. An evaluation of the evidence in a story is related to the number and expertise of the sources cited. And our judgment of those sources affects our sense of whether an account is complete. But it is useful to set out the questions separately to become more conscious of the process. And even though we may move through this process more seamlessly than step-by-step, the sequence offered here has some logic to it. We usually derive a sense of whether an account is complete before we judge if it is believable; we usually look at sources before examining the evidence they are offering.

And one concept guides the search for the truth. Scientists, law enforcement personnel, intelligence professionals, and journalists share a basic definition of what "truth" means. For all of them, truth is provisional but also empirical:

Truth is a statement of what is most probable in proportion to the evidence available at the time.[5]

Truth also can evolve over time in the face of new evidence. Truth, in the realm of understanding public life in that sense is also a process that may become clearer over time. It is the same in the realm of understanding science. (For example, Pluto was once considered a planet, but in 2006 scientists declared it to be a dwarf planet, one that did not dominate the area around its orbit as only a true planet does.) What should guide the way of skeptical knowing, the signal of work that is more reliable or less, is the amount of effort we can detect that the journalist or presenter made to comb through the sources and the evidence and the degree to which they did so with an open and skeptical mind.

If anything, our expectations about how much we should know about a journalist's sources, evidence, and process are rising. For many years, journalists tended to offer little in the way of information about sources. The fact that a trusted news organization thought the source was worthy of quoting was considered enough. "Gee, the newspaper or the TV network wouldn't be quoting this guy if it didn't think he knew what he was talking about, would it?" we tended to believe. Consider that Walter Cronkite, rated in 1970s polls as the "most trusted man in America," used to conclude his newscast with a signature sign-off: "And that's the way it is." And we took Walter's word for it.

That bygone era might best be described as the "trust me" era of news.

Today, when the news comes from all kinds of sources, in all styles and formats, from journalists and nonjournalists, we need more. We need to be able to know why we should believe the sources relied on to offer facts or to comment on them. Now we tend to think, "Give me enough information to judge this source for myself."

We operate today, in other words, in what might be described as the "show me" era of news.

And notice that the "me" in these two phrases has shifted. The "me" in "trust me" refers to the journalist. The "me" in "show me" refers to the audience, the news consumer. That reflects the power shift in the digital age from the journalist as gatekeeper to the consumer or citizen as his or her own editor. With that shift the consumer has now acquired a greater responsibility to adopt and perfect a skeptical way of knowing.

This book, and the tradecraft of skeptical knowing that it outlines, might be considered the consumer formula for the show me era of citizenship and public life.

What Kind of Content Is This?

The first step in this effort is one of orientation: identifying what kind of content you are looking at. In the wilderness of an open and mixed media culture, the labels on information are often there to deceive rather than to illuminate. And not everything people encounter in the public media is news, even if it labeled as such. Nor is all news the same. Today, indeed, institutional brand names such as CNN or NBC News are no guarantee of a single set of norms, values, or approaches to quality.

Now we may find competing models of news delivery, with different implicit values, even on the same news channel, on the same Web site, and even within a single TV program.

This presents an obvious challenge to anyone who wants to know what to believe, but it begins the process of knowing what to believe.

What kind of content am I encountering?

In a class on news literacy developed for students at State University of New York at Stony Brook, former newspaper editor Howie Schneider calls this evaluation "knowing the neighborhood." Schneider tells his students to first identify whether what they are looking at or hearing is news, propaganda, advertising, publicity, entertainment, or raw information.

The lines between those types of media are blurring. Ads are embedded in movies through product placement. Publicity is embedded in news programs interviewing celebrities hawking movies or books. The ecosystem of news is splintering into different models of news with different values and purposes. And as consumers we need to be able to recognize them.

We identify four distinct models:

- *Journalism of Verification*, a traditional model that puts the highest value on accuracy and context
- *Journalism of Assertion*, a newer model that puts the highest value on immediacy and volume and in so doing tends to become a passive conduit of information
- *Journalism of Affirmation*, a new political media that builds loyalty less on accuracy, completeness, or verification than on affirming the beliefs of its audiences, and so tends to cherry-pick information that serves that purpose
- *Interest-group Journalism*, which includes targeted Web sites or pieces of work, often investigative, that are usually funded by special interests rather than media institutions and designed to look like news

Some may wonder about new media forms such as aggregation, blogging, social networking, tweeting, and texting, which we will discuss here as well. But these are *forms* of communication or activities—not models of content. And because these forms and activities instantly spread information across the Internet, they may involve all four core models of content.

Increasingly, wherever we encounter news it may be from any of these models today—traditional news headlines from a radio station followed by a political talk show host engaged in partisan affirmation. We may see a TV story that seems solidly reported followed by a piece of political propaganda that resembles a news story. Some media outlets offer content from more than one model. Our job, as consumers, is to evaluate each piece of content—each story or interview segment—on its own, though we may form judgments about a news channel, a program, or a publication from the cumulative nature of the content it provides. And certainly, there are hybrids forming in new media—Web sites that join partisanship content and traditional wire service news.

All this makes knowing how to discriminate among different pieces of content more critical. For the brand and the quality of the information we encounter increasingly is embedded in each piece of content itself. We can no longer entirely depend on institutional names as the basis of our trust. And only by understanding and recognizing these different models can we identify what we are looking at, the critical first step in understanding, deconstructing, and recognizing what we can trust.

In some cases, the people producing the material are not even aware of what model they are operating under, as they adapt to new technology, grope to maintain an audience, endeavor to innovate, and bow to financial pressure.

For there are no media rules. There is no law that requires labeling. The First Amendment protects the right of all of us to write or broadcast freely. What we are dealing with in the media culture is a function of the free flow of information, and a marketplace for an audience undergoing such profound disruption that there are few common norms anymore. In this market, as we pick and choose from what is available on cable, online, in our e-mail in-boxes, and elsewhere, we are each creating our own news package. And almost all of it lays claim to being true.

Some might argue that identifying the kind of news one gets is irrelevant. Useful information can come from anywhere anytime. The notion of categories and labels is quaint but out-of-date. Who cares where news comes from or how it is reported? If it is useful, it has value.

That argument seems appealing at first blush. Redefine the parameters of the discussion, and voilà, the problem vanishes.

But in the real world, context matters. If information is presented as factual and disinterested, you will have one set of expectations. If it is presented as an analysis or argument, you will have another. When encountering a news story, you will expect an independent description of what has happened, with the basic facts offered in a way that everyone could agree with. If there are controversies, you expect to hear a basic outline of the different viewpoints. When encountering an analysis or argument, you might actually have lower expectations for how complete the description will be. But you likely will expect the argument to be outlined more fully, with more evidence behind it and perhaps some anticipation of and response to any objections that might occur to the audience.

Let's take a closer look at these news models so we might more quickly know what questions to ask to assess the information's value and validity.

The Journalism of Verification

What most of us think of as journalism, or as traditional news, is what we call the journalism of verification. This model has its roots in the first professional journalism of the seventeenth century, began to flower in the late nineteenth century, and became more refined in the twentieth. It places the highest value on getting things right—on facts over opinion.

Perhaps nothing characterizes the ethos of the journalism of verification better than something taught to aspiring young reporters at the City News Bureau of Chicago, who were trained to fear getting things wrong. The CNS, the country's first cooperative news agency, covered local news. It became famous for an axiom that captures the grizzled skepticism of the old tutors lurking there, who accepted nothing at face value and terrorized every student to corroborate and verify even the most likely assertions they encountered: "Kid, if your mother says she loves you, check it out."

The promise of truthfulness became a hallmark of the modern press that developed alongside democratic governments. The first identifiable newspaper, published in seventeenth-century England, promised to rely "on the best and most certain intelligence."[6] Across the channel, the editor of the first newspaper in France promised to "yield to nobody" in his effort to get "the truth" for his reports.[7] As the press in America began to break from political parties in the nineteenth century, at times using sensationalism to build an audience, the "yellow journalism" of Joseph Pulitzer and William Randolph Hearst also promised accuracy to audiences, even if it sometimes provided readers more the impression of it than the reality.[8] As journalism began to suffer from a crisis of confidence, triggered by fragmenting technology and declining trust at the beginning of the twenty-first century, accuracy and verification were at the heart of the effort of newspeople to regain their sense of purpose. In 2000, for instance, when the Committee of Concerned Journalists surveyed journalists about what values they considered most important to their work, 100 percent answered, "Getting the facts right." Sorting out accurate information from false has been so consistent a goal of traditional journalism throughout history that when we codified the values of the profession in our book *The Elements of Journalism*, the journalist's obligation to the truth emerged as the first principle.[9]

When the stakes are highest, those who aspire to the journalism of verification have taken even greater pains to be cautious and to explain their verification process. In 1939, when the World War II was sweeping through Europe, the *New York Times* explained why its readers could believe the new flood of foreign news the paper was publishing each day. The *Times* ran full-page ads in its foreign-report section explaining how it received and edited foreign copy, along with printed examples.

Later in the century, as the intellectual underpinnings of journalism became clearer, notions of accuracy became even more refined. Simply publishing facts was thought of as insufficient. The context, the impression the facts created and the journalistic presentation of them, had to be accurate too. To a significant degree, when people encounter news, it is this journalism of verification that they expect. It is news in its simplest form—stories telling what's new—that they imagine they are encountering.

The journalism of verification thus puts a high value on completeness: answering questions that the facts of an event may suggest and attempting to put these facts in a complete context so that they can be understood as they happened. The journalism of verification aspires to fulfill the first requirement of news, as identified by the Commission on Freedom of the Press, known as the Hutchins Commission, in 1947: to provide "a truthful, comprehensive, and intelligent account of the day's events in a context which gives them meaning." The report went on to say, "The first requirement is that the media should be accurate. They should not lie." And it added that those facts should be presented in a way "that can be understood. It is no longer enough to report *the fact* truthfully, it is now necessary to report *the truth about the fact*." (Italics are in the original report.)

How can people identify this traditional journalism of verification? The basic telltale signs are these: Look for the effort of verification. The hallmarks of vetted news involve a multiplicity of sources and a skepticism of what those sources say, and evidence the journalists has not accepted things at face value but has gone through the process of digging down into what has happened.

Look for clear signals to the audience when the reporting is necessarily more speculative and the evidence less solid. Look for stories that do not claim to possess all the answers. Look for stories that clearly signal what is not yet known. And look for stories that maintain clear lines between the facts and the analysis of those facts into meaning. Look, in other words, for empiricism and humility.

The journalism of verification, in short, is that which provides the most complete answers to questions we ask in the skeptical way of knowing.

The Journalism of Assertion

Gradually, almost imperceptibly, in the 1980s and 1990s the journalism of verification that had become more refined earlier in the twentieth century began to lose ground to a different model.

A continuous news culture, one that was largely live and built on extemporanous and highly mobile news gathering, began to form. The inevitable bias of this 24/7 news culture is that it places a premium on getting things out there, passing them along as quickly as possible. That is the technology's competitive advantage. But that advantage also puts less value on vetting information before releasing it. And it became a place where news sources could more easily assert whatever they wanted with less vetting or filtering.

The new model, the Journalism of Assertion, planted its first seed with the creation of an initially little-regarded cable channel in Atlanta, Georgia. Ironically enough, the dream at Cable News Network, or CNN, was to re-create in style and ethos a network news operation like that of the old broadcasters at CBS. Without recognizing or intending it, CNN invented something else.

In part, the shift was a function of technology and speed. CNN is on the air continuously and live; there are 1,440 minutes of time to fill each day, which means there's less time for checking stories out—particularly relative to the 22 minutes of network evening news. And in part, the new model was a function of economics. As outlets offering news grew in number and expanded into new platforms, they often did so with limited resources—fewer people to check the facts. Another factor was also at play. During the early days at CNN (often derided as standing for "Chicken Noodle News"), there was a strong sense that the technology was the star, not any news anchor or journalist. Inevitably perhaps, the practitioners played with the technology of continuous live news to see what it could do. In the control room, director Bob Furnad loved to air multiple images, often of material that had not been vetted.

CNN cofounder Ted Turner's goal was to create a television channel devoted exclusively to delivering news from around the world on a continuous, real-time basis. The theoretical advantages of his concept were clear. Audiences no longer had to wait for the evening broadcast or the next day's paper to get the news. Journalists could hear it and immediately report it. Every new interview or factoid seemed to be a scoop. Every few minutes presented a new deadline. It was an adrenaline rush. The news seemed organic. Reese Schonfeld, who cofounded CNN with Turner and described himself as the network's "news professional," remembered that ethos: "Live news had never been the raison d'être for a network. Who knew how it would work? [But] live was our métier. If we knew where to put the camera, if we guessed right, then the whole world would watch us."[10] Technology, in other words, was not just a tool; it was the system.

In 1990, Ted Turner said, "Here at CNN, we are the only network where we might go to a correspondent who says into the camera, 'We're here, and nothing is going on.'"[11]

What the practitioners barely noticed was that they had shifted the values and paradigms, if at first only a little. No doubt they got better when they got bigger and more established. But putting such a high value on getting things out there meant a lower value was placed on checking them out and getting them right.

Most cable news is live. The Project for Excellence in Journalism has consistently found that roughly 60 percent of all the programming on cable news is extemporaneous and unscripted. By contrast, less than 10 percent of the network evening news broadcast is "live" or extemporaneous, while 92 percent is edited. The difference is enormous. In taped and edited story packages, the journalists can vet and verify the facts they present. The pictures and the words—the two elements that create coherence and understanding—can be matched to create a clear meaning. The correspondent and producers can check the words used to contextualize the sound bites to make sure the right meaning is conveyed. In cable news, virtually all those capacities are not only less evident, but for much of the air time, they also do not exist. Even before the age of the opinionated talk show, the medium of cable TV had all but abandoned what was once the primary element of television news: the written and edited story, in which scripts are vetted prior to air and pictures are matched to fit those words and their meaning.[12]

The effect of all this is profound. In the journalism of assertion, what were once the raw ingredients of journalism—the rumor, innuendo, allegation, accusation, charge, supposition, and hypothesis—get passed on to the audience directly. The ingredients become the product. Slowly, by degrees, being immediate, and thus presumably interesting and provocative, became the point.

How can one recognize the journalism of assertion? The hallmarks are easily identified. This journalism is fundamentally stenographic. Work in which the journalist is a conduit, an enabler for sources and newsmakers, is the heart of the matter. There is an inherent passivity.

On television, in print, or online, a telltale sign of the journalism of assertion is newsmakers reciting talking points without being challenged.

Consider Arizona senator Jon Kyl's claims on CNN in the fall of 2009 that the Obama healthcare reform "would involve a five-hundred-billion-dollar cut in Medicare." Would it really? Anchor John King didn't probe, because CNN wanted to move to another segment: "We are out of time on this day," he said.

Look for moderators watching helplessly as guests talk over each other in passionate but ultimately confusing or even incoherent moments of cross fire. On NBC's *Meet the Press*, there is liberal talk show host Rachel

Maddow arguing with former Republican House majority leader Dick Armey about whether the liberal group MoveOn.org had run ads comparing George W. Bush to Adolf Hitler:

"They never did that," Maddow argued.

"They did do it," Armey insisted.

"They didn't do that," Maddow repeated.

Meet the Press's host David Gregory had opened the program promising, "this morning, a special hour-long discussion making sense of health care . . . separating fact from fiction in the fight."

So did such ads run? Gregory never sorted it out. Or was Armey correct when he asserted, "Seniors today are captured by Medicare. They have no choice. They can't get out of it if they want to without being punished by the government"?[13] Gregory didn't probe. He simply turned to Maddow and said, "Rachel?" She went on to discuss something else.[14]

Also watch for so-called analysts, particularly those with partisan backgrounds who make broad analytical generalizations without being challenged. In late July 2009, Lawrence O'Donnell, a Democratic pundit appearing on MSNBC's *Morning Joe*, assessed Sarah Palin's political future as she announced her resignation as governor of Alaska.

"There is no mystery to her political future," O'Donnell said. "We have settled history on this. When you lose as the vice presidential candidate in America, your career is over. It's done. In the TV age, not one person who has lost in the vice president slot has ever accomplished anything again in politics. Not one."

Is that true? No. But in the rush of talk and the cozy chattiness, neither of the two journalists noticed or wanted to point out that O'Donnell was egregiously wrong. Even without knowing much history, it's absurd to suggest that two major vice presidential candidates, one recent and one currently still serving, will never accomplish "anything again in politics." Robert Dole of Kansas, the losing vice presidential candidate of 1976, later served as majority leader and then minority leader of the Senate. For many years, he was among the most respected and influential lawmakers in the United States. Perhaps no other legislator of his generation, other than Edward Kennedy, put his stamp on so much legislation or changed so many American lives. In 1996, Dole was chosen to head his party's presidential ticket.

And currently, Joe Lieberman of Connecticut remained in the Senate after his defeat in the vice presidential slot in the 2000 election and eventually became chairman of the Homeland Security and Government Affairs Committee, as well as an influence in both national political parties. He became a pivotal swing vote and a key bridge for Democrats to the Republican party Senate leader John McCain.

The culture of immediacy has also changed the relationship between people who cover the news and the newsmakers they cover. Power is ceded away from the journalists who produce the content and toward the sources of information they rely on to fill airtime. In the journalism of assertion, the sources are in a position to dictate the terms of use. That is why officials and sources who trying to control the message the public hears vastly prefer to appear on live broadcasts. They can say whatever they want, filibuster, spin, and lie, putting the host in the position of having to listen carefully for lies while at the same time having to be skillful in pointing out any perceived lies without looking like a bully for doing so. This problem is much bigger than it might seem.

The journalism of assertion is less of a filter and more of a conduit. The people who might manipulate the report (the sources) have more influence, more power. It is the difference between the live interview and the edited one. It is the difference between carrying the press conference live and reviewing it on tape and using only those quotes that are accurate. Even if one is skeptical of journalists' ability to verify or mediate facts from assertions, or is distrustful of how well this task has been performed in the past, if a news organizations is no longer trying, we need to recognize that it has abdicated this task and that we are on our own. The news organization itself is unlikely to admit it.

By the late 1990s, this journalism of assertion was on the rise, even though there was just one cable news channel. It gained even more force with the advent of the World Wide Web and the growth of additional cable news channels. The notion of posting first and letting the verification process occur after publication through audience reaction to the information became a standard, taking on influence even at the Web sites of older media.

The Web created the opportunity for organizations that had been largely limited to print to compete in an area they had lost a generation earlier: breaking news. Online, newspapers can rival television, radio, and cable as sources for live events. The *New York Times* Web site can, a little after nine A.M. on the East Coast, display tomorrow's story from the

Middle East atop its homepage. And as print newsrooms have shrunk, amid declining resources, they've cut back on copyediting. In 2008, for instance, the *Washington Post* instituted a "two-touch rule." Every story would be touched only twice between its submission by the reporter and its posting online or in print. Any further editing would be too costly and would slow the process down.

The new conditions that prevail in newsrooms are highlighted in this op-ed by Clark Hoyt, then *New York Times* public editor, about his exchange with Joe Sexton, the paper's metro editor, regarding an early post of *Times* reporting about Senator Edward Kennedy:

"'I don't think we should be driven to throw out any rules or standards for the sake of haste,'" [Sexton] said, 'and generally I don't think we do.' That's true [Hoyt replied] as far as it goes, but print deadlines are established, and journalists work all day toward them. The Web has no deadlines, just the anxiety that the guy down the street will beat you to the story, and you have to get yours published fast."[15]

Stories are posted online, and bloggers write quick accounts for their news organizations that might become fuller stories the next day. By and large, these accounts are not edited. In a 2008 study of newspapers, the Project for Excellence in Journalism found that even among blogs produced by papers' own staffers, only 18 percent were edited prior to being posted.

In a sense the bias toward speed over accuracy is built into the nature of the technology. It is something as close to a physical law as might exist in the realm of news and information: Speed, in news, is the enemy of accuracy. The less time one has to produce something, the more errors it will contain. Platforms such as cable television and live blogging are so oriented to instant transmission that there is no time for vetting those transmissions.

Those who practice the journalism of assertion, to the extent they are aware of doing so, argue that a postpublication vetting process occurs. With more sources, they claim, the truth will be sorted out over time—perhaps even more accurately than it would have been in the old journalism of verification. This might be called the pure marketplace view of truthfulness and accuracy. Implicit in this argument is that the truth has a way of making itself known in the end. In practice, something more nuanced occurs. The marketplace of truth works if the inquiry into a subject is robust and prolonged. For a good deal of news, perhaps the vast majority, the press and public attention simply move on—and in the era of assertion, the tendency to move on has accelerated.

A second complication to the marketplace-view-of-truth argument is that misinformation that has entered the marketplace is often sifted out over time and in a context that may function outside the realm of political events and sometimes even journalism itself. The Bush administration in 2002 and 2003, for instance, operated in the belief that Iraq was developing weapons of mass destruction. In a political atmosphere of support for going to war against Iraq, the press writ large did not challenge those claims, though some reporters and news organizations did. The truth about the weapons of mass destruction was discovered years later, after the political meaning of the truth had shifted markedly. In the journalism of assertion, such mistakes are more common. The same might be said of the causes and effects of the recent recession or the debate over health care reform. Sources of news in positions of established and official authority have a stronger hand. For them, it is easier to assert misinformation. Journalists devote less time to checking these sources' facts and more time to simply arranging content for dissemination. The press is more of a conduit, an enabler of its sources. And as the journalism of assertion grows, those tendencies grow with it, becoming more of a factor in what we know and how we know it.

The challenge for those who produce the news, and those who consume it, is to apply human values against the inherent bias of the technology. The people involved must assert the values of accuracy and verification. It is not inevitable that the journalism of verification will recede. But the technology will tend in that direction unless opposing pressure is applied.

Certainly there is value in instantaneous information. There are events that we simply want to see or hear for ourselves, even in summary form: What did the president say in his speech in the Middle East? How did the stock market close? Did my team win? Did the jury convict in that trial? What happened in the press conference? Did they find the wreckage of that plane? What are the latest headlines?

But this is a limited category of stories, and the transmission of some of them—airing live a president's speech or a press conference or a video of a car chase—is as much or more a matter of technology than it is journalism. Quickly, we may want more information: Why did my team lose? Are the charges made in the press conference true? How did the audience in Cairo react to the president's speech?

In the journalism of assertion, the reporters and hosts and anchors rarely provide answers. They arrange discussions. They pose questions. But fundamentally the mind-set here has shifted to partisan sources arguing over possible answers. The talking points on both sides are offered—though often only those from the polarized edges of the debate. But less often are these talking points examined for accuracy.

The Journalism of Affirmation

As the barriers to entry in news reporting fell, a journalism model emerged that at first glance seems rooted in the past, though in fact it is in many ways quite new and quite different than anything seen before.

It is a neo-partisan form of news—the news of the talk show star posing as an anchor, of one-sided or lopsided broadcast segments, of cherry-picked facts. We call this model the Journalism of Affirmation, for its appeal is in affirming the preconceptions of the audience, assuring them, gaining their loyalty, and then converting that loyalty into advertising revenue.

This is different from the eighteenth- and nineteenth-century partisan press in the United States, in which the newspapers were controlled by political figures and operated with little or no expectation of financial return. Their purpose was to rally political support, extend ideas, and influence the ballot box. Today, the new journalism of affirmation often occurs in a commercial context. The owners of these news outlets are typically corporations, and the hosts or writers usually must justify their product in economic terms; the viewpoints broadcast or published may or may not represent those of the corporate owners. It is hardly clear, for instance, that the executives who run General Electric agree with the progressivism of Ed Schultz or Rachel Maddow.

But there is generally a political purpose to the journalism of affirmation as well. The practitioners of this work—whether on the air or online or in print—are strongly ideological, often demagogic. And what they offer audiences usually falls more squarely into the arena of propaganda, persuasion, and manipulation than anything else. Verification is not its primary goal. Nor is it passive like the journalism of assertion.

Its economic model is based on delivering a product that affirms its audience's preconceptions.

The most immediate roots of this new commercial neo-partisan media are found in the rise of talk radio in the late 1980s and early 1990s and in figures like Rush Limbaugh. In 1996, when Fox News was launched, Fox News president and former GOP political consultant Roger Ailes recognized an important reality about his young network. Ailes knew his channel could not compete with CNN, given the fewer number of bureaus and staffers it had. But Ailes, who had started in television in the 1960s as a young producer of the highly successful daily talk and variety program *The Mike Douglas Show* in Cleveland, Ohio, was a brilliant TV producer. He recognized that the audience who listened to talk radio during the day could be persuaded to watch talk-radio-style TV at night. Ailes had tried and failed to make Limbaugh into a TV star before taking over Fox News. Limbaugh's syndicated half-hour TV program ran from 1992 to 1996 but never really took off. At Fox News, Ailes tried a new cast of prime-time hosts. One of them was an old TV hand, Bill O'Reilly, a former network correspondent who, after falling out at CBS and ABC, subsequently hosted two syndicated tabloid shows, *A Current Affair* and *Inside Edition*. Another was Sean Hannity, a relatively unknown radio talk show host whom Ailes had found in Atlanta and wanted to pair against some liberal host yet to be determined. Some other early shows, such as *The Crier Report* with former judge and CNN and ABC anchor Catherine Crier, did not survive.

Opinion news traditionally had been the province of print. Opinion journalism was dominated by the more intellectual press, by the *National Review*, the *American Spectator*, the *Nation*, the *New York Review of Books*. The op-ed pieces were heavily reported, and though they were not delivering the news, they were cogitating on it.

In the journalism of affirmation, however, the opinion press was delivering news in real time, and commenting on it as well. There was an intermingling of breaking news, opinion, and interviews that was new and fast.

In time, Fox's success building on opinion entertainment programming in talk radio led the way for MSNBC to find traction as a liberal opinion network with hosts like Keith Olbermann, Rachel Maddow, and Ed Schultz, the No. 1 rated liberal radio talk show host in the country. And something new was forming and shaping our politics.

In 1998, linguist Deborah Tannen coined a term for the kind of discourse she saw in the journalism of assertion. She called it the "Argument Culture," one that grew out of a conviction that opposition itself can lead to truth:

> In the argument culture, criticism, attack, or opposition are the predominant if not the only ways of responding to people or ideas . . . It is not the *automatic* nature of this response that I am calling attention to—and calling into question. Sometimes passionate opposition, strong verbal attack, are appropriate and called for . . . What I question is the ubiquity, the knee-jerk nature, of approaching almost any issue, problem, or public person in an adversarial way. One of the dangers of the habitual use of adversarial rhetoric is a kind of verbal inflation—a rhetorical boy who cried wolf: The legitimate, necessary denunciation is muted, even lost, in the general cacophony of oppositional shouting . . . The argument culture limits the information we get rather than broadening it.[16]

In the journalism of affirmation, the argument culture has given way to something else, the "Answer Culture." In this new incarnation, hosts are not staging *Crossfire*-style debates and are not neutral moderators. Their appeal is not in the questions they ask. It is in the answers they have already arrived at before the show has begun. They offer to the audience the illusion of putting things in order. They are not offering information, something people already are awash in. In the Answer Culture, the certitude and aggrievement of the radio talk show has come to the news show. They are offering answers.

The appeal of the journalism of affirmation is, in part, a response to the confusion of the 24/7 news culture. If information is coming quickly and overabundantly, knowledge, paradoxically, is harder to come by. When information is in greater supply, knowledge is harder, not easier, to create, because we have to sift through more facts, more assertions, more stuff, to arrive at it. An abundance of information often means more dissonance, more contradictions. The journalism of affirmation creates the impression that it is putting something in order, making sense of it, helping us understand what it means. The appeal of the journalism of affirmation is similar to that of the security and convenience offered by faith, as opposed to fact and empiricism.

Rush Limbaugh, the emerging media personality of the 1990s, may not have initially claimed to be a journalist. "I'm proud to be an entertainer. This is showbiz. At the same time, I believe everything I say," he has said, among various self-descriptions of his role.[17] But his followers in the new century, from Hannity to Olbermann, sometimes have claimed journalistic mantles. On election-night coverage on cable, in particular, it has become a source of controversy over whether characters like Olbermann, Lou Dobbs, and Chris Matthews should be allowed to host. (CNN used Dobbs briefly and pulled back. In 2008, MSNBC used Olbermann and Matthews, which drew public criticism from Republicans and private criticism from newspeople inside NBC.[18])

How do we recognize the journalism of affirmation? Look for an anchor tipping his hand by affirming one side of an argument or another. Look for graphics at the bottom of the screen that affirm a particular view of the news, even if the narrator sounds more neutral, such as the "Tea Party USA Growing Revolution" ticker on Fox's April 6 *America's Newsroom* daytime program. It is evident in programs whose hosts, such as Rachel Maddow, invite mostly guests they agree with. It is in segments that always allow one side to get the last word. It is occurring when an interviewer uses guests as foils or targets. And it is evident when a host battles guests whom he imagines the audience despises, asking "Do you still beat your wife?" style questions.

That is the kind of question, for instance, that Bill O'Reilly opened with in a 2008 interview with Massachusetts congressman Barney Frank on Fox News. Why, O'Reilly asked, didn't Frank resign his chairmanship of the House Finance Committee because of the economic collapse?

Frank dismissed the suggestion and said O'Reilly had the facts wrong, that he never encouraged people to invest in the stock market. O'Reilly, perhaps calculatingly, became enraged. And the conversation devolved into ad hominem attacks from both sides—a kind of entertaining combat that might have thrilled partisan audiences but that certainly represented something far different from journalistic inquiry.

"Oh, none of this was your fault! Oh, no. People lost millions of dollars. It wasn't your fault. Come on, you coward. Say the truth," O'Reilly screamed at Frank.

Frank responded, "What do you mean coward?"

O'Reilly said, "You're a coward. You blame everybody else. You're a coward."

Frank replied, "Bill, here's the problem with going on your show. You start ranting, and the only way to respond is to almost look as boorish as you."

The cross talk, at high decibel, went on for several minutes, with the frustration level rising on both sides. At one point O'Reilly suggested that Frank, who is gay, was not "man enough" to admit a mistake.

The journalism of affirmation is a netherworld of pseudo reality. Real life is too complex and too messy to toe a party line.

Some may wonder why we use the term journalism of affirmation. Isn't this new partisan media a variation of opinion journalism, like something in the *National Review* or the *Nation*, only now on television or the radio?

In our minds, they are distinctly different. One distinction is that traditional opinion journalism, as found in the *National Review*, the *Nation*, *Harper's*, and the *Weekly Standard*, is primarily engaged in the contemplation of news, not the coverage of it on a daily, let alone hourly, basis. Those magazines spend their effort primarily trying to cogitate and reflect on the implication of events. They do not also represent themselves as a platform for neutral or straight reporters to portray events in the first place, conduct interviews, offer daily news reports with a first-hand account. In the journalism of affirmation, the players have mingled the roles, offering daily delivery of news, while building their audience base largely around opinion. As news organizations, they raise expectations that they will cover the news comprehensively, in proportion, and without fear of alienating or favoring any one side—key elements of traditional news gathering. But they have built their prime time—their front page that most people see—around ideological affinity, and those two actions are often at odds.

Another difference is that the tradition of opinion journalism in the United States has sat squarely in the realm of the journalism of verification. That legacy, once again, begins above all with fidelity to getting the facts right and following them where they may lead. Because traditional opinion journalism is involved in contemplating the meaning of events after they have occurred, and usually at some remove, it typically allows more time and takes more care than even traditional daily journalism to ensure factual correctness. Indeed, this devotion to accuracy has tended to be sacred among opinion journalists and in the alternative press, both of which operate outside the notion of impartiality, precisely because accuracy, rather than neutrality, is the basis of their claim to fairness.[19]

The journalists who work in these traditional opinion models share the same aspiration as others who work in the journalism of verification: to inspire citizens to think. Their work is rooted in the facts they marshal to build the arguments on which the opinion they describe is based. That is a far different goal from that of activists or propagandists who populate talk radio and cable, whose aim is to forge a certain political result, or their talk show cousins, who want to gin up an audience and make a buck, however sincere their ideology. The goal of the opinion journalist is to develop public understanding by exploring facts. The media demagogues are exploiting facts on behalf of political faction or commercial ratings. And this difference, as we will describe in Chapter 7, can clearly be seen in the way affirmation journalists use evidence and their attitude toward those with whom they disagree.

Interest-Group Journalism

As traditional newsrooms have shrunk, political interest groups have found new openings to influence the political dialogue. These groups have recognized that they can create journalism of their own, control how it is put together, and send it out to get picked up in the more widely distributed mainstream press. A key element in this has been a shift in thinking in traditional newsrooms. As declining revenues led to budget cuts, newsrooms could no longer cover every story with their own staff. The technology of the Web has also made aggregation, or being a gateway to the work of others, something consumers expect and something more readily possible for news organizations to effect. At the same time, technology makes it possible for anyone to enter the news field, at fairly low cost, by producing their own content.

Into this shifting news landscape have come both citizens offering their own personal blogs and community news sites, what many call citizen journalism. However, the new environment has also attracted news political interest groups, whose primary purpose is not producing journalism but effecting political outcomes. Shaping the public discourse is a critical element in helping advance those outcomes. Think tanks, political groups, so-called public interest groups, often well financed, are increasingly creating their own Web sites and producing their own reporting.

BigGovernment.com, which produced the undercover exposés of the liberal group ACORN, is one example. Libertarian political activists who believe a large government is a drag on liberty and commerce created Watchdog.org, a network of Web sites, funded by a group called the Sam Adams Alliance, that produce reports on government waste, fraud, and abuse. Finding out Watchdog.org's origins, however, is complicated: The Web site says it is "a collection of independent journalists covering state-specific and local government activity." It also says the project is "the brainchild of the Franklin Center for Government & Public Integrity, a 501(c)3 non-profit organization dedicated to promoting new media journalism." With enough digging on the Franklin Center's site, one can see mention of the Sam Adams Alliance, a libertarian group. But this group's particular nonprofit status allows them not to disclose where that funding comes from, and the real purpose of Watchdog.org, by all practical purposes, is masked.

The work of such groups can substantially influence the media. The ACORN story was promoted heavily by Fox, became a major news event, and eventually influenced a vote in Congress. A Watchdog.org story that found some problems in states' accounting of how many jobs were created or saved by President Barack Obama's stimulus package was picked up by the Associated Press and others.

While the reporting in each individual story may be sound, consumers should be mindful of the intent behind the work, which can substantially affect the selection of what gets covered and what does not. If the subtext of every story on a Web site points in the same direction—that government is bad and inefficient, for instance, or that conservatives do not care about social justice—that is a sign of something important about the site's agenda, even if each story is produced in the seemingly neutral tones of a conventional wire service story. Often the reporting on these sites, like the ACORN exposés, have some or even many of the characteristics of a classic watchdog investigation. The larger tip-off is what the totality of the coverage conveys. In our book *The Elements of Journalism*, we note that a core principle of the traditional journalism of verification is that "the news should be comprehensive and proportional." That involves the notion that if a news organization really intends to cover a subject, it should do so fully, so the audience can get a fair and complete picture of what is portrayed, good and bad. As the Hutchins Commission suggested, news organizations should report not just the facts but also the truth about the facts in a broader context. A failure to do this is akin to a cartographer drawing a map but leaving out inconvenient details. While artful, a medieval rendering of the globe that only guessed about the New World or portrayed geography to fit a political worldview was less useful for actual navigation. This new genre of interest group journalism often fails to meet this full-coverage standard, precisely because a comprehensive, accurate map is not its goal. Political persuasion is.

What are the telltale signs that an outlet purporting to be a news organization is really a political interest group producing journalism? One sign is funding sources that aren't genuinely and thoroughly transparent. Another is that the stories all point in a single direction or to a single repetitive conclusion. If every story says the same thing, beware. Look at the full history of the people involved, where they have worked, and how much of their work has been political activism. Try to learn about the totality of the work that the funders and the groups involved do, and whether some of it is political in nature.

If the funding isn't genuinely transparent, if the people and even journalists involved have a political history, if the stories all move toward one conclusion and the connections of the organizations involved (to the extent one can detect) have more to do with politics than news, these are all red flags that you are in a zone of interest-group journalism.

The Journalism of Aggregation

A word must be offered about other forms of media that have emerged—if only to clarify what they represent and how they fit into the discussion. One of the most important new media forms is built not on producing news but on harnessing and organizing existing information. This is aggregation.

In our minds, aggregation is an act of journalism. It does not constitute a model, like the other four we have discussed, because it may involve many types of content. It is relevant, however, precisely because what one chooses to aggregate, to pass along, to recommend, to sort, involves normative evaluation of content. To aggregate well, one must know the other models.

Some might, at first blush, rankle at the idea that aggregation itself is a kind of journalism, thinking it just involves machines and algorithms searching for keywords. But aggregation is editing. It is making choices about relevance, value, and significance. And increasingly, each of us acts as our own editor, our own aggregator, assembling our own diet of news every day. We are also increasingly interacting with others about the news, about what we like and what we recommend and what we don't. The discussion that once occurred across the breakfast table with our family now occurs all day long with friends and even strangers, whether through the e-mails we send to friends, the summaries we upload at work, the recommendations we post on user sites like Reddit, or the material we post or follow on social networks.

News organizations themselves have shifted their view on aggregation. In the first years of the new century, traditional news organizations tended to dismiss aggregation as something merely mechanical. In truth, aggregation has always been an essential part of what journalists do; gathering what others have produced, organizing it, and making it more easily available—whether sports statistics from the professional sports leagues, or the stock tables from the various exchanges, or crime reports from the local precinct. Some journalists, defensive and sometimes impudent, had forgotten this. They had fallen into a common trap, confusing the techniques they tended to use most often—working the phones, face-to-face interviewing, attending events and meetings, bearing witness firsthand—with the larger purpose they were fulfilling: gathering information in whatever form and making it comprehensible and useful for audiences.

More recently—though to some extent late to the game—news organizations have come to inevitably recognize that with information so plentiful, organizing it was an act of journalism too. Even the most traditional news sites began to offer audiences not just original content but also highlights of other sites' content. Consider that a 2006 study found that only three of twenty-four Web sites from major traditional news organizations offered links to outside content. A year later, half of them did. By 2009, one could go to a *New York Times* article online and find links to the *Washington Post's* coverage of the same subject. Part of this change occurred because of a shift in understanding. Part of it was economic necessity. As traditional news organizations' resources shrank amid declining revenues, aggregation became an even more important part of the service journalists were offering. Unable to even pretend to do everything—to "cover the waterfront" in the classic language of the press—traditional news organizations focused on what they did best and borrowed or aggregated the rest. The bigger issue for those in the news business was not *whether* to aggregate but *how*. Were computer algorithms that gathered everything—in effect the Google News model—an effective form of aggregation? Or was employing some human sensibility, filtering out dubious things and recommending only the most trusted, a better approach?

As consumers, we are all aggregators. And the question of filtering is a matter of values. What kind of content do we choose or ignore? What do we include in our mix? What do we reject? It might be an amalgam of different models that we include in building "My News." Many of us may aggregate elements of all the four models of journalism enumerated above. So as we aggregate, how do we discriminate among the models? And we must discriminate, or the values of the press will become more confused, our ability to know what to believe will become more limited. Now, increasingly, it is up to each of us, as consumers, to practice the journalism of aggregation.

Our point here is that aggregation has a subjective and an ethical dimension. Just as we will help you identify what news is reliable and discern the different motives and norms of the different models of journalism, we also want you to recognize that how and from where you aggregate your news involves a qualitative and a normative choice.

Blogging and Social Media

Where do blogging and social media fit among the models of journalism?

Contrary to what some may think, bloggers do not fall squarely into any one model. Given the enthusiasm for interactive engagement, blogging is perhaps the most ubiquitous of the new forms of communication. But blogging does not describe a set of journalistic norms; it is only a form. Many of the blogs at traditional news sites operate by the same journalistic norms as the sites' other platforms, though the language may be more informal. But some blogs at these sites do not. There are blogs whose editorial content supports advocacy, including activist blogs such as Daily Kos. There are blogs, such as those produced by Brian Williams at NBC, that are largely about explaining journalistic decision making.

Some blogs are much closer to opinion columns, such as Andrew Sullivan's. Others are very close to traditional citizen-community-service journalism, such as Baltimore Grows, which tracks the progress and financing of different real estate projects in Baltimore, Maryland. At Myreporter.com, professional journalists answer reader-submitted questions about coastal North Carolina, like "What is the telephone-size pole about one mile south of Midway Road on Route 211?"

Then there are niche blogs such as Techcrunch (www.techcrunch.com), an extremely successful site about technology issues, including breaking business news (it broke a story about a new Google-designed phone), public issues like net neutrality, and gadget reviews. And then there are some that are hard to categorize at all, such as Boing Boing (http://boingboing .net), a popular blog that has news and information about everything from technology to celebrities, art, and culture. The reason Boing Boing is interesting is because of what it unearths and writes about. It has a unique voice that readers return to. This Week in Education (www.thisweekineducation .com) is a good example of a niche blog that is public-issues focused, covering education policy, both federal and local, and general education news. Thousands of such blogs about public issues exist, covering tax policy, government waste, the military, etc.

In a sense, blogs are like muffins. They are one shape, but the batter that goes into it might run the gamut from chocolate cake to bran. The same is true of social media forms such as Twitter or social network sites. They are ways of conveying information, but they do not dictate the nature of the content conveyed.

The New Hybrid

Some news outlets increasingly mix different kinds of content. Huffington Post began as a salon of different bloggers and has moved into aggregation and even has a smattering of original exposés, though the outlet has a political orientation. Talking Points Memo, a liberal blog that moved toward a kind of synthesis and analysis of journalism (more than actual shoe-leather reporting), has adapted aggregation. When you find a news outlet that's hard to categorize, look at the totality of the work and draw a general impression of both the effort made and its purpose. There may be works in the journalism of verification there. There may be instances of fast, assertive journalism. There may be ideological blogging and commentary that is close to a journalism of affirmation. Probe the content to get a clear sense of who the authors are and what their real purpose is. For hybrid sites or outlets, you need to ask an additional question: What is the bulk of effort made up of here? Is this mainly an aggregation site with a little bit of reporting? Is it mainly ideological blogging, with some wire-copy headlines attached?

Identifying what you are reading is not simply a matter of buyer beware. You must learn to discriminate, to know what kind of journalism it represents, to discover the norms and motives lurking in the work—what the journalists are trying to do. It is the first step, but a critical one, in knowing what to trust. Once you have done this, then comes the work of knowing how to navigate, of walking the other steps of the skeptical way of knowing.

CHAPTER 4

Completeness: What Is Here and What Is Missing?

At a conference of science writers in the 1990s, reporter John Crewdson ruffled a few feathers by describing the kind of journalism he did *not* produce. He was not a "stenographer interviewing people and dutifully writing down what they said."

Indeed not. Crewdson has made a career of producing work that challenges conventional understanding and explodes myths about various subjects, from science to transportation. In 1989, at the *Chicago Tribune*, he produced a fifty-thousand-word history about the discovery of the AIDS virus. It took months of research and earned him the science writing award from the American Association for the Advancement of Science. It also earned him the enmity of a great portion of the American scientific community and a good many science writers as well. Crewdson's dogged research had led him to challenge the self-promoting claim of Dr. Robert Gallo, a scientist at the National Institutes of Health in Washington, D.C., who claimed he had discovered the AIDS virus. Following a lead by another scientist who doubted Gallos, Crewdson dug through mountains of research documents and medical journals and interviewed researchers to educate himself on the subject. He compiled a compelling case that two French scientists, Luc Montagnier and Françoise Barré-Sinoussi at the Pasteur Institute in Paris, were the first to isolate and identify the virus. Twenty years later, the 2008 Nobel Prize was awarded to Montagnier and Barré-Sinoussi, in recognition that "these two persons awarded today made the discovery. They provided the virus."

While working on the Gallo story, Crewdson frequently flew back and forth to Paris. On one flight, an announcement asking if a doctor was on board came over the PA system. Crewdson began wondering about the relative risk of having a serious illness tens of thousands of feet in the air over the middle of the ocean and about what precautions airlines took for such a risk. After finishing the Gallo story, Crewdson did a search for flight attendants who had posted a personal profile on AOL and sent a blanket e-mail to those he found asking what happened when people got sick on an airplane. One attendant responded that she had been on a flight on which a passenger had died, and the story she told Crewdson set him on the trail of another groundbreaking area of reporting.

The passenger, Steven Paul Somes, vice president of State Street Research and Management in Boston, had died October 18, 1995, after suffering heart failure on a flight to California. A few details of the incident made clear to Crewdson that it could be a teaching moment of risk and reward.[1] Crewdson set about reconstructing the events. Somes lay flat on his back on the floor of United Airlines Flight 32 as it soared over the Rocky Mountains surrounded by three physicians, a nurse, and a paramedic, who were also on the flight. Why should a man die in the midst of as much medical help as could have been assembled by the average hospital emergency room? Crewdson wondered. He discovered that the dramatic and frantic effort to save Somes's life was futile because there were no cardiac drugs or defibrillator equipment on the plane.

"They had literally the right people on board," Somes's personal doctor said when told of the circumstances of his patient's death. "He was better off having this happen in the airplane than if it had happened in his living room. The bottom line is that they couldn't change the outcome because they didn't have some of the things they needed."

Neither the Federal Aviation Administration nor the airlines, Crewdson reported, could say how many people got sick in American airplanes or even how many died. They didn't know because the airlines weren't required to report such information. As one official told him, the FAA is an "*Aviation*" agency. "We're interested in accidents not heart attacks."

Crewdson dug up data that neither airlines nor government regulators had ever gathered about domestic and foreign carriers. What he uncovered showed that more than seven hundred emergency medical landings had been made each year in the United States, more than twelve thousand in-flight emergencies had occurred, and at least 114 and maybe as many as 360 people had died annually in flight. Passengers, he discovered, were more likely to die of a heart attack or illness in flight than in a crash.

"In cases of cardiac arrest the best hope for survival, and often the only hope, is immediate defibrillation," he reported. "But despite the increasing affordability of portable electronic defibrillators only two international airlines currently carry the lifesaving machines."

Airlines had long taken the position that the best thing they could do for a sick passenger was to make a fast landing at the nearest airport. The problem was, Crewdson established, that the vast majority of in-flight medical emergencies did not result in an unscheduled landing. The American Transport Association, representing the airline industry, had aggressively lobbied against requiring more sophisticated medical emergency equipment and training. Its argument: Airplanes "cannot be flying hospitals."

Then Crewdson went further. He explored how other countries had drawn different conclusions about medical care in flight. The doctor who worked to place the first defibrillators on British airliners, for instance, dismissed the U.S. carriers' concerns about the difficulty of training nonmedical personnel to use them: "You can teach a milkman how to do a defibrillation in 20 minutes."

Crewdson compared two life-threatening emergencies that had occurred on air carriers from different countries: a United Airlines flight on which the passenger died and a British Airways flight on which the passenger survived. The doctor who treated the British Airways passenger said that the medical kits on U.S. airlines were so limited that he would never have attempted to perform a life-saving procedure with them. In contrast with those then carried on U.S. airlines, the medical kits aboard many international airlines were smaller than an ordinary suitcase and stocked with most of the same cardiac drugs found in hospital emergency rooms, along with medications for seizures, pain relief, narcotic overdoses, and psychotic behavior. Such kits on British Airways, Lufthansa, Air France, Quantas, Alitalia, and other international airlines had saved numerous lives.

"It might seem gratuitous to question the wisdom of installing a

$1,100 medical kit or even a $3,000 defibrillator on a $170 million air-
plane, the price of the newest Boeing 747," Crewdson wrote to introduce
a ten-page story devoted to an item-by-item analysis of the cost that
would be involved in supplying every airliner in the United States with
life-saving medical kits and equipment and training staff in their use.
"The total needed for outfitting every U.S. commercial jet with medical
kits and defibrillators—about $56 million over the next 10 years—could
be raised by adding two cents to the price of every airline ticket sold."

The report, in the June 30, 1996, edition of the *Chicago Tribune*, ended
with his cost-benefit analysis: "Medical kits and defibrillators would be
economically justified if they saved just 3 lives each year."

The story became a national event. As public awareness of the health
risk of the lack of medical equipment spread, an industry that had aggressively resisted change began to act. Within a year, American Airlines
put defibrillators aboard its planes. The other airlines' lawyers suggested
that their clients should follow suit or face negligence lawsuits. Officials
at O'Hare International Airport in Chicago installed defibrillators in the
terminals, where people had died running to make their flight. Other
airports followed O'Hare's lead, and soon defibrillators began to appear
in public spaces across the country.

In a simple but dramatic way, Crewdson's journalism demonstrates the
value of facts gathered from multiple sources, transparently documented,
all leading to the same conclusion. The question that occurred to him as
he flew across the ocean is the kind of question that all of us have asked
ourselves at one time or another. As a journalist, he was able to go further,
gathering data and interviewing experts and officials. His questioning
approach was so thorough, his reporting so complete, and his case so well
documented that his analysis couldn't be ignored. Ten years after first installing defibrillators on its aircraft, American Airlines reported that
eighty lives had been saved by the devices.

The first question we should ask when encountering news and information is what kind of content it is. The second question we should ask
relates to another broad issue:

Is the information complete; and if not, what is missing?

Most journalism, indeed most information we encounter as consumers,
does not operate at the level of Crewdson's deep inquiry into airline

medical equipment or the discovery of AIDS. Much of it is more steno-graphic and incremental—by necessity. What happened today at the White House? Did the stock market rise or fall?

Yet we should ask about the completeness of any news content we en-counter. Are we getting from it what we should realistically expect?

On the first day of an introductory journalism class—the traditional trade-school approach of teaching the craft—students are usually ac-quainted with some basic catechism about thoroughness. Often this is distilled into the idea of "the five Ws and one H": the idea that all stories should explain the Who, What, When, Where, Why, and How of the story. Put more plainly, every news story should tell us who did what, when they did it, where they did it, why they did it, and how they did it. Though basic, the questions are a helpful starting point.

Let's apply them to the most basic kind of news story.

Straight News Accounts: Facts About Events

The simplest story we are likely to encounter is the "straight news" ac-count of a single unfolding event. Straight news is content that offers us new facts about what happened, what was learned yesterday, or what is scheduled to take place today. It is a simple recitation of facts, like those found in a brief radio- or TV-headline summary. "The president said this today." "The Pirates won four to two." "The House passed the bill they had been debating last night along a party-line vote." Often it is the first account of something, about which the details have yet to fully emerge or play out. "The mayor promised a new plan for building roads, which he will reveal next week."

Straight news is the kind of "commodity" that often is so ubiquitous we don't have to seek it out: It comes to us almost by osmosis. Once you've heard about a piece of straight news from a friend, on a car radio, or from a glance at a news Web site, you might not bother to learn more about it. It is the type of news we are likely to see aggregated on Web sites coming from wire services.

Our expectations about such stories' completeness are the simplest and easiest to comprehend. Take for example this headline in the Metro Section of the *Washington Post,* May 7, 2009:

"Burst Pipe Floods Homes in District," "Water Main Break in Adams Morgan Disrupts Traffic."

The story begins: "A 20-inch water main in the Adams Morgan neighborhood broke yesterday during the morning rush hour, flooding homes and businesses and triggering traffic problems that extended into the evening."[2]

The lead paragraph contains three of the five Ws—what happened (a pipe broke), where (the Adams Morgan neighborhood in D.C.), and when (May 6, 2009). The Who of the story (the fire department and the victims of the flood) are quoted later, starting in the second paragraph. The Why of the story is dealt with in the fourth paragraph (the fire department isn't sure why the pipe burst but guesses it was because of a combination of age, fluctuating temperature, and corrosive soil conditions). The How is self evident: The pipe broke, the water gushed, the roads and buildings were flooded. No H is required. How complete is the story? Not bad.

The five Ws and one H are useful as far as they go. But there is another question here that people might want answered about the water main break. In the months prior to this story, pipes had been breaking all over Washington, D.C., and nearby counties. Why were so many breaking all of a sudden? What are the authorities doing about the trend? What, for that matter, can be done? Those questions are not dealt with in this brief news story.[3]

Add Q—Questions Raised

In trying to address how complete a story or news account or any piece of content is, we would add one other element to the five Ws and one H. Call it the Q of the story: Are any *questions* raised about the event in the audience's mind? And are those questions mentioned in some way?

As we will discuss, the Q of the story may be the most important part of thinking about the story's completeness. The questions that the news opens for us are as important as the answers the news may provide. Questions open inquiry.

There is another important point in the matter of the Q, or the questions raised. For years, journalists have been taught to make their stories seem airtight, even omniscient. Many have been taught the axiom "Never raise a question in a story you cannot answer." The idea is that this makes the story seem more authoritative and less speculative. In fact, this advice is a mistake, even perhaps a delusion. We call it false omniscience. Questions will arise in the audience's mind. The facts raise the questions by themselves, and the thinking reader or viewer will inevitably wonder.

A story that fails to make clear what the next questions are is less complete than one that does. Journalism should open inquiry. Its purpose, ultimately, is deliberation of public life. And modern journalism, which is more dialogue than lecture, must do this even more.

So consider, as you encounter even the most basic stories, what questions the events raise. Look for journalism that has the humility to ask questions that cannot yet be answered, that acknowledges what it does not know, and that does not infer conclusions it cannot prove. Such stories are more complete, not less.

The Importance of Facts

The issues of completeness, straight news, and the five Ws and one H raise another point that deserves some attention. The news, and our inquiry as citizens, should be built on a foundation of facts.

So in examining a story, report, or news account in any form, we should begin with what facts are offered. In our list of the questions that make up the tradecraft of verification and active skepticism, there is an inevitable overlap. Checking whether something is complete involves looking at sources, evidence, potential bias, and more. But all that inquiry stems from whether the content brings forward facts and documents them. If it doesn't, it is by definition moving toward something less trustworthy.

Given the immediacy and pace of the journalism of assertion, even straight news accounts are often incomplete and fragmentary. That is the model's weakness. When you see fragments, but lack the whole picture, that is a tip-off that you are in the neighborhood of assertion rather than verification.

In the journalism of affirmation, the signs are different still. As we will discuss in more detail in Chapter 7, often the stories move too quickly to speculation and opinion, and there is an absence of facts, or a careful cherry picking of facts, to make a simple case. And the questions the account raises are often rhetorical: "Isn't it interesting that we have not been told X." Or, "Now I would really like to know what was said in that meeting where they decided Y." Or, "How could that political party simply be opposed to this bill without offering any meaningful alternative." These are not really questions at all.

Straight news represents a shrinking part of what consumers encounter in the modern information culture, even from traditional content providers.

In addition, most news stories report on things more complicated than a water main break and very quickly test the limits of these seven elements of completeness, our five Ws, one H, and Q. In the May 7, 2009, *New York Times*, on the day of the water main break in the *Washington Post*, for instance, there were thirty-nine stories in the first section, sixteen of which were straight news accounts of something that had happened the day before. The rest were more-complex conceptual stories, trend stories, features, or profiles. What's more, none of the sixteen straight news accounts was on the front page (which was made up entirely of more-complex stories), and only five covered a single physical event, such as the water main flood (a car bombing in Iraq; the Senate's passing of a bill; a riot in Tblisi, Georgia; the Russians expelling two NATO diplomats; and a Centers for Disease Control and Prevention announcement about a new finding involving the swine flu pandemic). The other straight news stories were more complicated procedural accounts about government activities or announcements—what social scientists would call "created news events"—whose significance had to be untangled and explained.

This accounting of one day's newspaper reveals something else that a skeptical consumer of information and news needs to reckon with. Just as there are different models of delivering information, there are also different types of news stories. And how we answer the key questions related to their reliability differs somewhat depending on the type of story and content. Even within the fairly narrow boundaries of traditional venues like the *New York Times*, the notion of "news" encompasses several layers.

Most people probably have a single definition for the word *news*. The classic one, learned in grammar school, may be "*news* is whatever is happening that you didn't know." The word *news* implies things that are new and from all around—North, East, West, and South; the points on a compass spell out the word *news*.

In real life, however, and particularly in modern media, this single definition is insufficient, as our run down of one section of the *New York Times* on one day above suggests. To evaluate whether something is reliable or believable, it's important to know what kind of news you are looking at.

Sense-Making News: The Meaning of Facts

Once radio news began to spread in the 1930s and television news began to dominate in the 1960s, journalists in other media began to change the way that they presented news. It was no longer sufficient for a morning newspaper to merely repeat what people had heard the anchor say on TV the night before. News executives began to strategize that the morning newspaper, to add value, had to put news into a larger context or to move it forward somehow, to say where things might be going. With the advent of cable news in the 1980s, and the beginning of twenty-four-hour TV news, the push toward analysis became even more pronounced. Stories became more interpretative, more analytical, with more context. This was particularly true for print stories, but even executives for the network nightly newscasts wanted the two-minute stories that appeared at dinnertime to be interpretive.

Broadly, a new news category emerged. We call it sense-making news. It includes stories that don't just tell you what the mayor said to the garden club yesterday but also tell you how that speech fits into what he'd said before, and perhaps offer some reporting on why the mayor had chosen just those words or had changed his view.

At their best, sense-making stories add some new element that helps make other news and facts take on a greater or deeper meaning. They give reporters a chance to share some of the insights they have gained over time. Sense-making stories make the tumblers click in the audience's mind and bring new recognition or understanding. They are not necessarily analytical stories. They may be explanatory. They may reveal the backstory behind news, and in that sense, be highly reportorial. They may add only one or two essential new facts, a missing piece or two of a news puzzle. But they are, generally, a higher order of news story than a simple account of an event, contextualizing facts so the audience can begin to derive some meaning from them.

A short *Washington Post* story in 2005, for example, explained why people might not be able to identify the names of the cabinet members during President George W. Bush's second term: The president's agenda has been narrowed and most key decisions are now being made in the West Wing. Another example is a *New York Times* story on a woman who supports abortion but who, after getting genetic testing, decides to carry to term her Down syndrome baby. It explains how genetic testing can defy expectations.[4]

During the Iraq War, in 2003, dramatic stories of the combat action, wounds, capture, and eventual release of a soldier from West Virginia named Jessica Lynch made her the most famous female combat hero in American history. Months later, on November 11, 2003, the *Wall Street Journal* published a front-page article that put Lynch's fame into a broader context. The story, written by Jonathan Eig, appeared beneath the headline "Soldier's Stories: Why You've Heard of Jessica Lynch, not Zan Hornbuckle: As Sentiment About War Evolves, Victims Grab Attention, Not Fighters. It Wasn't Always So."

The story opened by telling of an attack on eighty U.S. troops outside Baghdad by three hundred Iraqi and Syrian fighters. The battle lasted eight hours.

> The U.S. counterattack killed an estimated 200 enemy fighters, according to the commanding officer who oversaw the battle. The American team had never trained or fought together, but all its men got out alive. The team was headed by Capt. Harry Alexander Hornbuckle, a 29-year-old staff officer who had never been in combat before. He was later awarded the Bronze Star, with a V for valor, for his efforts that day.

But, as the story reported, "Capt. Hornbuckle's name has never appeared in a newspaper or on television. He has received no book deals, no movie offers, no trips to Disneyland.

> By contrast, Lynch, who had killed no enemy combatants, became a celebrity. Publishing house Alfred A. Knopf signed her to a million-dollar book deal. *Saving Jessica Lynch*, a TV movie about her plight, was made. Why did she become the individual celebrated in popular culture and not one of the other men or women who distinguished themselves in combat?

The answer, Eig's story said, lay in changes in American culture:

> In World War I, Cpl. Alvin York gained fame for killing 25 Germans and capturing 132. In World War II, Second Lt. Audie Murphy was credited with 240 kills and went on to star in the movie "To Hell and Back," which told the story of his bravery.
>
> Military culture still celebrates the soldier who racks up a high body count. But since the Vietnam War, much of the country has tended to venerate survivors more than aggressors, the injured more than those who inflicted injuries.

The story went on to track the history of American war heroes and report experts' views about the evolving psyche of Americans and how we venerate different people. It answered something that many readers were wondering, if only in the back of their minds. Why is she our hero? What does that say about us?

As stories move from a largely straight factual account of an event to something more complex, such as the Lynch story, the notion of completeness becomes more involved. Largely, this is because the questions raised by the story—the new, or seventh, element involved in completeness—become a bigger element in assessing it. When a news provider becomes more interpretive—when it tries to help the audience contextualize or make sense of things—it induces a more sophisticated response in the audience than if it had simply informed them of what happened.

On May 7, 2009, the same day of the water main break in Washington, D.C., the lead story in the *New York Times* was a sense-making story, not a straight news story. A day earlier, reports had come out of Afghanistan that American airstrikes had killed possibly more than a hundred civilians. The *Times* story attempted to advance the matter by talking about the political implications of the civilian deaths.

It began: "American airstrikes that Afghan officials and villagers said Wednesday had killed more than 100 civilians in western Afghanistan threaten to stiffen Afghan opposition to the war just as the Obama administration is sending more than 20,000 more troops to the country."

The audience must recognize first that this is more than a news story. This piece is trying to make sense of this news event. The lead paragraph itself is a complicated one, going far beyond the five Ws and one H and leaning far more on the Q. It is not only telling us there were reports of civilians killed from a U.S. military bombing. It is also trying to assess the political fallout of the incident, at the same time that it is trying to pin down the basic facts on which that fallout would depend. It was an assessment that got ahead of the story.

The second paragraph indeed introduces yet another element: By co-incidence, there were talks in Washington on the day of the airstrike about the future of Afghanistan that included the Afghan president, the president of Iraq, and the president of the United States. "The reports of-fered a grim backdrop to talks on Wednesday afternoon in Washing-ton," the story said.

The problem is that the story's thesis—the bombing will hurt U.S. policy—is based on a variable that had yet to be established. The fallout of the bombing incident depends on how many civilians were actually killed. And that number is unknown and may never be known.

Most of the rest of the story, indeed, tries to sort out what that number might be, but a solid number is hard to pin down. The effort is made more difficult by an unavoidable reliance on secondary sources in trying to ascertain how many civilians died.

Of the twenty-six paragraphs that follow, just nine describe circum-stances that might lead to opposition to U.S. policy—most of them late in the story.

The *Times* reporting about the bombing was about as detailed as that in any paper that day. And months later, the article's supposition, that Afghan opposition to U.S. forces would harden and U.S. policy would become more complicated, was proved prescient. But the story was try-ing to accomplish a lot in a hurry and in a short amount of space. It was trying to tell us about the bombing, to pin down how many were killed, and infer its impact on a White House meeting. It was probably striving to cover too much before all the facts were clear.

We cite the story here not because it was wrong—it was proved to be right—but because it is an example in which sense making could not be supported, at least not at the time it was written. It shows how the judg-ments we make about sense-making content are different from those we make about simpler news accounts. Now the criterion of whether some-thing is reliable or useful becomes a matter of judging the logic of the analysis offered and the evidence to support it.

If a Web site or TV channel is genuinely trying to verify the news, one should expect to see a good deal more evidence. If the venue is engaged in the journalism of affirmation, in practice, an analysis designed to simply reinforce the audience's preconceptions may not bother with hard evidence.

Authentication Stories: What Can I Believe?

Sense-making stories began to appear more frequently starting in the 1960s and have grown more widespread since, while a third category of news, "authentication stories," is far newer. Authentication stories try to sort out for the audience what can or can't be believed about past events. These stories could be said to be sense making of a sort. But their primary purpose is not to provide new facts or put familiar ones in context to help audiences derive new meaning. Instead, these stories try to verify facts so that audiences can determine what facts or competing claims they can trust. These stories are about proof: What of the things I have heard or read can I believe? As such, the criteria for judging them leans more on their evidence and conclusiveness than on the quality of their interpretation.

Perhaps the most sustained examples of authentication news is offered by PolitiFact, a project of the Washington bureau of the *St. Petersburg Times* run by bureau chief Bill Adair. The project, which won a Pulitzer Prize in 2009, was launched to monitor the accuracy of the candidates' rhetoric during the 2008 presidential election but has gone on to fact-check the political debate in general. It rates accuracy of statements by national political players, including Barack Obama, Congressional leaders in both parties, and the two parties' national committees, as well as liberal filmmaker Michael Moore and various TV pundits from all sides of the political spectrum. It also monitors the White House's progress on presidential campaign promises. And it does all this in a nonpartisan, nonideological manner, aspiring to be is an honest broker in a traditional American journalistic manner.

PolitiFact built on a movement of fact-checking the political advertising that began in the early 1990s and in particular on the work of Fact Check.org, a project pioneered by former *Wall Street Journal* and CNN reporter Brooks Jackson and which is affiliated with the Annenberg School for Communication and Journalism at the University of Pennsylvania.

It also is increasingly common to see news stories that function in much the same way, in more detail, on specific subjects. On January 23, 2007, for example, CNN aired a story that sorted through, and eventually debunked, the allegations that Barack Obama had attended a radical Muslim school between 1969 and 1971 when he lived in Indonesia. *Insight on the News*, a magazine owned by the company that publishes the *Washington Times*, reported on its Web site that supporters of Obama's opponent in the presidential primary, Senator Hillary Clinton, had found proof of the allegation. Various media sources in turn cited *Insight*'s claim, including several Fox News hosts, the *New York Post*, Glenn Beck (then at CNN Headline News), and a number of political blogs. The allegation suggested not only that Obama had lied in his two autobiographies but also suggested, implicitly, that he was a kind of "Manchurian candidate," a secret Muslim trying to take over the nation. (The term "Manchurian candidate" comes from the 1959 book and two movies that depict a political assassin who has been secretly brainwashed by Korean communists.)

CNN sent a reporter to the school, where he interviewed school officials, observed the students and teachers, and interviewed Obama's former classmates. Throughout, the story presented the evidence the reporter uncovered, so the audience, in effect, could look over his shoulder as he pieced together the facts. "I've been to those madrasses in Pakistan," the correspondent, John Vause said, referring to schools that teach the political theology of Muslim extremism. "This school is nothing like that."

Authentication stories can even be more ambitious, and even be an ongoing process. In 2009, for instance, the media watchdog project Pro-Publica produced a series called Eye on the Stimulus. The project represented a whole body of authentication reporting investigating the impact of the government spending package designed to stimulate the economy and blunt the recession. Eye on the Stimulus, started in February 2009, shortly after passage of the stimulus bill, involves four reporters plus local independent reporters and citizens around the county who monitor local projects paid for with stimulus funds. Reporting focuses on job creation, spending, and transparency at the federal, state, and local levels. After the Obama administration pledged the program would save or create 3.5 million jobs, ProPublica reported on the dubious nature of making estimates on the number of jobs saved or created. Subsequently, using different accounting methods, the Obama administration revised its estimate to one million jobs, and ProPublica tracked those and compared them to the lower estimates at the state level.[5] Rather than issuing a static, one-time story, ProPublica created a living project with various elements that builds evidence and reacts to the administration's claims.

News organizations may also authenticate their own earlier reporting. In June 2009, for instance, the *New York Times* published a story that said its earlier estimates on the number of U.S. swine flu cases had been wrong. A spring article reported that there would be perhaps twenty-five hundred U.S. cases of swine flu by the end of May. But the Centers for Disease Control and Prevention estimated the correct number exceeded a hundred thousand. The later article went on to explain how and why the computer models used were so wrong; they were based on tracking how dollar bills circulated in the United States, not germs.

But the task of completeness in authentication stories is tougher. "You are marshalling evidence, and you are trying to prove a case," said Brooks Jackson. That means there must be enough evidence to prove a case, and where there are gaps, enough honesty to acknowledge them.

New-Paradigm Reporting

Closely related to authentication news are stories or content that try to establish new understanding about broader phenomena, that challenge conventional wisdom. This new-paradigm reporting goes beyond a single situation or event. It involves sifting through larger shafts of data and finding bigger patterns in events, institutions, or settings. This the kind of work John Crewdson does. Malcolm Gladwell's work in the *New Yorker* is another example. Gladwell's reporting on the research on concussions and football, for instance, began to change the way head injuries are dealt with in professional sports. The multipart series "Driven to Distraction," produced by reporter Matt Richtel in the *New York Times*, documenting empirically the dangers of people using cell phones and texting while driving, is another example. Within weeks of its publication, states began to change their laws in response.

Our expectations for this kind of paradigm-shifting reporting are higher still. Sense-making stories add facts to broaden our understanding of some event, and authentication stories prove a case, but paradigm-shifting reporting does more. It proves a much broader case, marshalling more evidence. Often, it is so persuasive that it has a direct impact on our lives.

Watchdog Reporting: Prosecutorial Journalism

Then there is the classic notion of investigative reporting, in which the news organization is a watchdog over powerful institutions and exposes wrongdoing.[6]

These are stories about malfeasance by public officials or institutions that affect people's lives. Watchdog journalism is not some new element of a modern press. It is deeply embedded in journalism's history, and in people's earliest expectations of what journalism hoped to offer and the function of the press in society. From the time that print periodicals first emerged in England in the seventeenth century until today, journalism has celebrated its ability to uncover wrongdoing. Watchdog journalism has set the value of this work apart from other forms of information.

Because most exposés imply that something isn't as it should be, this reporting demands high levels of transparency and greater detail about sources and methods to demonstrate its independence. The articles also require a higher standard of proof because of their prosecutorial nature. And all of this need for transparency and documentation is made more challenging because of the complexity of the reporting and the often sensitive nature of the sourcing.

The reporting that goes into watchdog journalism that exposes wrongdoing is often painstaking and can be the fruit of months or even years of slowly building a case. Not infrequently investigative reporting will start with a tip, a suspicion, or simply a question that cannot easily be answered or confirmed. "Tips for me that mattered were things I could document," and "the tips that I got that really mattered were about documents or trials," said Morton Mintz, who worked for thirty years at the *Washington Post* and uncovered such stories as the connection between the sedative thalidomide and birth defects; unsafe contraceptives; and General Motors' spying on automobile industry critic Ralph Nader. "I would go in assuming that everything that I would write would be lawyered. And that gives you a certain discipline."

Jim Risen, a multiple Pulitzer Prize winner, often talks about the need "to have patience," to "just talk to sources and not badger them," and to "find out the people who know what's going on and to get to know them well." Risen recommended reporters learn "to know who you can trust and who you cannot" and to "get to know closed subcultures." Those tasks, all painstaking ones, are the stuff of investigative reporting.

This is evident in the work by reporters Dana Priest and Anne Hull, with photographer Michel duCille, for the *Washington Post* that cataloged facts and assertions about the mistreatment of veterans at the Walter Reed Army Medical Center in 2008. Their stories were built on the accumulation of interviews, dramatic photographs of wounded soldiers, and official documents. So thorough were the details of the Walter Reed articles that they evoked a national outcry and federal officials immediately implemented widespread reforms at the hospital.

There is the accumulation of exhaustive on-the-record accounts, in such numbers that their similarity forms a pattern. There is combing through databases for quantitative evidence of patterns, and then augmenting that research with contextualizing interviews. There is following up on an anonymous tip by searching for independent eyewitness confirmation.

Whatever methods a journalist uses, the resulting story must display sufficient evidence to allow consumers to see the case for themselves and to understand why they should believe the evidence offered. Holding such information to a high standard can help us distinguish the exposés that have approached their subject with a dispassionate open mind, a dedication to accuracy, and a broad context from those that have been created with bias. Exposés produced by political or other special-interest groups tend to lack context, have a narrow focus, and ignore or underplay information that contradicts their assertions. The best exposés, as we will see, are the most skeptical of their own certainty.

Throughout this chapter we have discussed the ways to think about the completeness of different kinds of stories. Next we must begin to break down the other elements, and that process starts with looking at sources.

CHAPTER 5

Sources: Where Did This Come From?

In the spring of 2009 the on-again-off-again news reports about the health of Steve Jobs, the CEO and co-founder of Apple Computer Co., seemed to have settled down.

For nearly five years, rumors and speculative news stories about the technology wizard had periodically swirled through Silicon Valley, spooking the stock market. They had begun in 2004 when Jobs first disclosed he had received treatment of pancreatic cancer. He had initially calmed the technology markets by disclosing that he had received successful medical treatment for the problem. But when Jobs appeared on television to introduce the new iPhone 3G at the Apple Worldwide Developers Conference on June 9, 2008, his dramatically visible loss of weight re-ignited stories about his health.

For the next two months Apple's stock bounced up and down with each new report or rumor. Then, in January 2009, Jobs released a letter saying that his treatment for a hormone imbalance was more complicated than he had expected and that he was taking a six-month medical leave. Months passed, and a stream of Apple product and financial announcements suggested business as usual. A new iPhone, the 3GS, was launched; reports of better-than-expected sales of the new iPhones followed. Questions remained about Jobs's long-term prognosis, but when he announced his return in early June, it calmed erratic markets.

Then, on June 19, the *Wall Street Journal* ran a front-page story:

> Steve Jobs, who has been on medical leave from Apple Inc. since January to treat an undisclosed medical condition, received a liver transplant in Tennessee about two months ago. The chief executive has been recovering well and is expected to return to work on schedule later this month, though he may work part-time initially.
>
> Mr. Jobs didn't respond to an e-mail requesting comment. "Steve continues to look forward to returning at the end of June, and there's nothing further to say," said Apple spokeswoman Katie Cotton.

This eighteen-paragraph story in the *Journal* touched off an industry-wide scramble for more details about the health of Jobs, a key figure in the world economy of the twenty-first century; the creator of the iPhone, the iPod, and the Mac; the progenitor of the image of the teenage genius inventing the next big thing (the first home computer in Job's case) in the family garage; the original model of geek chic.

But the *Journal*'s scoop offered little hint of where to begin. The story cited no source for its information. There was only the vague hint of a source buried in one paragraph: "At least some Apple directors were aware of the CEO's surgery. As part of an agreement with Mr. Jobs in place before he went on leave, some board members have been briefed weekly on the CEO's condition by his physician."

Instead, the *Journal* used what some journalists call the "voice of God" approach to sourcing its story. The news organization, in effect, had taken on the role of being the source. The *Journal* was telling us directly, as if it knew this information on its own authority.

There might be many reasons why the *Journal* used that approach. The reporter and editors might have been protecting the actual source in hopes of keeping a line of communications open for future tips and stories. Apple is in a fiercely competitive industry and is well known among journalists as a company that highly values secrecy. Employees have been fired for disclosing information about upcoming products. Members of the company's board might have feared being removed for disclosing such information. Or the motive may have been to protect the value of the stock. It would have been interesting to know the paper's reason for the lack of sources.

But the voice of God approach is so unusual, and for the *Journal* so uncharacteristic, that it put in stark relief just how central the role of sources are in evaluating the reliability of news. Once you have identified what kind of content you are encountering, the next critical step involves thinking about the sourcing.

Who or what are the sources, and why should I believe them?

There are numerous components to evaluating the value of a given source. That process begins with identifying who or what the source or sources are. But there are many different kinds of sources, and dissecting precisely what type they are is vital.

Sourceless News: The Audience as Witness

An event that is public, for everyone to see, might require no special sourcing at all. An account of a presidential speech, by nature a public and likely televised event, might carry no attribution. The president is the source. If we watched the event on TV, indeed, we would be our own witness.

But most news we cannot see for ourselves. When we learn what the president said in private, why he delivered the speech he did, or what was left out, we must rely on the authority and reliability of others to be our eyes and ears. In these cases we must identify what kind of source we are relying on.

The Journalist as Witness

Often the best work we encounter, like Homer Bigart's Vietnam reporting, involves the reporter acting as our eyes and ears directly, seeing events for himself. This is the journalist as personal witness. Consider this May 7, 2009, piece by *New York Times* reporter Dexter Filkins:

> MARDAN, PAKISTAN—The dank and shadowed hallways of the Mardan Tuberculosis Hospital, crumbling relic of another age, were transformed here on Wednesday into a clinic of a more modern sort, when the refugees of nearby battles came streaming in the whole day long.

Hundreds first, then, thousands; tattered, woebegone, well dressed. They piled into the hospital courtyard, then into the hospital itself, moving down the hallways, sitting on the floors. It was mostly men who came but women did, too, nearly all of them lost and bewildered and wondering what fate awaited them next.

"Reza Mohammed, mother of five," said a voice behind a burqa; she was seated on the floor. She was offering her government identification card to an official in a chair. The hall was dark without electricity. "We came six days ago. Please take down my name."

For seventeen more paragraphs the story of the toll of battle is built detail by revealing detail to conclude: "Mr. Khan, the two-time refugee from Swat, ended a long conversation by reaching into his pocket and producing a 20-rupee note. It is worth about 25 cents; the only money he had.

"'God will not let me starve,' he said. 'But I will speak the truth.'"

Filkins is our eyewitness, our source, writing a story that says, in effect, "Come and see what I saw, hear what I heard." And he convinces us by the careful attention demonstrated to descriptive detail of place and people, several of whom he lets tell their story in their words.

Accounts such as Filkins's represent the height of reliable news. The reporter has seen it firsthand and can vouch for it. The fact that a reporter has been granted this access is frequently a hallmark of someone who has credibility, respect from sources, and has done the work to get inside. Such a reporter is not being held behind the rope line or sitting at a press briefing. Watch for such reporting, and if you see the same name appear frequently above such work, it is a sign of a reporter who, granted access like this before, is granted access again. Often it is a gold standard.

For if the reporter has seen it, she can show it to us, and we can come closer to seeing it ourselves and drawing our own conclusions.

The Journalist as Credentialed Expert

In some cases, journalists have such obvious expertise that we consider them a reporter-source based on their credentials alone. This is often the case with medical journalists, particularly those whose work we have come to know over time. Dr. Tim Johnson of ABC News, for instance, earned trust with viewers over decades and earned respect in the medical community as a practicing physician, a reporter, and a teacher at Harvard Medical School. Often in his reports, he simply offers his personal medical opinion or response to a news event, in the same way a personal doctor shares his medically informed judgments with a patient. Generally, however, the journalist expert is more the exception than the rule. And familiarity is important. A reporter we have not heard of before who is also a doctor, or an unfamiliar reporter who is not specially trained or credentialed, might not come close to satisfying our demand for a "recognized" source for a story.

More often, journalists build credibility for their stories through the sources they rely on for their information. The question we must ask in these cases is "Who are these sources and why we should believe them?" This implies not only knowing the sources and their supposed expertise but also the basis of their knowledge about a particular case. Credentials alone are insufficient. In a story about infectious diseases, for instance, it might not be enough to know the name of the doctor being interviewed and where she works. It might not be sufficient to know that she is a specialist in infectious diseases. It might be more important to know whether she has worked in the area of the particular disease in question. In other words, the more specificity we have about sources, the better.

This process, naturally, usually begins with knowing a source's name. That, however, is only a first step. And as we will see below in the discussion of anonymous sources, the name may be one of the least important elements in assessing a source's value. More important is deciding how authoritative or knowledgeable that person is about the events described in the story. How do these sources know what they are telling us about?

Sources as Witnesses: Firsthand Accounts

The *Washington Post* account of the water main break in Washington, D.C., cited in Chapter 4, is source rich. It includes a deputy fire chief and two named officials of the city's sewer and water authority providing the What, When, Where, Why, and How of the accident. It also provides details from two eyewitnesses in the neighborhood, who describe how the flooding water had affected their homes. All this is embedded in the description of the flooding and broken street pavement written by the two reporters.

In such cases, where sources are purporting to serve as witnesses (the residents with flooded homes), it is crucial for journalists, just as it is for police investigators or lawyers, to know whether a witness's account is firsthand. Was the source there personally? If so, did she see for herself what she is describing or is it something someone else told her? Is she an *eyewitness*?

Such shadings in distance from first- to secondhand knowledge can be subtle and easy to overlook when reading an article or viewing an account filled with dramatic and emotional detail.

In our discussion of sense-making stories in Chapter 4, we described an article by the *New York Times* that attempts to provide a broader context to a report of civilian deaths as a result of American airstrikes in Afghanistan. The headline of the article, "Civilian Deaths Imperil Support for Afghan War," makes that context clear. It was the lead story in the *Times* that day because editors considered the story to be the most important event it could provide for its readers.

American military officials confirmed an attack in the area but questioned reports that perhaps "more than 100 civilians" had been killed. The two reporters who wrote the story, although not on the scene, had extensive contacts in the region and were able to reach at least two people in the village who had been eyewitnesses and who gave graphic descriptions of body parts littering the ground.

The only other sourcing that might have established the extent of the damage came from a member of the Afghan parliament. He described two phone calls he had participated in, one with the mayor of the damaged city and the other with someone he knew in the area. The details the parliament member gleaned from those calls was thus two steps removed: The mayor was repeating what he was told by villagers who came to his office; the other caller reported seeing people buried, whom he was told were killed in the air attack. But these sources themselves were secondhand, and they in turn had talked to the parliament member who had talked to the reporters. Thus the reporters' source was thirdhand, and there was only one such thirdhand source, the parliament member, who might have altered the accounts to make them more consistent. So how do we judge sources who come at such a distance from events? We need not ignore them entirely. They may be the only sources we have. In such cases, it is useful to look for multiple sources who are independent of one another and to see if their stories all overlap with a consistency that begins to give them credibility. This is what skilled reporters do. They try, in effect, to "triangulate" multiple accounts to see if a reliable pattern emerges, much the same way scientists or researchers amass large amounts of data to see if the patterns form reliable conclusions. If multiple sources are unavailable, and the body of evidence is small, we need to view the accounts as less reliable—suggestive perhaps, but not proven.

As it turns out, subsequent investigations into what happened that day in Afghanistan proved difficult. Two months later, the core details of the story, how many civilians had been killed and how many had been killed by the bombing (not the firefight that preceded it), had still not been determined. The Afghan Independent Human Rights Commission reported eighty-six killed by the bombing. The U.S. government reported twenty-six civilian deaths could be attributed to a bombing around that time.[1]

In law, there are strict rules of evidence governing witnesses. They can offer testimony to what they have encountered directly—physical external facts, what was said, what was seen. But they cannot testify, generally, about what they imagine that the people they talked to might have been thinking or feeling, unless it was explicitly said to them. And secondhand accounts—what an eyewitness might have told them they saw—are usually also inadmissible. These are considered in law to be mere "hearsay," something allowed only in special circumstances. Journalists have no such strictures and rules of evidence. But, as consumers, we should know that they are hardly immune to the same problems that the law has tried to recognize.

Firsthand Witnesses and the Problem of Time

Even if a witness is firsthand, lawyers and police know that doesn't mean his or her account is reliable. For the moment, let's put aside the question of people who want to mislead or lie. Even people who have seen an event for themselves, and who want to be accurate and fair witnesses, can still have a faulty recollection. They may not have noticed certain things. They may want to appear more knowledgeable than they really are. And research by psychologists has consistently found that memory is highly suggestible. People are easily *reminded* of events that never happened, and having been *reminded*, may thereafter hold the false recollection as tenaciously as they would a true one.[2] Consequently, lawyers today closely question eyewitnesses regarding the accuracy of their memories and about any possible *assistance* from others in the formation of those memories.

A major factor, according to the psychological literature, is the immediacy of the recollection. Passage of time has a highly distorting effect on memory.[3] Thus one element in assessing the reliability of even an eyewitness source is how recent the event was.

One example of this is the case of a rape victim in a North Carolina who could not identify the man who raped her eleven years after the rape occurred. Though she had never doubted that the man she had originally identified was the rapist, eleven years later he was exonerated by DNA evidence.

"It was an utter shock, really," the detective in the case said when describing the victim's reaction to CBS correspondent Lesley Stahl on a *60 Minutes* segment on eyewitness testimony. "No, that can't be true. It's not possible . . . There's no question in my mind," the victim had said.

"Now that DNA has exonerated more than two hundred thirty men in mostly sex crimes and murder cases," Stahl said, "criminologists have been able to go back and study what went wrong in those investigations."

"What they've honed in on," Stahl said, "is faulty eyewitness testimony. Over seventy-five percent of these innocent men were convicted in part because an eyewitness fingered the wrong person."[4]

A second element in assessing the reliability of a source who claims to be an eyewitness is whether that account has been corroborated by others. This gets into the realm of number of sources. A story or account in which the same event is described similarly by more than one source is likely more reliable than an account that relies on a single source. In our work conducting content analysis of the news at the Project for Excellence in Journalism, we have used the number of sources cited as one sign of evidence of a story's authoritativeness.

Multiple sources are important because accounts can differ, particularly if the event happened in the distant past. Yet even when there are multiple accounts, there are limits to what can be ascertained. Many news events are controversial and politically charged, making recollections even more complicated.

One such case occurred in 2009, when Speaker of the House Nancy Pelosi became embroiled in an argument with the CIA over what she had or had not been told in a briefing seven years earlier.

The argument over how much congressional leaders knew of the U.S.

government's use of waterboarding and other harsh interrogation measures was touched off by a CIA report sent to Capitol Hill that said leaders had been briefed on these issues forty times since September 4, 2002. Pelosi said she had attended only one briefing, on September 4, 2002, and was never told waterboarding and other harsh measures were actually being used on prisoners. She was, she said, "briefed on interrogation techniques the administration was considering using in the future and that the techniques were determined to be legal." For two weeks after the CIA report was issued, journalists could find members of Congress on each side of the aisle prepared to assert with great certainty what they had been told and what they had not been told in those briefings. Cautious reporters and consumers were careful to look for many and varied sources for information about the dispute. They knew they were dealing with an event that took place seven years earlier and that was still, to some extent, legally classified as secret.

The episode showed not only the fragility of memory but also the hothouse atmosphere—one marked by self-protective and self-selected recollection—in which sources often interact with reporters. Even the director of the CIA warned about recollections based on notes made years earlier: "In the end, you and the committee will have to determine whether this information is an accurate summary of what actually happened."

Corroboration of Eyewitness Sources: The Two-Source Rule

In the 1970s, many Americans certainly heard Benjamin C. Bradlee, the executive editor of the *Washington Post*, talk of the "two-source rule" during Watergate. The concept, as Bradlee intended it, was that the *Post* would not go with an anonymously sourced story unless it was corroborated by a second source.

But the concept of corroboration is more involved than it might at first seem. For one thing, the corroborating sources need to be independent of each other. That means they can't be parroting the same secondhand account that they heard from the same person.

Few events have called as much attention to the problem of corroboration of secondhand witnesses as the affair between President Bill Clinton and a twenty-two-year-old intern in the White House named Monica Lewinsky.

One of the more controversial journalistic episodes involved what came to be called the "third-party witness" stories. A variety of news organizations reported that a third person had allegedly seen Clinton in an intimate encounter with Lewinsky. This would have provided proof that the president lied under oath in a deposition. Speculation over whether the story was unsourced or anonymously sourced and whether there was a witness or witnesses swirled through the media. One account mentioned a White House steward who was said to have testified before a grand jury that he had seen Clinton and Lewinsky together in a compromising situation. Other stories reported a Secret Service agent would provide similar testimony.

In the end, the stories proved inaccurate—and the problem was a matter of secondhand sources corroborating the same misunderstood account. A White House steward had encountered soiled towels. He talked to Secret Service agents, who complained to colleagues, who told their lawyers. The news organizations that reported on the story, some of which later retracted it, were getting at least some of their information from a lawyer representing the Secret Service agents. But the steward did not talk to reporters. And no one, contrary to the reports, had actually seen the president and Lewinsky together.

As the Project for Excellence in Journalism reported in a study of this episode, "journalists have acknowledged privately that at least some of the sources for some of these press accounts were not those directly involved in seeing the president and Lewinsky or even the investigators or prosecutors directly involved in the case. While a news organization may have two sources on a story, how much direct knowledge do those sources need to have before one can trust that a story has been verified?"[5]

The *New York Times*, on the brink of reporting the story, pulled back only at the last minute, when staffers began to mull over the question of whether their sources had direct knowledge or it was second- or thirdhand. The story seemed solid. It had multiple sources. It was slated to be prominently displayed on the front page of the paper. The early-edition deadline was looming. The story's two reporters kept working on it, trying to determine just how solid their sourcing was.

At six P.M. they walked into the office of then–Washington Bureau chief Mike Oreskes and said, "Mike, we've been thinking this through, and we realize our sources are secondhand. They did not themselves see the president and Lewinsky together. They talked to people who said they saw them together. We really wonder if that is good enough to call the president a liar."[6]

Oreskes called New York editors and said he thought they should hold the story. New York editors argued that it was going to get out anyway—the *Dallas Morning News* and the *Wall Street Journal* had both published such stories on their Web sites—but Oreskes held firm. It was a pivotal moment. The *Morning News* and the *Journal* retracted their accounts, but other news organizations that ran the story did not.

Sometimes the second source may be secondhand, while the first source is an eyewitness. But a potential problem is that the corroborating source could be repeating what the first source told him. That is not true corroboration. We must watch for these nuances, and if they are undetectable we need to be wary.

Participants But Not Witnesses

The next level of sourcing, after eyewitness, is a source who is a direct participant in the story but not a witness. Examples are a police officer who is investigating a murder, a firefighter who is investigating how a fire started, a paramedic who had rushed to the scene after the accident.

One step removed from this level is the police spokesperson, that articulate and often telegenic person who talks to the press, or the White House press secretary, who wasn't in the room when the meeting was held but was briefed on it by others so she could describe it to the press. There are good reasons that institutions use spokespersons, beyond the fact that these people can help control the message. We might not want the police officers investigating a murder, for instance, to expend time talking to reporters, letting the trail of leads go cold. But as consumers of news and information, we need to recognize that the spokesperson usually isn't investigating the incident herself but instead has been briefed on it. Did she talk to the investigating officer directly, or was she briefed in turn by someone else? Is this secondhand, or third- or fourth-hand? Rarely do reporters seem to ask this or is it conveyed to us as consumers. But the question is pertinent.

Expert Sources and Analysts

That brings us to the next level of sourcing: the source who isn't directly involved in the story but is called in as an expert to provide context or analysis. In an age when the discussion-oriented part of the media is growing, and the reportorial element of the media is shrinking, we hear more and more from these "experts" rather than sources directly involved. And much of what these experts offer is analysis—not facts directly describing the events. Analysis, by its nature, is more speculative. Thus, we should be more cautious of it. In sense-making stories that are trying to establish context, or trying to sift among competing facts to authenticate conclusions, we should expect more sources, more evidence, because establishing the case is more difficult. Ironically, the opposite often occurs. Since people are offering opinions, journalists, and perhaps even consumers, seem to expect less.

From these stories, which make up much of the talk that passes today as news presentations, we should at a minimum expect more information about who the experts talking to us are and what their real role is in relation to the events they are analyzing. Are they really dispassionate experts removed from the events they are assessing? Or are they interested players—the former prosecutor, the political strategist, the columnist— who pose as disinterested experts or authorities to give themselves more credibility? Too often, the purported experts are actually activists of a party, faction, or interest group who pose as outside experts so they can persuade and manipulate audiences. It is a false kind of affirmation that we should be on guard against.

Such activist experts appear almost daily on the politicized talk shows on cable TV, even on those in which the hosts are themselves not ideological. Let's look at the lineup on CNN on May 6, 2008, for instance, the night Barack Obama defeated Hillary Clinton in the North Carolina primary. Obama's victory was a critical one because it proved he could win in a Southern state, and it proved to be a turning point on Obama's road to the White House. But much would depend on how the victory was interpreted. CNN organized two prime-time panels to analyze the primary results. One aired at eight P.M., just after the polls had closed. The other aired at ten P.M., when the outcome was clear. The panel members and the way they are identified included Jamal Simmons,

Democratic strategist; Lanny Davis, former White House counsel; David Gergen, CNN special political analyst; Paul Begala, CNN political analyst; Alex Castellanos, Republican strategist; Bill Bennett, CNN contributor; and Donna Brazile, CNN political analyst. Anderson Cooper moderated the discussion.

The identifying descriptions of the panelists are pretty typical for a cable news panel program. Little other than a title or institutional affiliation is usually offered. Often that is not enough.

On this night, for instance, Jamal Simmons was identified as a Democrat and Alex Castellanos as a Republican and both as political strategists. It would have been useful to know that Simmons had worked in three presidential campaigns for Democratic candidates, including that of Senator Clinton's husband, and thus was hardly a disinterested Democrat. It was also not clarified that Lanny Davis had been counsel to the Clinton White House. It also would have been helpful to know that Castellanos had advised George W. Bush's campaign and was once called a "father of the modern attack ad." The hidden agendas of CNN's own analysts also was less than clear. Paul Begala had been a key strategist in President Bill Clinton's campaign and was a supporter of Senator Clinton. Donna Brazile, who participated in both panels, had already been appointed as a superdelegate for the Democratic National Convention, though it would be revealed months later that she had been backing Obama for quite some time. Their assessment was thus slanted. David Gergen is a rare political figure who has worked in White House advisory roles in both Republican and Democratic administrations, and Bill Bennett was a staunch conservative and is now a provocative talk show host. All of this additional information would have provided the audience with a better sense of the biases and agendas at play. In fact, none of these people was simply an analyst, with the possible exception of Gergen. Each was a player who would be active in the fight for the White House and, in some cases, directly in the battle between Obama and Clinton, though they presented themselves as dispassionate observers and their specific loyalties were not made clear.

In addition to asking whether the identification of a source is clear and complete, there is one other question worth asking about so-called expert sources: What kind of information is the moderator or reporter seeking from these experts? If the sources are being asked questions of fact, that is a sign that the inquiry is part of the journalism of verification. If they are being asked only for their opinions, that is a sign that we are in a different realm. If the questions themselves seem loaded to yield a certain response, that is a sign that the guests are foils, that we are encountering not inquiry but, more likely, persuasion—that we are encountering the journalism of affirmation.

Sometimes the absurdity of the guest as a foil for a host whose purpose is something other than inquiry is obvious. Consider an encounter between former Bush administration press secretary Ari Fleischer and former Senate Democratic press secretary turned talk show host Chris Matthews on the latter's MSNBC program *Hardball* four months after the 2008 election. The segment opened showing a split screen with the smiling faces of Matthews and Fleischer.

"Ari Fleischer!" Matthews announced, as though surprised to see his guest. "What are you doing here? Is this the hundred days of Napoleon's return from Crawford? What is going on with this former network of Bushies—current Bushies, I should say—singing the old song . . ."

"Chris, I'm here because you invited me to be here."

The answer stopped Matthews for a quick beat, but he plowed ahead. For the next five minutes, Matthews put forth a staccato barrage of questions, cutting off Fleischer or talking over him when the former press secretary tried to answer.

Eight minutes into the show, Fleischer called a halt: "Chris, you should not interrupt your guests. Or is that what you like to do?" Only then did Fleischer win himself a minute on a full screen to make his point.

Anonymous Sourcing

What are we to make of stories that do not include named sources, only anonymous ones? How, as consumers, are we supposed to evaluate those stories?

There are good reasons why journalists might use anonymous sourcing. Often the most sensitive material comes from sources who must remain anonymous to protect themselves. A whistleblower who reveals that the mayor is stealing public funds might lose her job or be punished for disloyalty. An anonymous source might be the best kind of public servant, and his whistleblowing might well be an act of patriotism. Congress, indeed, has passed a law to protect whistleblowers for just this reason.

But there is also evidence, as even many journalists acknowledge, that the practice has become more widespread than necessary. Many press secretaries on Capitol Hill, for instance, insist that they should always be quoted "on background," the journalistic term for describing someone's role but not naming them. The reason they typically give for wanting to remain anonymous, even though they are paid with public funds, is they do not wish to trump their bosses in the press. The journalists who accede to this request in exchange for access are passively robbing the public of accountability from public servants.

As consumers, we need to be able to distinguish between a justifiable use of anonymous sources and an unnecessary use. So how should we evaluate anonymous sources we encounter in news stories?

First, we have the right to expect some information about why the source is anonymous. If the answer to "Who is this source?" is "We can't tell you," as citizens we should expect a good reason why the source cannot be revealed. After that, we should ask why we should accept the source's information as credible. Unless we are given some additional information, how are we to know the source is in a position to know what he is talking about? News organizations should offer us some sense of a source's credibility, even without identifying the source. It is no longer sufficient for a news organization to say "CBS has learned," or "Sources tell the *Bugle*." In today's news environment, we want to know why the *Bugle* believes the sources, so that we decide whether we should believe them. A news account should do what it can to answer these questions without compromising a source who deserves protection. Journalists might grumble that this is cumbersome. They might even point to awkward shorthanded phrases that journalists use, like "a source who requested anonymity." Fine. We know it was requested. But why was it granted? "A source with firsthand knowledge of the affair, but who risked his or her job by talking to the *Bugle* about it" tells us much more. The journalist might consider such language self-evident. Most members of the public would find it informative.

If reasons for quoting anonymous sources are not given, you would be wise to reserve judgment until further evidence detailed in the story supports the information. If it isn't forthcoming, beware.

In recent years some news organizations have established stricter internal rules about when to grant sources anonymity. Clark Hoyt, then public editor of the *New York Times*, shared some of the new rules in place at that paper in February 2009. Among the factors the reporters and editors have to weigh, Hoyt explained, is whether the source is in a position to really know the information she offers, whether the information is truly newsworthy, whether the information can be acquired some other way, and whether the source has a record of reliability. All of those are proper criteria worth weighing. But as consumers, we will consider such an account more credible when information on the reason for anonymity can be hinted at or in some way shared with us as well.

One other factor is worth mentioning. Using anonymous sources for factual material that can be corroborated is far more valuable than using anonymous sources to offer opinions. When she was Washington editor of Newhouse newspapers, the late Deborah Howell required that confidential sources be used only for facts, not for opinions. If a journalist quotes anonymous sources offering a personal criticism of someone, you should be wary. "One Democratic consultant said the Congressman, a Republican from Alabama, had the kind of personality that was difficult to work with and people didn't like him. So he probably won't get the votes in the end." Why would the news organization allow a Democrat to personally criticize a Republican anonymously? This is an opinion, not an empirical matter. The information is useful only to the source and not really to public understanding. It certainly doesn't deserve to have the news organization sanction it by granting the source protection. Max Frankel, the former editor of the *New York Times*, called this kind of quote "the anonymous pejorative." The journalist has simply allowed the source to insult someone and protected the source in doing so.

Sources and the Manipulation of Talking Points

No discussion of sources, corroboration, and the disguise of propaganda and news is complete without a mention of the phenomenon of talking points and the concept of the coordinated message that permeate modern media. Talking points are preconfigured phrases and political-marketing buzzwords developed by communications specialists to manipulate public perception and designed to avoid conflicting descriptions of a program, idea, belief, or a product. They are a weapon that overwhelms the passive journalist of assertion, and they are wielded as a cudgel by the journalist of affirmation.

In the assumption that continuous repetition may convert assertion into belief, if not quite fact, the use of talking points has become standard procedure in Washington, where the administration and competing centers of political interest struggle each day to shape the language of the continuing debate of ideas and issues. These centers produce daily memos summarizing points for use in public talks or private meetings. The White House often distributes a "message of the day" to all government departments to saturate the public conversation on a policy or program. The Pentagon even provides public information officers with talking-point wallet cards. Often these phrases are crafted with the help of survey-tested data about which phrases resonate and research into the emotional impact of language. Their issuers want to put their message or product in a context that will promote a positive public opinion.

The term "talking points" has become so accepted that it has even lost its connotation as something designed to manipulate. Bill O'Reilly's Web site at Fox News has an archive of his talking points, a digest of his argument on a given day. Americans for the Arts' Web site has a series of talking points on issues such as arts funding, the economic impact of the arts, and arts and tourism that can be downloaded for use by those promoting public support and funding for the arts. The liberal Web site Talking Points Memo is an amalgam of partisan blogging, news aggregation, and even some interpretative reporting, usually synthesizing or analyzing original reporting conducted by others.

Marketing and Code Words

As wary consumers, we should be mindful of telltale signs that information is being sanitized: One signal is the use of words in new or unusual ways. A key of modern talking points is unusual or memorable phrasing that is designed to manipulate the audience.

One example of this is coded words. The term "clean coal" is designed to offset the image of coal itself and the black smoke burning coal produces in the face of a public more sensitive to the growing danger of increased carbon dioxide levels in the atmosphere. In economic circles, as the country was plunged into economic free-fall, unsecured loans were described neutrally as "subprime mortgages" or aggressively as "toxic assets," depending on how the user hoped the public would react.

How can we beware of such language? First, watch for words that you don't usually see together being connected. Consider "death tax," "pro-life" or "pro-choice," "welfare mothers." These are labels that are effectively meaningless but by repetition take on a meaning that is designed to persuade rather than to communicate. No one should be taxed for dying, right? But a death tax is also called an "inheritance tax." Should a rich person be allowed to pass on inheritance without the state taxing it? "Pro-life" also means anti-abortion. And "pro-choice" also means pro-abortion. We should expect our journalists to be committed to clarity and opposed to buzzwords. And we should expect newspeople never to employ them themselves. But we should not let the failure of the press dull our responsibility to be sensitized to Orwellian language. We should expect our journalists to be on guard against it, but we must as well.

The Repetition of Loaded Language

When multiple sources use the same language to describe an issue or event, we should be alert to the likelihood of manipulation. Descriptive language in lockstep is a sign of something other than corroboration.

To an experienced news gatherer, and news consumers, when sources use the same language, it is a sign they are hearing talking points concocted for them by communications strategists.

One of the better monitors of this controlled politicalspeak is not a news organization but a comedy program, *The Daily Show with Jon Stewart*. Consider how it skewered the talking points issued by the George W. Bush administration in an effort to silence critics of its war policies in Iraq.

The House of Representatives, controlled by the Democrats, was discussing timetables for withdrawing troops and even a resolution arguing that Bush's Iraq policy was no longer in the country's best interest.

Republicans responded with talking points they had used for months, all using the same word, "embolden," to denounce the debate. No Republican used a word like *encourage*, or *animate*, or *inspire*, or any of a dozen other words that could have been used to make the same point. All used the same construction: The criticisms of the president "emboldened" the enemy.

"All of these options that are being talked about on the Hill embolden terrorists in every part of the world," House minority leader John Boehner said on January 23, 2007.

"The withdrawal from Iraq will embolden the terrorists," White House spokesman Tony Snow told reporters on September 12, 2006.

"Retreat from Iraq before the job is done would embolden the enemy," President Bush said on November 6, 2006. And, "All timetables do is embolden the enemy," the president said on January 17, 2007. "You can embolden the enemy by sending mixed messages," he had said as early as July 22, 2005.

Mainstream media had aired the talking points, in effect enabling them. It fell to Stewart and his comedy program to link the examples and put them together in one cogent, revealing piece.

Sources, Motive, and Bias

Whether a source is anonymous or not, the source's motives may well be hidden, or at least not self-evident. We need to question why a source is offering the information and what ax they might be trying to grind in delivering it.

The fact that a source has a motive—that she is not purely disinterested—is not by itself a reason not to believe the information offend. But neither is it irrelevant to how we evaluate it.

Investigative reporters try to build into their work approaches that will reduce the level of bias in their reporting. Jim Risen, who has written important articles on intelligence communities for both the *Los Angeles Times* and the *New York Times*, prepared himself to cover those communities by interviewing former agents to learn how people in those agencies think and talk.

Risen, like reporter Seymour Hersh, prefers to get to know midlevel people in government, not those people at the top. "I always think of it as dealing with Rosencranz and Guildenstern—people backstage cynically talking about public policy," he said. "My approach is to just talk to a source, have a conversation, and not pressure them . . . The kind of people I deal with, my sources, are all people who talk about important people with power; they are not the important people."

This approach develops sources who come with information at some risk to themselves and often no obvious benefit to be gained. From these sources, Risen collects supporting or contradicting evidence. By working his way up an institution, he begins with those not wed to policy outcomes and thus more likely to offer different opinions from those of their superiors. Gathering information from those at various levels creates more opportunities to recognize a personal or political bias.

Risen's approach differs from that of reporters such as Bob Woodward, who tends to focus on policy makers and cabinet-level figures. The advantage Woodward has is that he gets exclusive information, perhaps known only to a few direct participants. The risk is that these people are most likely to be invested in protecting policy, well versed in spin, and interested in blaming rivals. There are also fewer such sources to corroborate accounts. This worries some of Woodward's sources. One of them described his concerns to us on background, and we have granted him anonymity so that he can maintain good relations with Woodward and other reporters in the future. But we found his insights worth sharing. They raise a concern about Woodward's technique that a reader can evaluate. They are not a personal attack. "I like Bob, and I respect him, and I think he is a great reporter. But I worry, in the books I have been a source with him on, that his version of events is easily skewed by who is willing to talk with him and who isn't. Sometimes the books have a Rashomon quality. Events look the way they do not because that's how they were but because this guy talked and this other guy didn't. But because everything is unsourced, the reader doesn't know what is missing, what version isn't there."

We should not expect that the sources cited in the news, even anonymous sources, be unbiased. That is impossible. Instead, we should expect the journalists or news providers to share with us any biases their sources might have and give us some sense of why the information is still reliable. One measure of a journalist's reliability is the degree to which they help us assess the sources they present rather than simply use them for their own purposes.

The nature of the source is one matter. The evidence the source offers, and how the person presenting the news has vetted or tested the information, in many ways is even more important. This is the matter to take up next—evidence.

CHAPTER 6

Evidence and the Journalism
of Verification

Seymour Hersh needed a moment to place the voice on the other end of the phone. Then it registered. The man was a professional from the intelligence community on whom Hersh had relied as a source during the cold war. He remembered the man as solid and reliable, a moralist who occasionally talked to the press confidentially as a way to keep the government honest. When they met later in Hersh's office, the man outlined a chilling tale of how the Central Intelligence Agency was employing torture techniques in the war on terror that went beyond anything known to the public.

Explosive exposés were not new to Seymour Hersh. Perhaps no journalist in American history has exposed more official misconduct or provoked more controversy through the disclosure of government secrets. The first had come in 1969, when Hersh discovered that the U.S. Army was covering up the alleged massacre by its troops of nearly five hundred Vietnamese civilians in the village of My Lai. He learned that the military had conducted a secret investigation of the massacre and chosen to indict one man, Lieutenant William Calley, who was taking the fall for many, and that the whole case was being hushed up. Hersh eventually found Calley and got him to talk. The revelations created a national outcry that led to the indictment of twenty-five other officers and enlisted men and contributed to a further drop in public support for the war. Hersh won a Pulitzer Prize for his reporting.

It was only the beginning. Hersh went on to uncover the secret bombings in Cambodia, the secret U.S. backing of the Pinochet coup in Chile, the secret U.S. efforts to help Israel develop atomic weapons, the secret spying by the FBI and CIA on American citizens, President Ronald Reagan's involvement in the secret program to circumvent a congressional ban on sending arms to the Contra rebels in Nicaragua, the drug-running background of U.S.-backed Panamanian dictator Manuel Noriega, and more. During Watergate, Bob Woodward and Carl Bernstein, recognizing how many major Watergate stories Hersh broke in the *New York Times*, referred to him as "the competition."[1]

Hersh also become something of a lightning rod for his reporting on the war on terror. When the Pentagon described the first major ground operations in Afghanistan as "overall successful," Hersh wrote a minutely detailed criticism for the *New Yorker* magazine that called the operations "a near disaster" and challenged the notion of the Taliban as vanquished. He also cast "extreme doubt" on reports of Iraq's weapons of mass destruction and connections to al-Qaeda. He was quickly condemned for both conclusions. Slate.com columnist Jack Shafer called Hersh's assessments of Afghanistan "boneheaded-dumb wrong" and went so far as to predict that, after Hersh's reporting on Iraq, he expected to see presentation of weapons of mass destruction and direct links with al-Qaeda "within the next two weeks." Time in both cases proved Hersh's reporting right.

Hersh's approach to reporting, inculcated over long years, is simple: a painstaking accumulation of detail and facts. It is a philosophy of empiricism instilled by an editor at the City News Bureau in Chicago where Hersh worked as a young reporter in the 1950s. Covering a story about an apparent suicide, Hersh was sent back to the police station time after time to get more detail on the victim's clothes, then sent back again because he hadn't adequately described the tie the victim was wearing, then sent back yet again to look for any sign the victim had been drinking. Each time he went back in search of additional facts proved more embarrassing for Hersh and irritating to the police. The last visit, Hersh recalled, brought him all the way up to the precinct captain, who finally "grabbed me by my shirt and pulled me up to his face and said, 'Kid! It is not my practice to stick my nose in the face of every fuckin' suicide.'"

Hersh developed something akin to a reverence for the importance of detail, and he turned that into a method that involves a systematic chain of reporting. "It taught me to work bottom-up," he explained. "Never jump up the chain. Learn everything you can from people below or around the story. Every step, get every document you can squeeze out of them. Then go back and review what you've got before you go on. Go back to earlier sources to check what they said against what you learned from later interviews or documents."[2]

As Hersh looked at the man in front of him bearing stories of CIA torture, he was once again wary. The reputed victim of the torture, described as the most-wanted terrorist suspect in Southeast Asia, had been captured in Thailand in August 2003. His name was Riduan Isamuddin, but he was known as Hambali by those he led in attacks against the United States and its interests. President Bush called him "one of the world's most lethal terrorists." Government agents were sent to Thailand to take part in his interrogation. In the succeeding months, fragmented leaks made their way into news reports that the interrogation of Hambali had produced important intelligence. He was transferred from Thailand to Jordan and eventually to Guantánamo, where he was still being held in 2005. But his name had largely dropped out of the news when Hersh got that source's first phone call in January 2006.

The information the source had provided Hersh in the past had always checked out. The man was no crazy. He was an idealist. And as he talked to Hersh, the reporter recalled later, "he was really upset. Outraged about behavior he thought immoral."

He proceeded to tell Hersh how the CIA agent who was sent to Thailand to lead the interrogation of Hambali was openly bragging back at CIA headquarters. Among other things, the agents said he had strapped a helmet filled with fire ants on Hambali's head, a technique "the Apaches used," as the agent described it. "Within five minutes they're attacking his eyes and up his nose, and he's screaming and crying his guts out," the source quoted the agent as telling his colleagues. "But," the source added, "they don't know if the intel he got is good or bad."

Hersh filled his legal pad with notes: names of others who had heard the stories; details of written complaints that had been filed about the behavior on which no action appeared to have been taken.

For the next three months, Hersh labored to verify and document the allegations. He interviewed more than fifty people and amassed every document he could find about the arrest and interrogation of Hambali. The fruits of the reporting are preserved in a collection of legal pads and documents that form a stack nearly a foot high in Hersh's office. "Facts, facts, more facts. That's what I was taught." Hersh said. "And at every step try to get a document to back up the facts. I contacted the police who originally arrested Hambali and documented all that, and I get hold of some files on the intel."

Five months after the source's initial phone call, Hersh had verified twenty salient points of what the original source had told him, and he confronted the CIA with the information he had. "I tell them what I've got and get a flat denial," Hersh said. "'Hambali was waterboarded, but not that other stuff.' Categorical denial. Everything I got tells me it's true. But my problem is I can't get a second source."

He was able to confirm some things. "I found three other people inside who confirm that everything my guy is telling me he was telling the agency in real time," Hersh said. The corroborating sources confirmed that Hersh's source had reported to the inspector general the same thing that he had told Hersh. Several people also confirmed that the interrogator himself had told them of using the same technique. Still, Hersh did not have anyone who had seen the insect torture for themselves. What he had, in other words, was still secondhand. And he had a flat denial from senior officials. As a result, he said he decided, "I can't go with my story."

Three years later, in April 2009, some of the legal memos written during the Bush administration outlining interrogation methods were released to the public. The memos included approval of the use of "insects," but did not specify what kind of insects and did not mention fire ants. But that was no consolation for Hersh.

"After that report came out," Hersh said ruefully, "a couple of the guys I talked to inside the agency thought the mention of 'insects' was hilarious. They told me they were having drinks and laughing about how I fell for that 'nothing but waterboarding line.' But, you know, the one thing they beat into me at the City News Bureau, where I first worked, was 'Don't write anything you don't know for sure.'"[3]

It is a deceptively simple but challenging idea. Write what you can prove, not what you believe to be true. Be skeptical, even of what you think you understand and of what the evidence might suggest. It is not enough to be almost certain, to "know" something must be true. You have to be able to show it, to establish it, to defend it, to prove it, including to a skeptical public and against official scorn.

The story of the story that Seymour Hersh didn't write is a window into the fourth question in trying to ascertain what to trust as reliable information:

What evidence is presented, and how was it tested or vetted?

The question of evidence is inevitably the most complex, challenging, and important element of sifting through the news about the world around us. It requires discipline and patience. It is where testing and vetting information comes into play, as well as the even more complex matter of trying to discern meaning from evidence, not just establishing facts. The journalist-turned-novelist Gabriel García Márquez put it this way: "Our only route to the truth is by means of evidence . . . and the concept of truth applies to the *results* of inquiry . . . and what we have a duty to do is observe the right procedures."[4]

Inevitably, evidence is interlinked with sources, the matter discussed in the previous chapter. The quality of sources cited in the news, their expertise, their vantage point, and the directness of their knowledge are a form of evidence. But knowing the source alone is insufficient in determining whether what they are telling us is reliable. We need to know how to identify and evaluate the evidence those sources are offering to answer our questions. Good sources who have proven themselves reliable and trustworthy in the past can be wrong. So can documents. On some occasions even honorable people may lie. A source's reputation, his or her past record, can tell us whether they are worth talking to, but it does not mean what they tell us is correct. It is not sufficient—for those reporting the news or consuming it—to simply take someone's word for something if it can be independently confirmed. If something can be proven, the proof should be sought.

In an age when we are our own editors, in the "show me" versus "trust me" age of information, the act of evaluating evidence falls more directly on us as consumers. Looking for and knowing how to understand evidence is how we can distinguish more-reliable information providers from those less reliable. It is the dividing point between knowing what is believable and simply believing. And we should expect more proof than we once might have from news organizations and other information sources claiming to serve the public.

There is an element of intuition and common sense to sorting through evidence, of course, to knowing what is meaningful in what context. In talking to people in different realms—in science, law, journalism, law enforcement–we have found what amounts to a shared set of steps or ideas about how to examine and evaluate evidence, although these professionals may use different vocabulary to describe them:

- Identify what evidence is offered and understand the nature of that evidence (much as we parsed through the basis of how a source might know something).
- Know how that evidence was vetted or tested and whether the countervailing evidence has been explored.
- Identify what conclusions have been drawn from the evidence (explicitly and implicitly), and whether or not those conclusions are supported.
- Ask whether this evidence could be used to draw different conclusions.

This is how you differentiate between evidence and inference. Evidence establishes something is true. Inference is believing it must be so before actually proving it.

One important element to look for is the use of implicit conclusions. Journalists sometimes use the neutral or independent voice of journalism as a cloak to make implicit or indirect points—to steer the audience to a conclusion. They may do this in the quotes they select, the sources they seek out, and the adjectives they employ. Knowing the telltale signs of such abuses, and how to deconstruct them, is important.

In the remainder of this chapter, and the next, we will walk through how to undertake this process as consumers of news, to be a skeptical editor. In this chapter we examine the evaluation of evidence in what we have called the journalism of verification, that realm of news most focused on trying to establish what has happened, with getting the facts right—the more *reportorial* kind of news. In the next chapter, we will show how the absence of this vetting is the hallmark of the more passive kinds of journalism, what we have called the journalism of assertion.

Then we will show how something beyond passivity, the actual cherry-picking and manipulation of evidence, is the hallmark of the journalism designed to affirm rather than genuinely explore, what we call the journalism of affirmation.

With any news content we encounter, this process of evaluating evidence should begin with recognizing what kind of news story or content it is. Is it a straight news account, one essentially just presenting what has happened? If so, we are looking for evidence that its facts are true, for proof of what happened. If we are looking at more-complex kinds of stories—sense-making news or even more ambitious paradigm-shifting or watchdog reporting—we will want proof not only that the facts are accurate but also that the interpretation is correct and that we can see the evidence for ourselves and make up our own minds.

Even establishing facts involves layers of complexity. We may be satisfied with less evidence, for instance, if the information in question is simple and uncontroversial. If we are trying to learn what the president said in a large meeting, with many witnesses and no implied controversy about what happened, we might accept the word of a single White House spokesperson, even if that spokesperson was not personally at the meeting. There is no reason for the spokesperson to evade the truth, and any incorrect statements about the meeting could easily be found out. The nature of the information and the context, in other words, influence our level of skepticism. If a statement is more damaging, we should want more proof. And if the question at hand is not what was said but why, the motive, we might require still more evidence. Establishing a motive, an "interior truth," is more complicated. Establishing why an administration compromised on its previous position on some important policy would probably require talking to more than two people. And the White House spokesperson might not be close to a sufficient source for getting the true story.

Evidence and Breaking News

To break this process down, let's start with an example involving the simplest kind of story: that water main break in Washington, D.C. Some of the evidence (the water on the street) is right in front of us. For most of us, immediacy isn't critical—learning about it later, or even the next day, would be sufficient. No one was at risk; the biggest problem was basements flooded. As a result, we expect a fairly complete account of a relatively simple event that has passed.

What evidence does the *Washington Post* article offer? Reading the story closely, it is apparent that the *Post* reporters were not eyewitnesses. The descriptions of the scene are attributed to official sources. "A lot of the homes suffered pretty significant water damage," the deputy fire chief is quoted as saying. But the *Post* reporters who worked on it demonstrate an impressive level of reporting for a story only a few hundred words long. Five different sources are quoted by name—a respectable number for so brief an account—three of them officials and two residents of the neighborhood where the incident occurred. The officials quoted are directly responsible for dealing with the problem, not spokespeople one step removed. The residents quoted corroborate information from those officials and provide added detail. In the overlapping accounts, the story offers a sense of what happened, why, and what it felt like. The nature of the event, something relatively minor, shapes what we consider adequate evidence.

Now let's examine reporting about a different kind of event, one more lethal, occurring during a busy commute and threatening hundreds of people. This is an event we would want to know about instantly while events are still unfolding, and given that, we might forgive a certain amount of uncertainty and confusion.

This is the story of two Washington, D.C., subway trains that collided during rush hour in the summer of 2009. How many have died and are injured? The first account, on a local television news program, suggests three people are dead. A *Washington Post* story published online a few hours later suggests six have died. Late that evening, the number has risen to nine. How did the accident happen? It isn't yet clear.

As consumers, we understand that the story might be incomplete. Events are fluid; details are chaotic. The scene must be controlled by first responders trying to save lives. We appreciate that journalists might be kept at some distance. We understand that not everyone knows what is going on and that, with victims being taken to different hospitals, the counts of injured and dead are unclear.

But we are also more urgently interested in this story than in the report about the water main break, since this is about something more serious. We might have loved ones on the trains or caught on another train stopped somewhere farther down the line. So we want to know whatever we can immediately, understanding there is much we cannot know. The event—and our urgent desire for information—alter our expectations about completeness and accuracy.

Now we are looking for signs of certainty in an uncertain situation. We want to know what information is solid and, most important, what information is not. We are even more keenly attuned to the source of the evidence—is it an authority, an eyewitness, a secondhand account? How carefully is our news provider distinguishing among rumor, hearsay, and firsthand knowledge, and how much is it sorting out differing accounts, as opposed to just ferrying along anything it hears? In a fluid situation, we demand to know what cannot be known, so that we are not misled or led astray by panic.

The medium Americans turn to most for news is local TV. One station on this day featured its anchorperson on the phone with a spokesperson from the subway authority. Another station interviewed a passenger from one of the crashed trains on a cell phone. A third station had a reporter on the scene, who had initially gotten quite close to the accident site but was sent by authorities to stand farther away.

At first glance the three reports might not seem that different in value. After all, the station with the transit authority spokesperson on the phone had an official on the air. The second channel had an eyewitness to the accident. The third channel had someone on camera at the scene.

But in reality, the accounts on the air at that moment were of three distinctly different values. On the first channel, the official transit authority spokesperson wasn't at the scene. She had gotten her information secondhand, and it wasn't much. She was clear about what she knew and didn't know, but after repeating that people should not rush to the scene and that the cause of the crash was uncertain, she had little to offer. But she was the best source the station had at the time, so they kept her on the air.

Click to the next station, and the second channel had one eyewitness on a cell phone who was trying to be helpful. She was at the rear of a crashed train. She described what it was like to be in the crash. Her description was emotionally riveting. She had seen someone who looked badly hurt. But she could describe only what she could see. It was one view, one witness, though the station interviewed her for a long time because she was highly emotional.

The third station offered substantively more. While its journalist had arrived after the incident had occurred, he had talked to multiple sources, including more than one eyewitness. So even though he was not a direct participant, an official, or a witness to the accident as it was occurring, he had information from all these sources. He also had access to first responders, and he reported what they had told him. He was precise about what had come from witnesses versus what had come from officials. And he described what he had seen for himself. And importantly, he offered caveats about what was solid and what was not—what information was likely to change—and by offering multiple forms of evidence, he was able to triangulate differing accounts.

It was this multiplicity of evidence, and the reporter's transparency about its strengths and weaknesses, that made this report most useful. It was broader in its scope and offered the advantages of both of the other two stations' reports.

All this touches on the first two elements we naturally ask: How much evidence is offered and of what nature?

But the skeptical way of knowing, Homer Bigart's notion of portable ignorance, demands that we ask more too, that we test the evidence offered. How do we assess whether something that seems like evidence is meaningful? Do the facts prove what they might suggest? Does seeing equal knowing? Is this evidence or inference?

Evidence, Skepticism, and Vetting: Seeing versus Knowing

To get at this notion of a higher expectation of evidence, let's consider a breaking story that played out over a longer period of time and was reported by national news organizations communicating to a more distant audience.

In the early morning hours of Monday, January 2, 2006, in an unused portion of the Sago Mine near Buckhannon in the coal country of West Virginia, something triggered an underground methane explosion. Even now, it isn't clear what started it, but the explosion was powerful enough to break through the walls that sealed off the closed section of the mine and send smoke, dust, and carbon monoxide into working sections of the mine.

It happened at six thirty A.M., the day after the New Year's holiday. Twenty-nine men had just entered the mine to start working. Sixteen escaped immediately. In the moments that followed, word quickly spread that thirteen men were still below—whether trapped or dead, no one knew. Within minutes, the town near Sago and the rest of the country, thanks to national media coverage, began to keep anxious vigil.

There were reasons for both hope and worry. The damage to the mine appeared to be limited. There were no cave-ins or accumulations of rubble. Some concrete walls built to direct airflow, however, were damaged, as were the seals designed to keep out carbon monoxide. The colorless, odorless gas could kill a person in less than fifteen minutes if it spread in high enough concentrations. The miners were trained to seek out air pockets and seal themselves off, and they carried "rescuers," tanks that would give them an hour of oxygen.

Above ground, the national media gathered, and the country and the world waited, watching, reading, and listening on TV, the Internet, and radio. Progress was slow. Hours passed before any formally trained rescue teams entered the mine. It then took those teams a day to travel the first two thousand feet, one sixth of the way to where the explosion had occurred. The rescuers had to work painstakingly, testing the air and repairing the ventilation as they went. They wanted to avoid releasing trapped methane, which could induce a second explosion. They also had to worry about weakening the roof as they dug and causing a cave-in. By Tuesday night, the gas readings were rising, in some cases to ten times the amount considered safe—ominous news. With only an hour of oxygen, the miners could not possibly have survived unless they found a pocket of safe air and then sealed themselves off. As the hours went by and the media offered background, reports mounted of safety violations at the mine, things that went unfixed after being discovered, and of lax monitoring of the mining industry in general, particularly in recent years.

Finally, Tuesday evening, rescuers found the body of a lone miner deep in, 11,200 feet from the mine entrance. The cause of death was unclear. The body was just a few hundred feet from a vehicle that had transported the team into the mine early that Monday morning, the first group to head in after the New Year's holiday. Tests showed the carbon monoxide levels around the body were high. Where were the other twelve miners?

Overnight, the answer came, and the news media rushed the story. The January 4 *Washington Post* front-page story was typical. The headline read "12 Found Alive in W.Va. Coal Mine."

A dozen miners trapped 12,000 feet into a mountainside since early Monday were found alive Tuesday night just hours after rescuers found the body of a 13th man . . .

The bells at the Sago Baptist Church pealed, and joyous relatives rushed outside to celebrate their miracle: miners surfacing after being in the cold, damp Sago Mine for 41 hours. Gov. Joe Manchin III said some would need medical attention. "Everybody ran from the church screaming, 'They're alive! They're coming!'" said Loretta Ables, whose fiancé, Fred Ware, was among the missing miners. She had lost hope when she learned about the dangerously high levels of carbon monoxide in the mine, but she was elated as she waited outside the church. "I feel great, very great."

The miners had apparently done what they had been taught to do: barricaded themselves in a pocket with breathable air and awaited rescue.

Apparently. Except for one thing. It was all wrong. Only one miner survived.

The official report to the governor on the tragedy six months later and press reconstructions correcting the mistake largely agree about how the press got it wrong. Both describe a communication process shaped by hope rather than skepticism. After nearly forty hours, mine officials were anxious to get good news from the rescue teams. They believed they had that news at eleven forty-five P.M., when the rescuers finally came upon the trapped miners. In the command center aboveground, officials believed they heard rescue team members, who were wearing oxygen masks and reporting through cell phones and walkie-talkies, tell them that the miners were alive. Without waiting for confirmation from the emergency medical technicians or to see the men safely aboveground, people in the command center erupted in celebration. Within seconds, someone in the command center leaked word out to the family members waiting in the nearby Sago Baptist Church. Against all expectations, apparently the men were miraculously safe. They were coming up. Ringing church bells, tears of joy, and shouts of thanks suddenly washed away the funereal pall over the town. Reporters, stationed with the families at the church, busily recorded the cheers and shouts of thanks from families and friends and assumed that the news must be true.

But several elements that would have been required for confirmation were missing. There was no official word from the only authority on the scene formally authorized to provide information. Virtually all the facts that preceded the celebration pointed to the almost certain reality that the miners had perished. Journalists reported the comments of a state official who was at the church, but they failed to recognize that he had not received any official word either; he was just reacting to everyone else. Had they been stationed at the hospital they would have seen a different story. Had they arranged direct contact with anyone in the command center, they would have known a different story. Had they been able to station themselves near the mine entrance, rather than staying in the church with the families, they would have had a different story. Ultimately, everything they knew was hearsay, second- or thirdhand. The message to the command center hadn't been conveyed clearly.

At midnight, just fifteen minutes after they found the miners, the rescue teams established that only one miner had survived. At twelve thirty, rescue teams brought the one survivor out of the mine, who was rushed by ambulance to the hospital—one man, one ambulance. The state report on the incident becomes curiously vague about what happened next. At one forty-five A.M., embarrassed and probably scared, mine officials "attempt[ed] to send a message to the families at the church via the state police, asking an officer to relay word to the clergy to the effect that the command center has conflicting reports on survivors and the initial reports may have been too optimistic," the report describes awkwardly.[5] "The message is reportedly relayed but does not reach the families." It is another hour before the families in the church, and the reporters with them, get the formal announcement.

In reality, what had transpired was exactly what the evidence for hours had suggested was almost certain to have occurred. The carbon monoxide levels in the mine were far too high. The one hour of oxygen that each miner carried had been used up a day and a half before. Handwritten notes the rescuers found in two of the miners' hands offered grim testimony. Most of the miners had probably died on Monday afternoon, before any rescue team even entered the mine and more than a day before the bodies were actually located. The journalists covering this knew all this, or should have. The fact that one young miner had survived was miraculous.

We are using the Sago case as an example precisely because it is such a challenging one. People in the church believed the miners were alive. They were celebrating. And there were government officials among them. These are the factors cited by journalists who later defended their mistaken Sago reporting. "We have to rely on the facts as we gather them, all the sources we have access to," CNN's Anderson Cooper said the next day. "We were tightly controlled physically . . . No officials came to talk to us. There's only so much one can do."

Cooper's argument seems sensible—at first blush. He reported what he could see and what the people around him believed. But Cooper and other reporters—not all on the scene—also failed to note what was missing: that they lacked official confirmation, that they had no confirmation from area hospitals, that they had not seen anything for themselves. The journalists who got it wrong at Sago, in other words, fell victim to believing what they saw, ignoring what they already knew, and failing to notice what was missing.

It is seductive, in the era of television and particularly live cable television, to be tricked into the simplicity of imagining that seeing is believing, and that believing equals truth. This is the aftereffect of the journalism of assertion's large presence in our culture.

But the skeptical way of knowing demands more. Seeing is not knowing. Sorting out what is true involves more than having one or two facts and passing them on. Distinguishing between fact and truth involves knowing how to weigh the value of different facts—in other words, knowing how to sort and evaluate evidence.

Our distance from an event also plays a role in our expectations and how much we might forgive journalists for making errors. If we were residents of Sago, who stayed up all night and watched local news, we might be forgiving of a reporter who described the joy in the streets for the first half hour, but we would be more grateful if a reporter had also noted the absence of official confirmation, and if the news station had sent someone to the hospital to report on the miners' conditions. When we are close to an event we are likely to be paying closer attention.

Yet for a national news organization, whose audience is likely farther away and paying less constant attention, the reporting mistake is arguably worse. The viewer of CNN or MSNBC is more likely to turn off the television set upon hearing word that the miners are alive and go to bed. The reader of the *Washington Post* is more likely not to read the story the day after. The more distant the audience, and the more disinterested, the more the press should be expected to give a vetted finished product of news, because we are less likely to consume everything about the event.

While Sago may be a hard case, and a wrenching one, mistakes like it are increasingly common. In the age of continuous live news, we frequently see the reporting of "facts" that appear to suggest something but have not been verified. On September 11, 2009, President Obama was at the Pentagon, just across the Potomac River from Washington, to commemorate the people who died there in the attacks eight years earlier. Shortly after Obama left the ceremony, a CNN staffer monitoring a Coast Guard radio frequency heard the local Coast Guard unit conduct a training drill, one that was repeated four times a week. The staffer mistook the training drill for something real. A call was put into the Coast Guard for confirmation, but before the Coast Guard could disabuse the anxious cable channel, CNN went on the air with the following report.

"We have seen at least one boat come up the Potomac and challenge the Coast Guard," CNN correspondent Jeanne Meserve reported, adding the Coast Guard "sent a transmission saying they expended ten rounds." The caption onscreen read "Coast Guard fires on boat on the Potomac River." Seven minutes later, Reuters news service, attributing CNN, sent out a news bulletin across the Internet marked URGENT: "Coast Guard Fired on Suspicious Boat on Potomac River in Central Washington, D.C.—CNN." A few minutes later Fox News repeated the story, citing Reuters as its source.

After it became clear the report was untrue, CNN Washington bureau chief David Bohrman told the *Washington Post*, "We didn't just leap onto the air." The decision to air the report, he said, came "after 20 minutes of trying to get some confirmation from the Coast Guard and being told nothing was going on. It would have been wrong for us not to report this was happening." A written CNN statement offered almost precisely the same wording: "Given the circumstances, it would have been irresponsible not to report on what we were hearing and seeing."

CNN argued, in effect, that it was not only justified and excusable for it to pass along false and unverified information. It also had an obligation to do so.

The press was left in the awkward position of being lectured on journalistic ethics by the White House press secretary. "My only caution would be that before we report things like this, checking it out would be good," Robert Gibbs told reporters.

In the age of continuous news, when information comes from many sources, checking it out *would* be good. And as consumers of news, we should be looking for the telltale signs that this checking has occurred. What is known? What has been verified? What has not? Does it comport with what we already know? What is missing?

Evidence, Analysis, and Meaning

The cases above all involved breaking news and illustrate the challenges of establishing even the most basic realm of evidence: What are the facts and what do they actually establish about what might have happened?

The evidentiary issues are largely a matter of corroboration and confirmation from knowledgeable sources. And this is challenging enough.

But given that so much media moves beyond simply establishing facts and enters the realm of analysis and interpretation, we need to go further. What kind of evidence do we require in those instances when the news is not unfolding in real time and when an outlet offering us news purports to weave together those facts to provide a deeper sense of meaning? How do we identify whether the evidence really supports the conclusions contained in the story and whether the news that aspires to analyze and interpret events is providing evidence or just inference. Those are the questions we must take up next.

On February 21, 2007, the triumphant campaign of Arizona senator John McCain awoke to a crisis. McCain was on the verge of capturing the Republican presidential nomination. By then, four of his five opponents had dropped out of the race, and McCain had gathered three quarters of the delegates needed to clinch the nomination. The apparent triumph was all the more remarkable given that only a few months earlier, McCain had been dismissed as a candidate, out of money, just having fired his staff, his campaign presumed all but over.

The comeback was another in a dazzling career marked by a string of political resurrections—and tenacity that served him through his capture and torture in a Vietnamese prison camp and triumphant postwar life in politics. In his early days in the Senate, McCain survived a scandal that nearly ended his political career when he and his wife, Cindy, had become political and personal friends with a Phoenix real estate developer and financier named Charles Keating. Keating and his friends had contributed heavily to McCain's election to the Senate, and Cindy McCain had invested in an Arizona shopping mall with Keating. But as the owner of Lincoln Savings and Loan Association, Keating also had used federally insured deposits to make risky but high-yield investments. During McCain's first Senate term, investments at Lincoln Savings were beginning to turn sour. Government regulators began to raise questions. Along with four other senators who later would become known as the Keating Five, McCain held two private meetings with regulators, trying to get them to ease up on Keating and other savings and loan companies. By 1989, Keating's bank had collapsed as a result of his risky investments. It cost taxpayers $3.4 billion to bail out Lincoln Savings.

McCain's colleagues in the Senate reprimanded him for "poor judgment" in his meetings with government regulators. The episode, McCain would later say, cost him "something very important"—his reputation and his personal sense of integrity.

Afterward, McCain became an outspoken critic of congressional earmarks. He attacked the corrupting influence of political fund-raising and helped push through a major campaign-finance law, the McCain-Feingold Act. McCain's drive to pass the reform, Feingold said, "had to do with his sense of honor. He saw this stuff as cheating."

Now, with the maverick Republican on the brink of winning his party's nomination for president, a story in the *New York Times*—a paper that had endorsed McCain's candidacy in the Republican primary only a month before—threatened to undermine him. The story was headlined "For McCain, Self-Confidence on Ethics Poses Its Own Risk."

> Early in Senator John McCain's first run for the White House eight years ago, waves of anxiety swept through his small circle of advisers.
>
> A female lobbyist had been turning up with him at fundraisers, visiting his offices and accompanying him on a client's corporate jet. Convinced the relationship had become romantic some of his top advisers intervened to protect the candidate from himself—instructing staff members to block the woman's access, privately warning her away and repeatedly confronting

him, several people involved in the campaign said on the condition of anonymity.

Both McCain and the lobbyist, Vicki Iseman, denied they ever had a romantic relationship. "But to his advisers," the article said, "even the appearance of a close bond with a lobbyist whose clients often had business before the Senate committee Mr. McCain led threatened the story of redemption and rectitude that defined his political identity."

The *Times* piece was long, sixty paragraphs, roughly a full page of the newspaper, and it went on to offer a lengthy account of McCain's earlier ethical conflict with Lincoln Savings and Loan before returning to McCain's relationship with Iseman. When it did come back to the original subject, the story asserted that "Mr. McCain's confidence in his ability to distinguish personal friendships from compromising connections was at the center of questions advisers raised about Ms. Iseman."

After describing how clients of Iseman in the telecommunications industry had contributed "tens of thousands" of dollars to McCain's campaigns and his Commerce Committee, the article enumerated staff concerns. "Why is she always around?" the *Times* reported one staffer as asking. One staff member, it said, was "instructed to keep Ms. Iseman away from the senator at public events": "A top McCain aide met with Ms. Iseman at Union Station in Washington to ask her to stay away from the senator."

"It is not clear what effect the warnings had," this portion of the article concluded, "and the associates said their concerns receded in the heat of the [earlier] campaign."

The last two paragraphs of the article quoted a statement from McCain's campaign headquarters:

> It is a shame that the *New York Times* has lowered its standards to engage in a hit-and-run smear campaign. John McCain has a 24-year record of serving our country with honor and integrity. He has never violated the public trust, never done favors for special interests or lobbyists, and he will not allow a smear campaign to distract from the issues at stake in this election.
>
> Americans are sick and tired of this kind of gutter politics, and there is nothing in this story to suggest that John McCain has ever violated the principles that have guided his career.

The article also triggered charges that the *Times* harbored politically biased motives to hurt McCain. Those charges, *Times* editor Bill Keller said in an editor's note in the paper the next day, "surprised me by their volume" and by "how lopsided the opinion was against [my decision] to publish." Keller should not have been surprised. In the George W. Bush years in the White House in particular, the *New York Times* had become a lightning rod for conservatives. Now, during one of the longest presidential campaigns in history, criticism of the paper as a mouthpiece for Democrats had become a common and harsh reaction to unfavorable stories.

In the wake of criticism, Keller insisted that the story had never implied a romantic relationship between McCain and Iseman. The story, he contended, was about the senator's blind spot to his own relationship with special interests. A year later, as part of the disposition of a legal action by Iseman, the *Times* even published a "Note to Readers" declaring that the article "did not state, and the *Times* did not intend to conclude, that Ms. Iseman had engaged in a romantic affair with Senator McCain or an unethical relationship on behalf of her clients in breach of the public trust."

The McCain story is a lesson in evidence, meaning, and audience. Regardless of what the *Times* "intend[ed] to conclude," readers correctly saw the piece as accusing McCain of an affair. That was the lead, and while the story also covered a good deal of other material, many readers—as we did on first reading—scanned quickly through that long intervening section of old material looking for a return to the lead and proof of what had been implied.

Most of the rest of the media certainly thought the news here was the implied affair. "Presidential Candidate John McCain Accused of Having an Affair with Lobbyist," read the headline in *Daily Mail* in England. As a long exploration of the piece in the *New Republic* put it more cautiously, "the piece . . . explores the possibility that the Republican presidential candidate may have had an affair with the 40-year-old blond-haired lobbyist for the telecommunications industry." The *Boston Globe*, owned by the *New York Times*, declined to run the *Times* story, opting instead to run one by the rival *Washington Post* dealing with the fact that McCain, like other presidential candidates, had lobbyists working on his campaign.

The *Times* story hung on the "anxiety" and "concerns" of anonymous sources who were worried that their boss, John McCain, was romantically involved. The *Times*, however, could not verify whether those anxieties were justified, at least not with any facts the paper could print. As the *Times*' own watchdog, public editor Clark Hoyt, concluded after looking into reader complaints about the fairness of the article, "it is wrong to report the suppositions or concerns of anonymous aides about whether the boss is getting into the wrong bed."

The failure here goes to the difference between fact and meaning. What was the *Times* telling its readers with this story? Beyond the facts offered, what was the *Times* story really saying?

In the field of semiotics—the study of understanding language and symbol—scholars talk about information having three levels of meaning. Those levels are worth discussing briefly, for they apply well to understanding how we confront the news.

At the basic level is the most direct or literal definition, or "signification," of information. This is the meaning derived from the dictionary definition of the words, without much context or inference. This basic level of meaning is called "denotative." In defending the paper, Keller limited himself to this denotative level of meaning. Taking things literally, the *Times* did not report that McCain had an affair but only that some of his staff were "convinced" of it, suffered "waves of anxiety" about it, and intervened to keep the lobbyist and the senator apart. It did not go further. But was that really *all* the *Times* was reporting? If we stick to this basic level of meaning, there is almost a kind of willful naïveté to the argument, which also smacks of a legalistic literalism.

The second level of meaning is the "connotative." The connotation of words in semiotics is their extended meaning: what the words suggest in our minds in the context they are written or spoken. As those who study semiotics see it, people decipher most texts by the connotation of the words and pictures, and it is a central part of how we derive meaning from most creative endeavors. How did most of the rest of the media react to the *Times* piece? They did so by recognizing *what the* Times *was saying* in the piece—its connotation, the implication of the words and the story in context. This is a less-lawyerly meaning but in many ways more real. This is what made the story explosive, what made it controversial, what made people read it.

The third level of meaning is what semiotics calls emotive, or "annotative." In plain terms, the annotative meaning is the value we place on what we are learning, whether we consider it good or bad. How do we react to the implication that John McCain had an affair, or even that he has personal blind spots when it comes to his own behavior? Are we appalled that the *Times* has intruded on this private space? Or do we cringe that an admired candidate and public figure might be vulnerable because of it (as the anonymous aides reportedly were)? Or do we think that the story exposes McCain as a hypocrite? Or do we think that the *Times* has rushed out with a story it cannot prove? And if the latter, do we think the paper did so out of liberal ideological zeal or journalistic blundering?

In news, the annotative meaning relates to the tone of an article, to the subtext, to whether the story is signaling something positive or negative in our minds. To understand this idea, imagine someone talking. Think of how the tone of voice used reveals what the speaker is saying. The words "You've got to be kidding," for instance, might be uttered in a way that conveys amazement. The same words, spoken in a different tone, might imply sarcasm. Or those words could be spoken in a way that communicates anger, or perhaps disappointment. The meaning depends on the speaker's inflection.

As consumers of information, we understand annotative meaning almost intuitively. We know by the fact that the story was published in the first place, for instance, that the people producing the news must think it's important. We sense something about the news organization's attitude about the story in whether the story is at the top of the newspaper or Web page or at the bottom, in the size of the headline or placement in the newscast. We also sense something about meaning from the way the story was written. The annotative meaning of news is the level of meaning we think about when we ask ourselves, *What do they really think they are telling us? What did they have in mind? What's their motive?* Beneath the dry toneless presentation of the news, what do the people who produced the story think it means? These questions are an inescapable and integral part of meaning of any kind of communication.

As we navigate trying to know what to believe, what to trust, we inevitably judge what we encounter at all three of these levels of meaning.

The *Times* piece failed to prove what it was conveying connotatively, what the words implied, and what most people thought the story was really saying—its annotative meaning. Was this a story only about McCain's personal blind spots regarding his own integrity, as Keller argued? If so, the paper's failure to write the story in a way that accomplished this was a blunder. Or was the story really about the senator's having an affair, which became so blatant that staffers put a stop to it? If so, the story failed to prove its case with evidence.

To be fully reliable, news stories should succeed at all three levels of meaning. The words and pictures should clearly convey meaning. The implications of those facts should be plainly established. And we should understand explicitly what the conveyers of the news had in mind. In short, the meaning of news should be manifest and clear so consumers can trust it.

Keeping an Open Mind:
How to Apply Meaning to News

It may seem unfair to put all the responsibility for making evidence and meaning clear on the shoulders of journalists. What about audiences? How do we, as consumers, arrive at meaning in news? How well do we navigate the borders between fact and belief, between empiricism and our own preconceptions?

Survey data suggest that consumers increasingly infer ill motive to the press, particularly political bias.[6] And as consumers, we are certainly capable of jumping to conclusions based on limited evidence. A quote in a news story from a politician we don't like may inspire us to send the story to a friend in an e-mail with an epithet about what a clown the guy is, even if no such evidence is contained in the story itself. Certainly any journalist who has pored through reader e-mails can relate examples of audiences missing the point of stories, making strong inferences based on scant evidence, or complaining about the story missing something it actually contained.

As consumers in the new age of information, we need to bring something akin to the skepticism we ourselves once expected of journalists as we navigate the information currents. And that can mean demanding to know, even when we see statistics cited from so-called authorities, evidence of where that data came from.

The best journalists we know have what might be described as a disciplined humility about what they see. They have trained themselves not to let preconceptions distort their observation and not to jump to conclusions about what they see might mean or imply. They don't rush to judgment or rush to establish meaning. They ask themselves whether they really know and understand what they think they are seeing. Author and journalist David Shipler, who spent decades digging for facts and meaning in war zones for the *New York Times*, describes this as "getting my mind into a state where I enjoyed having my assumptions challenged because there are many truths."

This kind of disciplined humility can be an important attribute of the skeptical consumer as well. To develop it, we need to maintain a skepticism about our own knowledge and understanding. When we exercise that kind of discipline, we begin to bring a more scientific mentality to our observations about public life and events. We become better at trying to understand facts and don't take their meaning on faith. It engenders more curiosity, and it demands that our curiosity be guided by empiricism. Not all journalists have it, though they should. As consumers, we are often far less likely to employ it.

How, as consumers of news and information, can we develop this discipline and apply the formula of "show me," or "prove it," or "why should I believe it" to evidence—particularly to evidence that may challenge our own beliefs?

In science, the most basic manner of developing this discipline is the scientific method—or the process of setting up an experiment designed to test a hypothesis or educated guess. In the social sciences, where the scientific method may be harder to execute, researchers use various procedures to test whether evidence really proves their hypotheses, or might actually indicate something else. The most common of these tests for determining the significance of observations or findings is called the null hypothesis. In layman's terms, it is a formal method of maintaining an open mind.

The process works like this: Researchers begin with a hypothesis that they want to examine. They then arrange their experiment, or gather their evidence, to test whether they can prove that their proposition is true. But this process involves recognizing that they could be wrong, that indeed the opposite of what they imagine could be true. This opposite proposition is the null hypothesis.

We use this kind of thinking in our daily lives all the time. Imagine you have a plumbing leak in your home—water is coming into the kitchen through the ceiling. You quickly recognize there are three possible sources of water in the rooms above, two bathrooms—one of which is just above kitchen—and the pipes carrying water up from the basement. You check the bathroom above the kitchen first, and if you find no leaking pipes there, you recognize there are still two more possibiles sources to check out. In scientific terms, your hypothesis is that the water is coming from the bathroom just above. But you also have in mind a null hypothesis—that you're wrong, and it's coming from someplace else. And you keep testing until you discover the source of the leak, until you have proof that you have found it. We are involved in the same method of thinking when we go to the doctor to undergo batteries of tests—eliminating possibilities of what might be wrong until we identify the problem.

At its core, this kind of hypothesis testing creates mental discipline, and that discipline forces us to be open-minded. It requires that we consider other possibilities, a null hypothesis. Then it demands that we ask whether something contains enough evidence to challenge conventional wisdom or belief.

It is also the fifth question in the checklist for assessing whether information is true and reliable.

What might be an alternative explanation or understanding?

As consumers, we should ask this of ourselves. And in the news we consume, we should also look for signs that authors or producers of the news have asked it as well. Have they explored the null hypothesis? And have they demonstrated sufficient reason to discard it?

Just as we employ this open-minded humility, or lay version of the null hypothesis, more in certain realms of our lives than in others, we believe people tend to bring this kind of discipline to certain kinds of news more than to others. People tend to be more discriminating, we believe, when they encounter stories in which they have some personal experience and knowledge—stories, for example, in which their company or their profession or their children's school is involved. It is also easier to bring this kind of cold eye or discipline to stories that aspire to higher levels of proof—authentication stories, paradigm-shifting stories, and exposés. These types of stories tend to be more thorough about organizing evidence, because they are more explicit about trying to prove a case.

And consumers *should* have higher expectations, or more refined questions, for stories or content that fall into the realm of authentication, sense making, or exposé.

First, *we should expect that there be enough evidence to reasonably prove the case.* That means we should expect to see the proof for ourselves, to see the evidence shown to us. We should not have to take the word of the news organization. If the information is presented in such a way that we are being told, in effect, "we checked it out, and the real story is X," that is not authentication. It is merely another voice taking a side. In an earlier era, some might complain that providing a simple and clear narrative and offering proof at the same time were hard to balance. A story, after all, is not an academic treatise. In the age of the Internet, however, where hyperlinks can function as both footnotes and instant access to original documents, and space is unlimited, that argument crumbles.

Second, in stories that aspire to prove something, *we should expect that the accounts being disproved be given a fair hearing.* We should, in other words, see evidence that the null hypothesis or alternative understanding of events has been explored. This exploration of alternative arguments also should be more than lip service. If the alternative explanation is an argument, for instance, we should hear the strongest case for it. If we are hearing something that came from different people, some more reliable than others, we should hear both the strong versions and the weak ones, so not all are discredited equally. The authenticator should not pick the one version that was erroneous as representation of the whole side.

Third, *we should expect that unanswered or unclear elements be acknowledged.* What is unknown, still to be explored, or not yet authenticated is as important as what is known or authenticated, and acknowledging the unknown adds to the authority of the group that is claiming to be dispelling the fog.

Fourth, *we should expect the coverage of a subject to continue in some form to keep us informed of what impact, if any, its disclosure has had.* This, in the end, becomes the best test of the quality of the information. Watchdogs often bark at innocent sounds in the night. So, too, careless or misguided efforts at investigative journalism often come to light only when they have no discernible effect. We should expect to see a response to the disclosure. And if it is not forthcoming, we should expect continued reporting that explains the lack of reaction.

Finally, it also may be useful, given the complexity of the issue, to review what we have discussed about evidence and the journalism of verification.

It is not enough to know the source of information. We need to know what evidence is offered—the proof. When evaluating that evidence, context matters: Facts that are incontrovertible and uncontroversial may require less evidence to satisfy us.

We may tolerate more uncertainty about news that is unfolding in front of our eyes—those chaotic, breaking news stories—but we should expect transparency and evidence of journalists' humility and acknowledgment about any information that may be in doubt.

And as time passes after an event, or our need for information becomes less urgent, we should expect more certainty about the information we receive and more effort on the part of journalists to confirm facts. We naturally will also have less tolerance for things that are simply asserted. And we should expect that any news that might create panic be treated more carefully by a news provider.

As news moves toward sense making and trying to arrive at meaning, the burden of proof and our expectation of evidence should rise even further. Ironically, the opposite often happens. The penalty exacted for faulty analysis and interpretation of news actually tends to be lower. Generally, no one demands a correction when an analysis is wrong. Mea culpas tend to be offered only for mistakes that are more black and white, even if they are more innocent—misspellings, misidentifications, typos in addresses, and the like.

Any assertions in stories should be backed by evidence, and whenever possible, any evidence should be corroborated.

News should meet the tests of imparting the literal meaning of the facts and also support the connotative and the annotative meaning as well.

And we should look for signs that alternative meanings, or null hypotheses, have been explored. There are many potential truths and meanings to stories. Have we been shown that alternatives have been considered?

All these are reasonable expectations when we encounter the most traditional kind of news—the journalism of verification, those stories that try to establish and vet facts. But as traditional newsrooms shrink, and audiences fragment across platforms and channels, this kind of carefully reported material is increasingly competing with other kinds of journalistic material that are less costly to produce. Evidence tends to operate quite differently in the other arenas of news—the growing realm of the journalism of assertion and the more ideological media of the journalism of affirmation.

That is the question that we must take up next.

CHAPTER 7

Assertion, Affirmation: Where's the Evidence?

Evidence can do more than reveal the nuances of a story or prove a case. How a news outlet handles evidence is also one of the most useful ways of identifying what kind of journalism you are encountering, which is the first step in determining its reliability.

Is the news content really engaged in open-minded inquiry that is trying to get to the bottom of things? Or is it just passing things along, unvetted and unchecked? Or is it doing something else altogether, such as using evidence for political or even propagandistic purposes?

In the previous chapter, we discussed evidence in the realm of news in which journalists are clearly trying to vet facts and establish accuracy. They may not always succeed, but their efforts are signs of their intention.

Now we take up how evidence is used in the newer models of journalism we encounter with increasing frequency today, the journalism of assertion and the journalism of affirmation, along with a variant of the latter, the partisan watchdog media. In these models, the behavior of journalists in relation to evidence is strikingly different. And recognizing it is one of the key ways in which we can distinguish which kind of media content we are encountering.

Evidence and the Journalism of Assertion

In the summer of 2009, American politics seemed to be reaching toward a new level of polarization. In town-hall-style meetings across the country, angry citizens clashed with Washington lawmakers in emotional and angry encounters that seemed to suggest deliberative democratic discussion might be becoming impossible. The most colorful and bizarre exchanges, some staged and some spontaneous, were videotaped by citizens and activists, and those videos turned up on YouTube and then found their way to cable news. In effect, politics was becoming a new kind of reality programming in which people staged angry encounters and then recorded them to make news. At one such meeting Congressman Barney Frank, a Massachusetts Democrat, became so resentful of one angry woman that he told her, "Trying to have a conversation with you would be like trying to argue with a dining room table. I have no interest in doing that."

Some in television news responded by arranging quasi-debates of experts to sort out both the town hall meetings and the legislative debates. One of these debates occurred on PBS's *NewsHour* on August 13. On one side of the table was Dick Armey, chairman of the organization that rallied opponents of the health care reform plan to turn out at town halls. On the other side was Richard Kirsch, national manager of a group that organized supporters of health care reform for the meetings. The moderator was Judy Woodruff, one of the most serious and respected journalists in television news.

For several minutes viewers were treated to a confusing exchange of contradictory assertions and conflicting details. Armey warned of "sheer abject waste." Kirsch worried about "tremendous insecurity" in the health care system.

Then Armey said something that would lead to a barrage of complaints from PBS viewers:

> But the fact of the matter is there is a large and growing number
> of Americans that . . . see this as a hostile government takeover
> of all health care, where they will be forced into a government-
> run program . . . If you're over sixty-five years old in America
> today, you have no choice but to be in Medicare. Even if you
> want out of Medicare, you have to forfeit your Social Security to
> get out of it. Even if you're a Christian Scientist, you have to give

up your Social Security. That's pretty heavy-handed, and people fear that.

Woodruff turned to Kirsch to respond: "What about this charge?"

Kirsch ignored her question and instead accused Armey of alleging something that the Republican had not said. "Dick Armey . . . doesn't think Medicare should exist. Basically, Medicare is the system that provides a guarantee of good coverage for seniors in this country. It is, in fact, what is meant—your old age means you don't have to worry about not getting the health care you need. That's the same thing we need to do for everybody in this country, but we need to do it in a system that provides choices between regulated private insurance or public insurance. And the point is we need that guarantee for people to have affordable health coverage."

The charges and countercharges of prearranged talking points continued, the points moving too fast to be sorted out. The bickering continued until each declared his side would win in the end. Woodruff finally announced, "We hear you both loud and clear."

Afterward, Michael Getler, the ombudsman for PBS, received an outpouring of complaints from liberals who were upset that Woodruff did not question Armey's statement about Medicare after Kirsch had failed to do so.

"Ms. Woodruff allowed Mr. Armey to lie about these very important facts," wrote one viewer.

"I understand that individuals that appear on the program have a right to their own opinion but that does not give them the right to lie and certainly does not give PBS carte blanche to accept everything they say as factually correct," wrote another.

Linda Winslow, executive producer of the program, told Getler that the viewers were asking for something Woodruff could not be expected to provide: "Judy was the moderator, not the judge." Nor were these viewers upset that Kirsch, too, had dissembled and exaggerated.

To PBS ombudsman Getler, however, there was a larger issue at play. The point was "not on Woodruff, personally, who did seek to get a rebuttal or challenge on these points," he wrote. "Rather it is on the broader need for journalists to question and challenge points that they know, or suspect, to be factually wrong."

Getler checked the accuracy of Armey's assertion with the Social

Security Administration. He learned that Medicare is a voluntary program, which made that part of Armey's assertion a misstatement. But if
a person signs up for Medicare and Social Security, the two are tied together. If you then drop Medicare, you lose the Social Security, which
made that part of the statement true.

Then Getler posted his own assessment of PBS's responsibility, given
that it had chosen such an interview, or debate, format, using the words
of another viewer, Tom Tonon, of Princeton, New Jersey. "In cases like
this," Tonon had written, "when an interviewer fails to challenge an inaccurate or misleading statement there thus arises an important question on the role of an interviewer on public television; to wit, is this role
only to allow interviewees a platform to state whatever they want to
state, regardless of the truth or validity or accuracy of their statements?
My own opinion is no, but rather, the interviewer must make an effort to
ensure that the truth/untruth of statements be measured or acknowledged in some way."

What the viewers noticed, however, is a primary signature of the journalism of assertion when it comes to the matter of evidence: the absence
of vetting—a failure to challenge assertions, ask for evidence, and then
test that evidence.

This example is important not because it is unusual or egregious but
rather because it has become so prevalent. We can see similar and indeed far-more-acute examples of it every day in our news culture, especially on television. Woodruff at least tried to get her guests to challenge
each other's claims. She didn't succeed. But many television interviewers
today do not even try. *NewsHour* segments are also longer and more
detailed than most on TV. And *NewsHour* is rare among television
news operations for having an ombudsman who would even take up the
issue.

"Almost everybody agrees that we can save between one hundred and
two hundred billion dollars if we had effective malpractice reform," Republican senator Jon Kyl of Arizona told CNN interviewer John King on
October 2, 2009.

Kyl's assertion was absurd on its face. It was hardly accurate that "almost everybody agrees" with that estimate. How much might be saved
in insurance costs by limiting medical liability was a matter of significant dispute, which King should well have known. And Kyl's math was a
common conservative talking point, not something that should have

caught a journalist off guard. But King did not ask Kyl what evidence he had to back his claim, or point out that the number was a matter of disagreement. He simply ended the segment, saying they were out of time. Seven days later, the Congressional Budget Office issued a report saying the real number was closer to eleven billion dollars the first year, and fifty-four billion dollars over ten years.

It need not be something as specific as a number. On September 29, 2009, Republican senator Orrin Hatch suggested that President Obama's real goal with health care reform was to socialize the American medical system: "What they're doing is, they are trying to do it in increments . . . until they finally get us to the point where you're going to have socialized medicine," which would destroy the greatest health care system in the world.

The idea that the president secretly intended to slowly and incrementally socialize the U.S. health care system was a significant talking point among opponents of health care reform that one could find repeated on various Web sites devoted to opposing the plan, including that of the Republican National Committee. The Democratic party scoffed at this notion. For all practical purposes, in effect, Senator Hatch was accusing the president of lying to the American people.

What was CNN anchor Tony Harris's response? Did he ask Hatch what evidence he had for such a claim? Did he point out that the Utah senator was effectively accusing the president of dishonesty? Did he make any attempt to vet this talking point, or even evince any skepticism about an assertion issued without any proof?

Harris, like King, simply uttered CNN's signature line for ending a discussion: "All right, let's leave it there."

When you see this passivity, be wary. Bring your own skepticism if not to the politician to the journalist. The journalists here, be they hosts, interviewers, or bloggers, are not demanding a high level of verification or even inquiry. Instead, they are operating more as conduits and enablers.

At its most acute, this kind of journalism of assertion occurs in staged formats, such as talk show segments in which guests are booked to simply offer their take on things. What might appear to be an analytical segment is really little more than a moderator or host letting guests spin and spout, with little effort to check what they are saying or to ask for evidence or much of anything else, other than to move things along.

The problem is that these conversations increasingly are occurring without a structure for fact-checking. The conversation creates a foundation of public understanding that may or may not be built on any knowledge of what is true or what is not. Facts, by the structure of this culture, are devalued. They are not foundation stones but incidentals. When everything is unchecked, all assertions become equal—those that are accurate and those that are not. The news, and journalism, becomes more of an argument than a depiction of accurate events that argument, debate, and compromise can build upon.

Yet most of this unchallenged talk passes unnoticed, filling hours on our television screens, accepted as a form of journalism like any other. An enormous amount of the programming on television news now employs the format of the live interview.[1]

One reason journalists on television have become more passive, and the journalism of assertion has gained momentum, is structural. Though people are often unaware of it, the modern "live" TV interview has severe limitations that cede control of the encounter away from the interviewer and toward the person supposedly being questioned.

First, by giving up the ability to edit, the news operation is incapable of checking for accuracy and context any facts asserted—at least during the interview. In practice, we also rarely see news operations correcting at a later time misstatements made by guests. Second, in live settings the person being questioned can more easily control the time—roll out prepared talking points, dissemble, evade, toss out questionable numbers or assertions, or filibuster. This is why most political consultants and public relations people like their clients to do live interviews. "We always prefer to do live interviews, especially cable," the vice president of communications of one of ten largest corporations in the United States told us candidly, though he asked to remain anonymous so he did not antagonize the media. "Because it's unedited, we can really get the message out the way we want it." Even Mike Wallace, the CBS news correspondent who's considered perhaps the most fearsome of TV inquisitors, told us, "Live interviews, like live press conferences, are the easiest thing for a politician to control."[2]

These two basic structural limitations are exacerbated today by something else: Most of the live interviews we see in this age of 24/7 television programming are hastily arranged, with the journalist only marginally involved in that preparation. The basic structure of a television operation now is that a group of relatively young researchers called "bookers" find the guests, do some level of "pre-interviewing" to identify what the guests will say, and then write out possible questions and answers for the host. There is also an element of what some in television call "casting" to this—a phrase borrowed from Hollywood. The bookers, instructed by their producers, tend to look for guests to play certain roles or to take certain positions. Often they are casting to stage demi-debates, though on cable these conflicting viewpoints are now increasingly offered sequentially, with the officials and newsmakers interviewed alone rather than sharing airtime with their antagonists.

Adding to their lack of preparation, the hosts on these programs are often on the air for hours and move from interview to interview, topic to topic, over the course of a program. They operate as something of a reporter-of-all-trades, covering all topics, as well as an anchor. The guests they are interviewing, by contrast, generally are experts on the topic they are addressing, better prepared for this brief encounter than the person who is questioning them, and often skilled in media training.

In 2008, for instance, David Barstow of the *New York Times* produced a lengthy exposé on the lengths the Pentagon went to during the Bush administration to organize, prepare, and control the legion of former military officers who were interviewed by the media about the war on terrorism:

> To the public, the men are members of a familiar fraternity, presented tens of thousands of times on television and radio as "military analysts" whose long service has equipped them to give authoritative and unfettered judgments about the most pressing issues of the post-Sept. 11 world.
>
> Hidden behind that appearance of objectivity, though, is a Pentagon information apparatus that has used those analysts in a campaign to gain favorable news coverage of the administration's wartime performance.

Not only did these "military analysts" get special briefings and talking points from the Pentagon, but most also had ties to military contractors with vital interests in the activities and policies they were asked to assess. Yet the news organizations that sought them out largely didn't know and didn't take the time to ask about the conflicts and connections.

The hasty preparation by third-party bookers common today stands in sharp contrast to the kind of pre-interview reporting television journalists once engaged in. Before interviewing convicted Watergate conspirator H. R. Haldeman on camera in the mid-1970s, for instance, Mike Wallace spent fifty-five hours in preliminary conversations with Haldeman to hear his story and check the facts and be prepared to challenge him. That was in an era when TV news wasn't on all day long and newsrooms had larger staffs, giving journalists more time to do their research. Television in that era was also trying to prove that the medium could compete with the most-respected interviews in print.

In the 1950s and 1960s, in the pages of publications like the *Paris Review*, *Playboy*, and the *New Yorker*, the interview became something of an art form to explore the personalities of literary, social, and political celebrities. Those long-form interviews were frequently the result of deep research and preparation, and the interviews themselves were a process, not a single presentation. Alex Haley, an author and journalist who produced work for *Playboy*, used to go to his subjects' hometowns and interview the people who knew them as children before he ever encountered his subjects face-to-face. Eric Norden, who interviewed former Nazi minister Albert Speer for *Playboy*, spent six weeks studying his subject before they sat down, and their interview lasted ten days and nights. Journalist Robert Scheer's famous interview with then-presidential-candidate Jimmy Carter in 1976 involved five separate meetings over the course of three months.

In television's early years, some analysts imagined the camera as a kind of psychic "X-ray," an almost magical device, whose "piercing stare" would expose the truth about the people being interviewed.[3] This is the kind of imagery that inspired CBS's unblinking-eye logo. The present-day live TV interviews on cable or the local morning news may bear the same name as these past encounters—both are called interviews—but few involve anything resembling the kind of preparation that gave interviewing its reputation.

Another limitation to the modern live TV interview is that newsmakers now can pick and choose friendly outlets, or at least avoid unfriendly ones. This is true even for people who may want to publicize their work—analysts, authors, or others who want to get their name or product out there. It is doubly true for newsmakers who want to deliver messages but do not need to saturate the airwaves. There are simply so many outlets now that journalists frequently barter and negotiate terms with newsmakers. Many interview subjects have lawyers representing them, negotiating the parameters of what can be asked and what cannot. Booking an important person for an interview on TV is now called "The Get," and TV correspondents and anchors can make their reputations if they are successful at the art of "The Get," even when it involves bowing and scraping.

Consider what happened, for instance, when South Carolina governor Mark Sanford, seven days after mysteriously disappearing from his job, reappeared in his state and became the subject of national press fascination. The forty-nine-year-old governor, a social and fiscal conservative and the head of the Republican Governors Association, was on the short list of those expected to run for president in 2012. But when the married father of four sons held a news conference to admit that he had spent the "last five days of my life crying in Argentina," trying to break off an affair with his Argentine mistress, his chances for national office likely evaporated, and he became the hottest "get" in the TV interview business. So salacious was his story that the competition to land an exclusive interview wasn't left to young bookers. Joel Sawyer, the governor's press secretary, was flooded with e-mails from top network anchors and correspondents, several of whom offered Sanford explicit and implicit deals that betrayed the new balance of power in TV news toward those who make the news rather than those who cover it.

On July 15, 2009, the *Post and Courier* newspaper, in Charleston, South Carolina, obtained these e-mails through a Freedom of Information Act request. The ones from TV correspondents showed them wooing the governor with something other than the prospect of hard-hitting journalism.

Griff Jenkins of Fox News e-mailed with hints of the controversy being dispelled: "If the Gov does an interview and its [sic] exclusive, it will make air on the TV channel and our radio news service all across the country . . . I work mostly for our primetime coverage Oreilly [sic], Hannity, Greta, Beck—so there would likely be primetime coverage as well for some soundbites of the Gov dispelling this flap."

David Gregory of NBC's *Meet the Press* suggested the governor would get to frame the conversation how he wanted: "Look, you guys have a lot of pitches . . . I get it and I know this is a tough situation . . . So coming on Meet the Press allows you to frame the conversation how you really want to . . . and then move on. You can see you have done your interview and then move on."

Even Comedy Central's Stephen Colbert e-mailed Sanford, but his was a parody of the posturing by the real journalists: "As you may know, I declared myself a South Carolinian last night. I went power mad for about 40 seconds before learning that Gov Sanford was returning today. If the Governor is looking for a friendly place to make light of what I think is a small story that got blown out of scale, I would be happy to have him on. In person here, on the phone, or in South Carolina. Stay Strong. Stephen."

The publication of the e-mails was a scandal in itself, one that revealed how modern news operations sometime prostrate themselves to newsmakers and explicitly offer the live interview as bait.

Perhaps most important, live interviews involve some strict boundaries beyond which the journalist cannot easily trespass and that make it difficult to dig too deep. From the 1980s into the twenty-first century, journalist Ted Koppel, the host of ABC's *Nightline*, was considered among the most skilled interviewers on television. At the peak of his popularity, in the 1990s, Koppel talked about those lines beyond which interviewers couldn't go. There is a natural affinity between the viewer and the host, he explained, a bond that you don't want to break. "The most fundamental rule is to keep the viewer identifying with you. You can lose that identification easily by losing control of the interview, or by being too aggressive or rude or by not asking the right type of questions," Koppel explained. To maintain that subtle relationship, Koppel thought it was important to let the person being interviewed have his or her own say on the first question or two. Then, at a certain point, if the person is going on too long or avoiding the question, and "everyone at home gets it," the interviewer has license from the viewer to become more aggressive. Koppel described it as if an alarm has gone off and the viewer is saying, "Ted, get in there." Even then, however, Koppel imagined strict limits. If the subject continues to be evasive, he said, "the best you can do is leave the audience with the impression that this person just doesn't want to answer the question." You can ask a question two or three times to "underscore that, underline it," Koppel said, but little more. Imagining that "you can wring the truth of someone who doesn't want to offer it is unrealistic."[4]

Even doing this in a live interview requires the interviewer to have knowledge of the subject and the ability to edit the interview in his or her own mind while it is going on, not just letting the subject roll through talking points. "The essence of journalism is editing," Koppel said. "And editing while you are on the air is extremely difficult. It means sifting out the extraneous from the relevant, the new from the old—in your head, while listening to the person talking, and thinking of the next question."

Assume the interviewer is knowledgeable enough to know when a subject is dissembling. Assume, too, the interviewer is skilled enough to do a mental edit during a live interview, while listening to the interviewee and perhaps to someone in the control room via a headset. Even then, the interview probably needs to be long enough for more to happen than the interviewee to simply roll through talking points. Yet the average interview on cable daytime news today, according to our research at the Project for Excellence in Journalism, is three and a half minutes long. The average interview on morning network news is two minutes and forty seconds. The outlier on television news today is *News-Hour* on PBS, where the average is almost seven minutes.

Given these enormous limitations—the difficulties in editing, the limitations on controlling the interviewee, the lack of preparation, the lack of broadcast time—most live interviews are less a revelatory encounter than a kind of ceremonial ritual, less a way for journalist to *gather* news than a way for newsmakers to *present* themselves and deliver messages. More than a decade ago, ABC's Diane Sawyer told us, "My husband [director Mike Nichols] calls live interviews 'performance masquerading as conversation.'" It seems even truer today.[5]

Why is a format that has so many limitations so prevalent? One reason is economic. Talk is cheap—or at least cheaper than reporting. With so many hours of programming to fill each day, it is simply less expensive for TV news operations to stack live-interview segments together than to have correspondents go out and produce stories in which they can check their facts. The guests arrive on the set, the host scans through a few questions prepared for them by young bookers, and a segment is born.

The other factor, which may be more of a rationalization of economics than any proven effect on audiences, is a prevalent notion among TV programmers that audiences prefer elements that are live to those on tape. In fact, taped programs have bigger audiences. The most popular

TV magazine, for instance, is *60 Minutes*, a show made up of carefully prepared taped segments. The three commercial nightly newscasts, which are made up of 70 percent taped segments, have much larger audiences than any individual news programs on cable. As of 2010, the worst-rated network nightly newscast, CBS's, had seven million viewers, according to data from Nielsen Media Research, twice that of the most popular cable news program, Bill O'Reilly's. The three network evening news-casts combined averaged twenty-one million viewers, four times that of all cable news combined.

Still, the live-interview segment has become a central feature of our television news landscape, thanks to the ease and cost of producing it—and with audiences fragmenting, it is only likely to grow.

That is why it is so important for consumers to recognize what is oc-curring in these segments.

Wherever you find the interlocutor, the journalist, or content provider simply letting people talk, without any effort to check facts or challenge assertions or ask for evidence, you have entered another sphere, one little recognized even by its practitioners. You have entered the realm of the journalism of assertion, and the content you are getting there is not a finished product, not a vetted assessment of information. And the fact that a journalist has let something pass is no guarantee it is correct.

Evidence and the Journalism of Affirmation

While a defining characteristic of the journalism of assertion is a lack of vetting of evidence, in the growing realm of journalism of affirmation, evidence is used more carefully: It tends to be preselected to prove a point. Rather than something to be sifted through in open-minded inquiry, it is a weapon, a tool, in an argument of persuasion.

Discerning consumers can detect this selection process if they look carefully at the presentation, the choice of stories and topics, the lineup of guests, and even the arc of the segments or interviews themselves. The treatment of evidence is one of the defining characteristics of this new partisan but commercial media and sometimes the most subtle. For the stories of this type are often carefully woven.

When it comes to presentation of evidence, there are many ways this selection process can occur, but four methods appear most often. If you detect them, you will know that what you are encountering, even it if looks like and calls itself reporting, is really something else.

Cherry-picking Facts: The Use and Misuse of Anecdotes

The first method is to cherry-pick facts that seemingly prove a case. These quotes, anecdotes, and statistics may well be presented in a deadpan neutral manner. The host or moderator or reporter may never explicitly say they prove some larger point. Or in more bombastic settings, say, in the hands of a Glenn Beck or a Rachel Maddow, the host may well connect the dots and shout about their nefarious meaning—that they show exactly what the audience has known all along. In such cherry-picked news, there is an absence of looking broadly to find out whether the anecdote is representative or the statistic really means what it might suggest. There is no attempt to interview the person being skewered or any of that person's supporters. There is no meaningful attempt to explore an alternative or null hypotheses. Such inquiry might intrude on the goal of trying to make a point.

By September 2009, the national debate over health care legislation proposed by President Obama began to be clarified as some basic provisions of the bill were spelled out in more detail. Solid Republican opposition to the legislation, aided by wavering conservative Democrats, was the subject of MSNBC's *The Ed Show*, hosted by Ed Schultz, on September 24.

Schultz introduced his opening segment with a short video clip of a woman at a town hall meeting on health care held by Republican House whip Eric Cantor in northern Virginia. The woman told the story of a friend in her early forties who had lost her job and then learned she had tumors that required surgery. Without employment—and therefore insurance—her friend was in a difficult financial and emotional situation.

Cantor told the woman he would need to know more about the friend's situation, "in terms of income eligibility and the existing programs that are out there right now, because, if you look at the uninsured, there is probably 23 percent or 24 percent of the unemployed right now that is probably already eligible for an existing government program. Beyond that, there are programs, there are charitable organizations, there are hospitals that do provide charity care."

The video stopped, and Ed Schultz said, "That is a classic my friends. Did you get all that? The woman's got issues. She's got cancer. She needs the surgery right now! This is a classic . . . because when you present the Republicans and the obstructionists with a real-life scenario, they don't have an answer.'"

Then Schultz became more animated: "They're still talking percentages. How would you like to be in the percentage where you're left out? You're just SOL. That's their reform. That's their answer. You know they're great at holding up the socialism, the communism, the Marxism, all kinds of 'isms.' But they don't have an answer for that woman. She's just at the wrong spot at the wrong time, and we've got to talk about the redistribution of wealth."

Schultz, however, had carefully selected his facts from the video. Cantor said he needed more facts in order to fully address a woman's concerns. To be helpful, the congressman had added that there were some ways to approach such emergencies. Even that limited segment of video opened up several areas Schultz might have explored to provide viewers with real knowledge. What programs were these 23 or 24 percent of unemployed eligible for? On what terms? How effective was such protection? Schultz conveniently ignored those prospects and zeroed in on the one statement that seemed to reinforce his point.

The cherry-picking that goes on in the partisan media may also include numbers and statistics. In those cases, when the evidence offered appears as data, with an aura of objectivity that implies, it may well still be partisan, more factlets than facts, more a stray number than data that might meet some test of statistical significance or meaning.

In May 2009, when Chrysler, then under the supervision of President Obama's auto-restructuring task force, announced it would close one quarter of its auto dealerships nationwide, Web sites were filled with bloggers looking for the heavy hand of partisan politics in the decision.

One blogger, a man named Joey Smith, got a lot of attention. Smith took five pages of the forty-page list of dealerships slated to be closed, and announced he was creating a new Web site "to determine if the surviving dealerships are being rewarded for their campaign donations to the Democrats and/or Obama since 2004." He found that the closed dealerships listed on those first five pages had given more than $130,000 to Republican campaigns and only $37,800 to Democratic campaigns. In the 2008 presidential race, the same dealerships had contributed a total of $7,150 to John McCain and $0 to Barack Obama.

Smith's work quickly became the go-to site for other bloggers. Among them was Doug Ross, who labeled Smith's work as "Obama's Dealergate" and rhetorically asked what the odds were that you would lose your dealerships if you were a big Democratic contributor? "Looks to be somewhere between slim and none" was his answer.

The flurry of accusatory blogging, including claims that President Obama had a "hit list" of dealerships, soon reached the White House, where press secretary Robert Gibbs disclaimed any government involvement in the decisions. "The president's task force on autos did not pick individual dealerships," Gibbs said. "It isn't involved in picking what plants may or may not be closed . . . That's the job of the individual car companies."

So what was the truth? Brooks Jackson, head of the Annenberg Political Fact Check Project (FactCheck.org), decided to look into the charges. As a journalist who had covered national politics for more than thirty years for the Associated Press, the *Wall Street Journal,* and CNN, Jackson has always been suspicious of instant judgment and quickly drawn conclusions. He knew, for example, that over the years he had covered politics, auto dealers as a group had long given Republican candidates much more in the way of campaign contributions than they had Democratic candidates. So Jackson studied the record of 2008 campaign contributions by all auto dealerships handling Chrysler brands, those that had closed and those that had not. What he found was that the contributions of those dealers were $10 to $1 in favor of Senator McCain: $26,200 to McCain and $2,700 to Obama.

"That leads us to think that if Chrysler dealers were chosen for closing purely at random, with no political thumb on the scales at all, we should see nearly $10 in McCain donations for every $1 of Obama donations, both from the dealers who were closed and the dealers who were not."

Anecdotes are important. They are the stories that add flesh and bone and a sense of reality to our understanding of things. They make numbers come alive. But when they appear alone as a foundation for an argument, they should be seen as a warning signal, a sign of a house built on a single load-bearing wall. Beware of stray anecdotes in isolation or even a seemingly elaborate analysis of a single number or statistic.

These are not evidence. Evidence must be surrounded by context and corroboration.

Serious journalists often express concern about one bit of shoddy newsroom tradecraft: You can find an example to illustrate anything. They remind themselves of a cynical journalistic axiom: If you can find three anecdotes showing the same thing, you can write a "trend story"—a piece supposedly illustrating some broader phenomenon—though you will have no idea if it's true. As a result, the best journalists are on guard not to use anecdotes as evidence without obtaining other proof.

In the new world of information and self-editing, we should be just as wary. Anecdotes illustrate; they do not prove. Single statistics hint, but they do not establish. Examples or stray numbers offered as proof are a red flag. When you see them, take care. They are a sign of cherry-picking, a hallmark of the journalism of affirmation.

Beware of the Fallacy of Evil Men

One of the most useful pieces of advice we're learned in our journalism careers is summed up in the phrase "Beware of the fallacy of evil men." It refers to the idea that when you are trying to understand a situation in public life, the likelihood that people did something because they are basically bad, or have vicious motives—because, in effect, they are evil—is almost always wrong and is even more suspicious when it is used to describe a large group. Using the explanation that someone is basically bad is a way of shutting down inquiry and turning information into fables— e.g., the CEO of Acme Widget Company took a bribe because he is a bad man, or that politician came to this conclusion because he is evil. The reason people do things, their motives, are invariably more complex— and more interesting. The story of a CEO who takes a bribe because his company, his life's work, and his vision of an invention that will help the world will not survive without it is a human story with an authenticity to it that the imputation of evil lacks. What's more, the solutions to problems, the points of compromise and agreement, are almost always found in those nuances. The idea that he did it simply because he was greedy and bad is a flat cartoon in one dimension.

There is an additional problem with imputing evil motive. As we noted earlier, journalism that focuses on the interior elements of the news—such as what a person thinks or what her motive might be—is inevitably harder to prove than journalism that deals in external facts, such as what the person said or was seen doing by others. Thus accounts that purport to deal in this kind of interior information require more evidence, not less. Yet precisely because motive is so difficult to prove, weaker forms of journalism often try to skate by with less evidence. After all, who could prove it was wrong?

The journalism of affirmation is saturated with examples of the fallacy of evil men. In affirming and comforting the preconceptions of an often angry audience, talk show hosts indulge in this notion so frequently that we have found it in nearly every transcript we have reviewed.

"What made this country great is the recognition by our founders that individuals are all created equal, endowed with certain inalienable rights, life, liberty, pursuit of happiness," Rush Limbaugh told fellow host Sean Hannity on January 22, 2009. "If you look at the Democratic Party, are they for life? Folks, they're the party of abortion. Liberty? These are the people that are trying to pass any law they can to restrict where you can go, what you can do when you get there, where you can eat, what you can eat, what you can smoke, when you can't smoke, what kind of baby you can have—all these things. Pursuit of happiness? I have yet to see a happy liberal."

Ed Schultz ended his discussion about the health care legislation and Eric Cantor with a similar condemnation. "The Republicans lie! They want to see you dead! They'd rather make money off your dead corpse. They kind of like it when that woman has cancer and they don't have anything for her. That's how the insurance companies make money—by denying the coverage."[6]

The suggestion of ill motives, and the lack of respectful dialogue that it leads to, serves a purpose that, again, has nothing to do with understanding or even analyzing the political scene. It has nothing to do with facts. It's strictly about affirming the audiences' preconceived beliefs.

Be on the lookout for the fallacy of evil men. When you see it, it is a sign that this isn't a journalism of inquiry but a media of persuasion built on prejudice and distrust.

The Ad Hominem Attack

Perhaps no device is as common in the journalism of affirmation as when a talk show host attempts to undermine a guest's argument by attacking the speaker instead of addressing the argument. What we may miss, in the heat of the shouting that ensues—the sense of combat, the vague shock of seeing such anger on a supposed news program—is that this is a classic example of flawed logic. It is an ad hominem attack, well known to any undergraduate class in rhetoric. It is also a diversion, often an insult, that moves the discussion away from inquiry. "Ad hominem arguments are easy to put forward as accusation, are difficult to refute, and often have an extremely powerful effect on persuading an audience to reject someone's argument . . . even when little or no evidence has been brought forward to support the allegation," author Douglas Walton wrote, describing the technique in a text on logic.[7]

In the journalism of affirmation, ad hominem attacks are often delivered in a preemptive way, to discredit an argument before it has even begun. Yet you may also see them when an ideological host encounters a guest who will not back down and the conversation devolves into butting heads. Here's an example from Fox host Bill O'Reilly, when he interviewed Salon.com editor Joan Walsh on June 15, 2009, about late-term abortions. The segment began with a substantive question and answer. O'Reilly asked Walsh, who supports legalized abortion, whether she felt "late-term fetuses deserve any protections at all?" Late-term procedures make up 1 percent of all abortions, Walsh answered, and most of those are to save the life of the mother or when the baby is about to die. O'Reilly agreed.

But the conversation then quickly devolved as the two began to argue over basic facts about abortion that should have been a matter of record. Walsh and O'Reilly repeatedly interrupted each other. "All right, you're filibustering, Ms. Walsh. Ms. Walsh, stop talking," O'Reilly said. The jousting for position continued, with Walsh refusing to concede a point she apparently considered a trap.

O'Reilly finally gave up trying to debate and simply attacked.

"You know who has blood on their hands. You. You don't care about these babies," O'Reilly said.

"That's ridiculous, Bill," Walsh said.

"It isn't ridiculous. You're the zealot," O'Reilly said.

"You're a piece of work," Walsh responded.

The segment ended, mercifully, with a commercial but without offering much understanding.

Such ad hominem attacks need not take place in person. Hurling personal insults about competing talk show hosts is also a staple of the journalism of affirmation. Here's Ed Schultz talking about Rush Limbaugh: "Apparently, the drug-ridden loser Rush Limbaugh, he thinks because he's got a lot of money and a lot of stations that he's a success in life. The guy who can't hear because he did so many drugs, that had no self-discipline and character has now taken his first shot at me . . . Come on, you fat pig. Let's get it on."[8]

And here's Limbaugh on October 8, 2009, talking about fellow Republican Joe Scarborough: He's a "neutered chickified moderate."

Scarborough fired back at Limbaugh the next day: "I would be careful if I had put my testicles in a blind trust for George W. Bush for eight years."

Such vitriol may pretend to toughness and appeal to angry audiences. But if you hear someone in the media engaging in this kind of demonization and playground machismo, remember that these insults are a diversion, not an argument.

Alternate Realities

The ethos of many ideological talk shows is a kind of netherworld, a TV salon in which the host, and often a like-minded guest, describes the landscape of public events as they see it, or as they wish it to be, and as they imagine the audience member wants to see it too. The ethos is reassuring, and at the same time, it exhorts listeners against the opposition, often using the techniques described above. On radio, the formula is often extreme, with the host as a champion of the average person, touching on some wound, some aggrievement, and identifying enemies. On television, those same elements of the formula are evident, but they are typically subtler. They emerge less in shouts or derisive sarcasm than in a conversation between a host and a guest who affirm and embolden each other in a mutual worldview, one most of their viewers hold too. They assure the viewer that worldview is right and correct.

We see this night after night on cable shows. For instance, here is Sean Hannity on February 5, 2009—the third week of the Obama administration—talking with one of his regular guests, Republican political communications professional Mary Matalin. He was looking for affirmation of his own view that President Obama was making things worse by telling people the economy is weak and encouraging Congress to pass a stimulus package. "Isn't this dangerous talking down the economy? What is the rest of the world thinking?" Hannity said.

Yes, Matalin agreed urgently: "There is so much of a problem of the economy that has to do with psychology. And ... I hear you talking about this every day, Sean. You have to give people a better sense of confidence. It's completely wrong, substantively and psychologically. It's not leadership."

Watch different channels on the same night and one can get a disorienting sense of alternate realities that is hard to reconcile.

Here is liberal host Rachel Maddow on November 9, 2009: "Since Barack Obama took office ten months ago, the Democratic Party went from having fifty-eight in the U.S. Senate to having sixty. Democrats went from carrying two hundred and fifty-seven seats in the House to now carrying two hundred and fifty-eight. And this weekend, the House grabbed the brass ring that president after president and Congress after Congress have wanted to grab and failed—health reform at last."

Here is conservative Sean Hannity the same time on the same night: "And the liberal takeover of your health system moved forward Saturday evening. When midnight struck in the garden of Nancy and Rahm, America was one step closer to a universal nightmare, or is it? ... some senators are already saying the bill is dead on arrival. But more importantly ... it appears that [House Speaker] Pelosi's arm-twisting has actually intensified the internal war within the Democratic Party."

In the end, neither Hannity's nor Maddow's assured but alternate reality was close to the mark. The country would prove increasingly unsure of the president as 2009 drew to a close, and health care almost foundered because a Republican won the seat opened up by the death of Democrat Edward Kennedy in Massachusetts. Yet it was revived in large part because Speaker Nancy Pelosi held her Democratic caucus in the House together.

The problem with the determined sense of reality is that it begins with a predetermined worldview and then picks evidence to support that view. It is fundamentally uninterested in evidence except that which can be used as a building block or tool to construct that worldview, and it is immune to any evidence that contradicts it.

All these techniques in their way are related. They are all evidence of a closed system of thinking about the news.

Other Techniques

Cherry-picking facts, imputing cartoonish evil motive to people, engaging in ad hominem attacks, and constructing reassuring, closed realities, are only four of the most common techniques used in the journalism of affirmation. But we must be on the lookout for other methods. Notice who gets the last word in a segment. If it is consistently given to one side of a debate, it is probably no accident. Notice the lineup of guests. Rachel Maddow and Sean Hannity do not regularly invite guests with alternate points of view.

And there is more subtle element of "casting." In television, producers talk about who is being cast in the role of a particular character in the drama or segment. If a partisan is on one side and a journalist trying to hew to neutrality and analysis is on the other, the segment has been cast this way, and the effect subtly portrays the press in an ideological role. If the advocate for one side is forceful and telegenic and the proponent of the other soft-spoken and less telegenic, it often was cast this way.

The larger point here is that the journalism of affirmation is a form of persuasion, or an appeal to an audience based on ideological loyalty rather than journalistic inquiry. That bond is carefully constructed. And to a much greater degree than is true in the fast-paced and often-haphazard environment of the journalism of assertion, the producers of this more ideological media have greater control over what they are doing.

How Evidence Separates Opinion Journalism from the Journalism of Affirmation

The use of evidence also distinguishes practitioners of the journalism of affirmation from other kinds of journalists who operate with a point of view but who fall more squarely into the traditions of accuracy, verification, fairness, and open-mindedness. These writers, whose work often appears in journals such as the *Atlantic*, the *National Review*, or the *Nation*, or who write newspaper columns, have traditionally been called opinion journalists. And as we noted in Chapter 3, because of their fidelity to traditional journalistic values, they operate within the journalism of verification. They are engaged in inquiry, even if they do not offer themselves as neutral or without a point of view. This notion, that the journalism of verification does not imply neutrality, is discussed at length in our book *The Elements of Journalism*.

Consider what conservative *New York Times* columnist David Brooks wrote, as Barack Obama took office, describing his view of the new president's agenda. "The political history of the 20th century is the history of social engineering projects executed by well-intentioned people that began well and ended badly. There were big errors like communism, but also lesser ones like a Vietnam War designed by the best and brightest." Now, Brooks wrote, "I fear that in trying to do everything at once, they [the Obama administration] will do nothing well . . . I worry that we're operating far beyond our economic knowledge." Brooks doesn't impute ill motive to Obama. Instead he infers good but misguided intentions. He fears the president is wrong, but he admits he cannot be entirely sure. As evidence, he cites past efforts of government hubris, from communism to Vietnam. He also does not denounce Obama, who is just taking office, as incompetent or dangerous, the way Hannity and Matalin have done.

Contrast that with right-wing radio host Alex Jones on the subject of the U.S. military being used to protect leaders at the G20 Summit in Pittsburgh: "Our military's been taken over. This is the end of our country . . . They'd love to kill ten thousand Americans . . . The republic is falling right now." Or Glenn Beck on the eve of the 2008 election, a commentary that comes up as number one on the "most popular" list on his Web site: "Gang, this is the final warning. I mean it . . . If this is out here and this man is elected, you are going to elect the most arrogant Marxist, who will not be stopped, because he came into office fully uncovered. Do not pretend to be shocked when we begin to see a Marxist, and who, I believe, will become a fascist president. And he will become fascist, because he will not understand how you suddenly don't want to become Marxist."

It's the continuing struggle between evidence and belief. Brooks offers evidence to help you understand why he finds Obama's agenda flawed. Jones and Beck have nothing to offer but the belief that their conclusions are right.

When William Safire died in 2009, his former fellow *New York Times* columnist Les Gelb, a liberal, wrote admiringly of his ideological foe: "He was always ready and willing to argue and to do so without rancor. He was willing to make points and to concede points if his opponent's facts and arguments were sound. There was no pretense or hatred in his give and take." What's more, Gelb noted, "he was always a reporter. He actually worked extremely hard to gather actual information. His columns weren't simply off the top of his head, which made his opinions all the more weighty."[9]

Safire, in his farewell op-ed column in the *New York Times*, on January 24, 2005, offered twelve tips on how to read a political column. The final tip exposed one of the differences between the journalists trying to explore ideas and arguments and the demagoguery of the ranters. "Scorn personal exchanges between columnists," Safire advised. "Observers presuming to be participants in debate remove the reader from the reality of controversy; theirs is merely a photo of a painting of a statue, or a towel-throwing contest between fight managers. Insist on columnists taking on only the truly powerful, and then only kicking 'em when they're up."

In Chapter 3, we talked about how the journalism of affirmation was part of something we call the "answer culture" of journalism, in which part of the persona of the talk show hosts who populate this new territory is that they present themselves as culture warriors, heroes of the forgotten and the aggrieved, soldiers in the war armed with all the answers. In that lack of humility, you see an indifference to evidence, for an examination of evidence would require the possibility of doubt.

That is why the journalism of affirmation almost always fails to meet the fifth test in our checklist for examining the veracity of something: exploring alternative explanations. The only alternative explanations the omniscient talk show hosts are interested in tend to be strawman arguments that they raise to be knocked down.

In the distinction between the two forms of point-of-view media—opinion versus affirmation—you see the difference between empiricism and propaganda, between journalism and activism. In their connections with their respective audiences, the difference is in the appeal to understanding and inquiry versus the appeal to belief.

Evidence and Interest-Group Journalism

Many of the same characteristics that apply to the use of evidence in the journalism of affirmation also apply to the new interest-group journalism evolving around the country—the category of news providers that are funded by political interest groups and activists. Many in this new category of news operations are online, many of them operating in state capitals. They are only now emerging, and the category, to be fair, describes a range of approaches. Some cover their subjects more comprehensively and with a straight-news approach. But a significant number of these sites, like those outlets that practice the journalism of affirmation, are political and partisan in nature, and their purpose is more persuasion than inquiry. There are, as we pointed out in Chapter 3, important differences between the interest-group news sources that are clearly political in nature and the journalism of affirmation outlets we have been discussing. Purveyors of the journalism of affirmation generally build their audience to make money. Interest-group journalism sites that are clearly political generally do not have profit as their primary motive. One result of this is that the more-commercial media of affirmation often has an entertainment dimension, even a kind of grandiose or oversize quality to its presentation. Glenn Beck, Ed Schultz, Rush Limbaugh, and even often flagrantly rhetorical bloggers like Michelle Malkin are mainstays in the journalism of affirmation. But there tend to be no such personae at sites like Old Dominion Watchdog. Such personae would be counterproductive. Much of the point of interest-group journalism is to seem as toneless and credible as possible, so that the reporting will be noticed or picked up by more traditional press outlets.

As a result, the more clearly political interest-group news Web sites tend instead to employ one use of evidence that we also see in the journalism of affirmation. They cherry-pick stories and sources that support their political purpose. Most of the content tends to convey a consistent message. It is a kind of subtext or master narrative that traces through the stories, headlines, and sourcing and creates a limited and consistent sense of reality. That master narrative is the real purpose of these political-interest-group news sites. At Watchdog.org, for instance, all the stories tend to point to government abuse or inefficiency or to evidence of the danger of taxes or other ideas that advance the message of the Sam Adams Alliance's interests of conservative libertarianism. The Pennsylvania Independent, funded by the conservative Commonwealth Foundation in Pennsylvania, shares many of those characteristics.

That could not be said so clearly in early 2010, in our opinion, of the Idaho Reporter, funded by the conservative Idaho Freedom Foundation, which offered a broad view of state politics. Nor would it so clearly characterize Fiscal Times, a news site focused on the federal budget funded by the Peter G. Peterson Foundation, which comprehensively covers the federal budget.

Examining how such sites use evidence, particularly how they select stories and sources, is one of the key ways to distinguish whether an interest-group-funded news operation is genuinely interested in covering a subject or is really trying to manipulate public understanding of it. This realm of news is so new at this point that no norms really exist. Traditional news organizations are still learning how to react to such sites and how, and if, to link to them. As consumers, we are largely on our own, and vigilance is required. In tone and presentation, a story found on these sites may seem in every way to resemble the most conventional wire story. But in reality, the funding, purpose, and thinking behind it is quite different.

This brings us to the final item on our checklist of ways to be a more conscious and careful news consumer. How to know whether our diet of news is a healthy one, and whether we are learning what we need, is what we must consider next.

CHAPTER 8

How to Find What Really Matters

Loretta Tofani thought her career as a journalist was over.

After twenty-three years, during which she had won a Pulitzer Prize for documenting gang rapes in Maryland jails, reported from China, and earned the admiration of her peers, the business had changed and Tofani wanted a change of pace. She took one of the growing number of buyouts offered by her newspaper, the *Philadelphia Inquirer*, and moved with her family to Salt Lake City, Utah, to begin a new career selling imported Chinese ethnic furniture.

For her new career, Tofani traveled back to China to visit furniture factories she might use as suppliers. Traveling as a potential buyer, she could tour factories without government escorts, something she never would have been permitted as a journalist. In the process, she saw a different side of Chinese capitalism. Workers sprayed lead-based paints in unventilated rooms without the protection of respirators. Other workers breathed fumes and handled materials that exposed their bodies to an array of toxic chemicals.

Curious and alarmed, she visited a hospital library, where she found medical journals filled with articles about Chinese factory workers who'd been injured or killed because of conditions in the workplace. The experience moved her. She felt she had encountered something too important to ignore. Eventually, as evidence grew of the dangers faced by the workers producing the furniture she was selling, Tofani closed her store back in Utah.

The professional journalist turned businesswoman was morphing into a citizen journalist. She had come across a story that had to be told. It was not her job, but it became her calling. With financial support from the Center for Investigative Reporting, she collected shipping documents like those she had for her own imports. They allowed her to tie goods shipped to the United States to specific factories. With that, she could locate individual workers whose products she could prove were purchased by consumers in the United States, thereby tying the lives of Americans to the plight of specific Chinese factory employees.

She returned to China, where labor rights organizations helped her locate the victims. Much as she had persuaded jail rape victims, and even their rapists, to tell their stories in her award-winning reporting as a professional, she now coaxed frightened Chinese workers into telling their stories about occupational diseases. She documented where they worked, the chemicals to which they were exposed, and the conditions under which they worked. She spoke to the doctors treating them, gathering documents along the way to prove their claims. Nothing was merely asserted. She did not simply unearth the claims of one side, balance them with the assertions of government officials and business leaders, and suggest that there might be a problem that should be scrutinized officially.

The results were published in 2007 in the *Salt Lake Tribune* under the headline "American Imports, Chinese Deaths,"

> With each new report of lead detected on a made-in-China toy, Americans express outrage: These toys could poison children. But Chinese workers making the toys—and countless other products for America—touch and inhale carcinogenic materials every day, all day long: Benzene. Lead. Cadmium. Toluene. Nickel. Mercury.
>
> Many are dying. They have fatal occupational diseases.
>
> Mostly they are young, in their 20s and 30s and 40s. But they are dying, slow difficult deaths, caused by the hazardous substances they use to make products for the world—and for America. Some say these workers are paying the real price for America's cheap goods from China.

"In terms of responsibility to Chinese society, this is a big problem for Americans," said Zhou Litai, a lawyer from the city of Chongqing who has represented tens of thousands of dying workers in Chinese courts.

The toxins and hazards exist in virtually every industry, including furniture, shoes, car parts, electronic items, jewelry, clothes, toys and batteries, interviews with workers confirm. The interviews were corroborated by legal documents, medical journal articles, medical records, import documents and official Chinese reports.

Other news organizations picked up her series, and it soon reached a worldwide audience. Reaction on Capitol Hill was followed by new language to be written into trade agreements designed to protect workers making imported products.

It would be difficult to overstate how pervasive and important products from China have become to life in the United States and the world. Every American consumer has a role in the safety of these Chinese workers. And the safety of those products affects virtually every American. According to the Federal Trade Commission's report in 2009, the United States imported twenty-four billion dollars' worth of products from China, while exporting four billion dollars to China in return.

It was a story so important Tofani felt she had to change her life to tell it.

Most citizens, if they happen to encounter some injustice, do not become investigative reporters. Few of us, even few journalists, have the skills or the opportunity to undertake the kind of global exposé Tofani was moved to produce. But each of us, as we each day navigate the expanding array of media available to us and decide how much time to devote to it and what to look at it, must engage in a calculus similar to, if less acute than, Tofani's. We must decide how important the events are, how much time we want to spend understanding them, and how we want to react. In other words, when we encounter information, we must ask something beyond simply whether what we are seeing is true. We must also wonder how much it matters. And over the course of many stories we must ask whether we are learning what we need to know about a given subject.

This question of navigation and selection is the last item in our check-list of what the empowered, conscious, and active citizen who encoun-ters and consumes news about the world must ask. In many ways it is also the most important.

Am I learning what I need to?

Answering this question involves putting together the skills we learned in answering the previous five elements of the checklist. It is where we ask ourselves, are we really finding out what we should—about our community, our children's schools, the debate over health care, the state of the environment or the economy, or a war abroad? If not, what are we missing? And where and how do we get that missing information?

In earlier eras, we did not have to think about this quite the same way. Editors did it for us. They ordered and preselected the news on our be-half, deciding which six or seven stories should be on the front page or which ten stories should make the lineup of that day's newscast. That preselection and ordering was an important part of the journalistic gate-keeping function, every bit as critical, and in some ways more so, than the editing and verification that occurred within each story.

Journalists still select, of course. But their choices have less impact on us. In the digital age, the front page of a Web site may easily have a hun-dred headlines, not six. Most of them are grouped by topic for us to choose from. We may well customize the front page of news Web sites we frequent according to our interests.[1] And much of the time we navi-gate the news not by turning to a news organization for its choices at all but by using a Web search to find stories we are interested in, or clicking on something a friend has sent us or that we have heard about on a social network. In effect, we consume the news now by topic and by story, and less by relying on the judgment of news institutions to select for us.[2]

We have always had some element of choice in our news consump-tion, of course. A newspaper has scores of stories each day, more than most of us actually read. Television reduced those choices when it be-came the most popular news medium in the last half of the twentieth century. Social scientists noted that television also increased the level of social consensus. Suddenly millions of Americans were seeing the same three national newscasts each night, with a limited menu of about ten to twelve stories. In the digital age, we are back to more choice again—far more.

All of this makes the question of knowing whether we are getting what we need more critical. What is it that most of us think we need to know about?

By and large, we are not all that conscious of the choices we make selecting news, or even how to make them. We tend to follow what interests us. But what does that mean? Surveys tell us the number-one reason that people get news (72 percent of adults cite it) is that they enjoy talking about it with friends, family, and work colleagues—news as a social act. That suggests they will follow stories their social cohort wants to talk about, be it sports, politics, schools, movies, etc. Almost as many Americans (69 percent) say they follow news because they have a civic responsibility to do so. This suggests they will try to look for things that they think will affect the life of their community in some manner. Third on the list of reasons people say they follow the news (cited by 61 percent) is to improve their lives—news they can use. Less than half, 44 percent, say news is diverting or entertaining by itself; and 19 percent say they follow it for their work. On local television, which is the most popular source of news in America, weather is the number-one topic, according to most audience research. In the morning, traffic news is critical. And on the list of what kind of news people say they are most likely to follow online, weather again is number one, followed by national news, medical news, business news, international news, and science and technology news.[3] There are hints here that the Internet, which makes it easier to access popular national and international Web sites such as Yahoo or that of the *New York Times*, as well as specialty sites like ESPN.com, may also be reducing interest in local news. On this list, news about one's local community came in ninth place.

The question we increasingly need to ask is how do we decide what we need to know about a given subject? Or put another way, how do we determine if what we are learning matters?

Certainly Americans also have growing doubts about the way the traditional media have determined significance on their behalf. Those doubts are seen in the declining levels of trust in the media and in the growing literature among scholars and awareness among everyday consumers about the ways that media "frame" stories—the media predilections toward building stories around conflict, or negativity, or drama, or through a political lens.[4] On a number of major stories in the past decades, there have been grave doubts about whether the media worked as an alert system. Significant questions were raised in the 1980s, for instance, about whether the press had done an adequate job of alerting us to the savings and loan crisis, and in the late 1990s to the technology-stock bubble bursting, and after 2001 to the run-up to the war in Iraq, and in 2008 to the collapse of the economy. And as newsrooms have shrunk dramatically because of declining revenue, it is worth asking whether any single news operation still has adequate resources to do this monitoring for us, to be our all-purpose gatekeeper.

As newspapers and other media began to lose their audience, many news organizations also stopped organizing and presenting the news strictly by significance. At the daily meeting at the *New York Times* in the 1960s, at which top management sat around for an hour to determine what stories should be put on the front page, only one question mattered: Out of the thousands of words filed to the paper that day, which seven or eight stories were the most important for most people to know? That notion— most important to most people—was the only question on the table. As television ate more deeply into newspapers' audience, and poll after poll revealed that the public trusted television stories more than print stories, that began to change. To compete with television news, newspaper editors at the *Times* and elsewhere began to stress bright writing. Space was opened up for accompanying images. Style, not just what the story was about, began to matter more than it had—and properly so. Since audiences had more choices for their news, journalists began to ask, Do we have something here to appeal to women? Is there sufficient diversity of subject matter? Is there a "good reader," a story that is artfully told? Is there a strong emotional appeal? Though most people do not realize it, the front page of a newspaper as an index of the importance of events began its slide to obsolescence two generations ago. This was well intended from a civic standpoint too. The notion of a homogeneous public that might agree on a single list of significance is debatable. Nonetheless, ironically, as the press began to worry more about how to please its audience, the audience began to have doubts about the professionalism of the press.

The concept that increasingly governs what news organizations choose to cover and emphasize in the twenty-first century is "brand," or developing certain franchise subject areas that audiences can find nowhere else. In that sense, in a time of declining resources and audience, almost every news organization is becoming a niche news organization. The development makes good economic sense, but it has altered the agenda-setting role of the press and only increases the demand on each of us, as consumers, to determine for ourselves what we need.[5]

To the degree the news has become so fragmented into so many different packages of information, in other words, we are, increasingly, on our own in determining significance.

Thus, the question we need to ask is how do we do this for ourselves.

To Find Reliable News, Look for a Method

Even in the era of aggregation, when we can scan the global information universe in seconds, most of us do not monitor the media in aggregate. Instead, we regularly rely on a few outlets and hope that they are monitoring the others on our behalf. Jeff Cole, director of the Center for the Digital Future at the University of Southern California's Annenberg School for Communication and Journalism, has found in his surveys that most Americans in the age of cable TV and the Internet watch six TV channels and visit fifteen Web sites—and that includes those sites we used for banking and shopping.[6] Research by the Project for Excellence in Journalism and the Pew Internet and American Life Project finds that most people regularly visit fewer than six Web sites for news. In an ongoing weekly study of more than a million blogs and social media, we've also found that even this universe of new media tends to rely on and link to a fairly limited number of fairly traditional media sources. The *New York Times*, the Associated Press, the BBC, Reuters, and other usual suspects dominate the list. In practice, even in the twenty-first century, in other words, we look for authorities we can rely on—even as the number of options and outlets to choose from expands daily.

So an essential step in efficiently seeking important coverage is to find outlets and individual reporters who do great work on a consistent basis—a network of trusted sources or brands we can look to regularly. How do we do that? There is no magic formula. But there are ways to develop your own methodogy, your own tradecraft, to identify those who consistently do exceptional work.

In our experience, the work of the best journalists tends to bear a

subtle signature. It is the product of a conscious and often highly personal method or approach that great journalists tend to bring to their
reporting. These exceptional journalists develop such methods because
it is a way of disciplining their curiosity. It is a way for them to go deeper
in their questioning, to hone their inquiry, and to avoid missing things.
The result is that they see more, ask other questions, look for patterns,
and derive more from the events they encounter than other journalists.
They are more likely to rise above the stenography of only reproducing
facts presented to them. They are more likely, because of their method,
to arrive at a deeper level of verification. They are more inclined to see
context and understand causes and thus produce genuine sense-making
stories, ones that point us toward real knowledge based on evidence, not
merely based on inference or the transitory hunchlike impressions that
fill so much of our so-called interpretative journalism. These are the fruits
of the way of skeptical knowing.

Even if you do not know what method a journalist uses, you can still
see signs of its existence in the work. Nuance, detail, and evidence of a
certain care make it stand out. Those elements are the telltale of a conscious approach. Look for them. This can be your first step to developing your own methodology to find the truth in a world of competing
information.

To give you a sense of what we mean, we offer examples of a handful
of exceptional journalists and describe their particular methods. The
point here is not to look for these specific methods but to look for work
that bears the sign of some method, work that rises above just describing events, that adds a deeper level, that ineffably seems to offer more
value.

The Sociologist as Journalist

Perhaps no other reporter in American history has challenged the notion
of how to cover a "beat"—the journalistic vernacular for a coverage area—
more completely, or to more dramatic effect, than David Burnham. Burnham worked at the *New York Times* from 1968 to 1989, and his coverage of
police led to the creation of the historic Knapp Commission on police
corruption in New York City, which led to major governmental reforms
and was depicted in the films *Serpico* and *Prince of the City*. When he
moved to the paper's Washington bureau, he covered the Atomic Energy

and Nuclear Regulatory commissions. And it was while on her way to provide Burnham with damaging information about the manufacture of faulty fuel rods by the Kerr-McGee Corporation that whistleblower Karen Silkwood was killed in a car crash; that controversial case was depicted in the film *Silkwood*. Burnham's reporting at an organization of investigative journalism he created called Transactional Records Access Clearinghouse (TRAC) has also examined whether we, as citizens, are getting what we should expect from the Federal Bureau of Investigation, the Internal Revenue Service, and even the Justice Department.

All of that work was the result of Burnham trying to cover his "beat" with a series of systemic questions that he had learned from prominent sociologists. Burnham, indeed, was really "a sociologist as journalist."

Before joining the *New York Times*, Burnham had worked for two years on a presidential commission on law enforcement. "It was like getting a master's in sociology," Burnham explained. Given what he had learned, he did not think much of the *Times'* coverage of law enforcement. "It was all anecdotal," Burnham recalled.[7] Asked what he would do instead, Burnham came up with a list of twenty stories heavily influenced by the sociologists he had met while working in government, "The list was all about systems and procedures." Once hired by the paper, Burnham sought out the experts and academics he had met in government and asked how he should approach his new job. One person in particular had a powerful effect on him, Alfred Blumstein at Carnegie Mellon University. "He said to me, 'Ask yourself whether the agency . . . is achieving its stated goals. And if not, why not?'"

"How do I do that?" Burnham asked Blumstein.

"If you study its output," Blumstein answered, "it tells its own story."

That angle of approach became a defining focus of Burnham's work for the next forty years. It involves five distinct steps:

- Identify the stated goals of the agency you are covering.
- Identify what information would help tell you whether the agency is meeting those stated goals (i.e., the agency's output).
- Follow what the data, the product of the agency, tells you.
- Measure whether the output suggests the agency is doing its job and, if not, ask why not and what job it is doing instead.
- Question the participants to get their views on what the evidence shows.

Though his reporting never explicitly mentioned these five steps, his systemic approach quickly led to his revolutionary coverage of law enforcement in New York City.

One of his first, and most groundbreaking, stories was about "cooping," police slang for sleeping on duty. It was sparked when Burnham interviewed Jim Curran, then a New York City policeman, who referred to someone being "in the coop," Burnham recalled.

"Someone, a source, drops a phrase on you. And at first you tend to nod, so you look informed, like you are in the know. The phrase is 'cooping.' But then you catch yourself. Don't try to pretend you know more than you do. That is a way to miss things," Burnham said

"What is 'the coop'?" Burnham asked Curran.

"You know . . . that is where everyone sleeps on duty from midnight to eight A.M."

After more questioning, Burnham heard that every day thousands upon thousands of New York police supposedly working the night shift were actually sleeping, stashed in coops all over the city, only to be awakened if a crime was discovered.

At first, a *Times* editor told him it was not the kind of story the paper did. So Burnham recruited a copyboy to go with him and take pictures during off hours. In the middle of the night they would drive around the city—to parks, piers, bridge underpasses, and other likely cooping hangouts—taking photographs of patrol cars with sleeping cops inside.

Then Burnham set out to interview cops, to provide a human dimension to the evidence he had found. Many of them told Burnham that "this was an old and fully honored tradition," he recalled. One cop told Burnham he carried an alarm clock to wake himself and his partner when it was time to roll again. Burnham learned that the Patrolmen's Benevolent Association had even pushed a "feather bedding" law through the state legislature in Albany requiring that the NYPD assign one third of all officers to be on duty for each shift. That meant too many cops were working the midnight to eight A.M. shift, when most New Yorkers were asleep, and not enough were working during the hours when more crimes were likely to be committed. Cooping was a natural result and a dramatic example of a city agency misusing its resources.

When the story broke, to huge effect, the police commissioner held a press conference to say the *Times* story was exaggerating the behavior of a few "rotten apples." A rival reporter at the *New York Daily News*, apparently reamed out by his editors for missing the story, confronted Burnham in a rage. "You son of a bitch. That's no fucking story. Everybody knows it," Burnham recalled him screaming. "And he was right," Burnham said. In a sense, that was the problem. People knew about the cooping and accepted it. That made it even bigger news.

The lessons of the cooping story became the basis of Burnham's method of how to approach a beat. The day after the story ran, a source called Burnham and challenged him to do a variation of the cooping story, only this time on more powerful people in the city than cops— judges. " 'Okay, Burnham, I know how the *New York Times* likes to take on lower-class Irish cops. But not upper-class Jewish judges," Burnham said the the source told him. Many of the judges in New York worked three days a week, taking Mondays and Fridays off. When Burnham asked how he could possibly prove such a thing, the source told him it was easy: average the number of cases disposed of on Mondays and Fridays and compare that with those disposed of on Tuesday through Thursday. Study, again, the output. The source was right. Many judges were working only three days a week, slowing the court system while thousands of defendants were awaiting trial on Rikers Island.

It took Burnham six months of fighting to get the story into the *Times*. A quantitative analysis that challenged the continuing behavior of judges, at least for journalism at the time, was too systemic, too much a challenge to the way things worked, the basic nature of how institutions operated. And when the story finally ran, editors had cut much of it out. But Burnham was on a roll, and his coverage would help transform policing in New York City. In time, Burnham applied the same systemic approach researching the Justice Department, Internal Revenue Service, and the Atomic Energy Commission, among others. He continues to do so with TRAC, which puts the results of the output of U.S. government work in justice and other agencies on a searchable database for other journalists and citizens to access.

His coverage stands out because it has been driven not by events but by questions.

Listening for Untold Stories

Diana K. Sugg, in our minds, is among the finest beat reporters in the country. She doesn't call herself a specialist, or a health writer, though she won a Pulitzer Prize for her coverage of that subject. She talks instead with the inspiration of the passionate believer in journalism about how to cover a beat—any beat.

Though she does not use this term herself, as we have read her work, and listened to her talk about it, we see a method in Sugg's approach that we call "listening for untold stories."

First, Sugg tries to make sure that she does not get distracted by all the small breaking news stories that other reporters are covering. "I wonder if I am doing my beat justice," she wrote, meaning to cover it in a way that the subject deserves.[8] To do that, she noted "it helps to articulate a vision for your beat"—some sense of the larger questions involving the subject, something affirmative that you are after to help you let those small stories go.

She also tries to gravitate toward stories she believes no one else will write, that are difficult, that seem to "call" to her. A writing teacher, she recalled, once told her to "do the stories only you can do . . . Mine your own emotional territory."[9] Sugg also writes stories that tell people things that they didn't know. This involves telling stories that aren't preordained from her own views or from her editors' back in the newsroom.

Sugg says her particular skill is listening, being patient with people and being herself with them, so that they begin to trust her. This has allowed her extraordinary access to people who were sick and at their most vulnerable, who told their stories because it might help others, even though it made their pain public. Her portfolio includes several series focused in the most intimate way on individuals whose agonizing illnesses tell larger and more important stories.

To get these stories and to earn and keep people's trust, Sugg has a sense that a journalist, as someone who makes things public, is acting in a public sphere themselves. "How you conduct yourself goes to the heart of how well you do," Sugg wrote.[10] "Realize that you are your own product, your own brand. When you're a reporter, your name is all you have . . . Are you the reporter who thinks he knows the story ahead of time, who forces the details into a preconceived mold, or do you listen to the people you're interviewing? Are you the reporter who confirms all the worst stereotypes about our business, or are you the one who surprises people with your honesty, integrity, and passion? Don't think for a minute that the public doesn't quickly figure out which category you're in and deal with you accordingly."

No story may have epitomized this notion of journalism as a public act, an act fraught with values and morality, as much as the series she produced with photographer Monica Lopossay called "The Angels Are Coming," about a dying twelve-year-old Baltimore boy named R. J. Voigt. The series, wrenching and raw, explored the issues medical professionals and families face in caring for dying children.

In a later essay about the series, she said she struggled with the line between covering people and exploiting them. We think that knowing where that line is, and treading it carefully, is the difference between stories that matter and stories that are voyeuristic, stories that people read and stories that change people's lives and help medical professionals and families make better choices.

"To get a great story, how much had I taken advantage of R.J. and his family?" Sugg wrote. "Would the story hurt his already devastated mother? What about all those other moms who'd fought to save their children? Had I been brave enough to tell the truth? Did I even know the truth? And in the end, how much would it really matter?"

Afterward, she remembered standing in an auditorium at the Johns Hopkins Hospital, which was packed to the rafters with physicians, nurses, and division chiefs, silent in their white coats, as she talked about what she had learned, and later when she spoke to the CEOs of the country's biggest health insurance companies. "From now on, every story I do, R.J. will be with me," she wrote. "A reminder of how far I can go as a journalist and how carefully I must tread."

Readers of Sugg's stories can easily sense something extraordinary in the work. It is manifestly the product of remarkable and substantial humility, care, and concern. She has simply thought through what she is doing more than most. You may not know what her method is, but you can detect its presence.

Saturation Reporting

David Halberstam, whose book *The Best and the Brightest* defined the Vietnam War period, often told young colleagues that the highest accolade he ever wanted was to be thought of as someone who didn't seem to know anything because he kept asking questions. He called it "saturation reporting." It is a process of building the world you're trying to describe from the ground up.

And when Halberstam was finished building, his reporting had such an authority and was so deep that his narrative was something much more than descriptive; it was explanatory. He had an unmistakable narrative voice, and the depth of his reporting was so clear to the reader, his understanding of the roots and reasons and implications of what he was writing so thorough, that he was able to simply explain what he had learned, what had occurred and why, how it fit in history, and what it said about the human condition. He used the voices of his sources as his proof. But his accuracy and evidence were never in doubt.

In *The Best and the Brightest*, a masterpiece that made his reputation as an author, Halberstam started with a question that had grown out of his time reporting in Vietnam: How had the people who were considered among the ablest people in government ended up with the worst tragedy since the Civil War?

Speaking to a group of Nieman Foundation fellows at Harvard University in 1996, he described the process of reporting this way:

> You figure out who do you know who could help unlock it [the answer]? Going out, figuring out what you'd want to know . . . And I remembered a guy I'd known in college who I'd given a briefing to when he first went to Vietnam . . . A guy named Daniel Ellsberg and I went out and spent three days with him in California. I came back . . . I had twenty-two pages of single-spaced notes . . .
>
> Then I started picking off other people, getting the people that are most likely to talk first, taking time with them, always asking them at the end of an interview, "Who else should I see? What else ought I to see? Who else is good on this? Who else knows?"

The interviews are incredibly thorough:

> I try to build a biography of the people I talk to. Ask them, How did you get to where you were that day? What was your background, your philosophy. What were the weeks and months like while you were involved? Who led, who was afraid, what were the vulnerabilities? Always building a ground work of information . . .
>
> Someone says, "Well, he seemed volatile." You, the reporter

say, "What do you mean, 'volatile'?" Explain that. Bring it out in a
story. Make them explain every phrase. Make them tell a story.
Some people can't express themselves anecdotally. But most
people can, particularly if they are talking about themselves . . .

There's a danger of reporters wanting to appear smart, of
wanting the other person to think you're smart. But your job is
to get people to talk. Make them go back. Make them explain.
It's OK to go very slowly."[11]

Halberstam was tireless when researching a book, his notebooks
stacking higher and his interviews more in-depth than even most journalists would imagine. At his funeral in 2007, several of his eulogists
were sources he had interviewed—a soldier from his book on the Korean
War, a firefighter from his book on his neighborhood firehouse. He had
come to know them that well.

Halberstam's readers probably did not know the term "saturation reporting," but they sensed its presence.

Finding the Voices That Tell the Story

The worldwide financial crisis that began in 2008 tested the ability of journalists and conventional journalism. The challenge was to make sense of a
complex and fast-moving story of deep public interest in a way that made
sense to people whose grasp of world markets, hedge funds, and securi-
tized mortgages was fuzzy at best.

This American Life, presented by Chicago Public Radio, is a weekly,
hour-long show hosted by Ira Glass unlike any other radio program. It
examines a single topic through personal stories told by a variety of people.
The approach—finding people who tell their own stories their way—
imposes a kind of discipline of its own: Who does this story affect? How?
Who can tell it? It is always interesting. On occasion, the effect is profound.

The episode "The Giant Pool of Money" was an exercise in nonfiction
storytelling put together by Alex Blumberg and Adam Davidson in April
2008, before the global economy went into meltdown. Using personal stories of those caught up in the panic, they teased apart a primary education for their audience on the subprime mortgage collapse. The stories of
a nervous mortgage holder, Wall Street bankers, mortgage bundlers—all

were used to demystify the arcane language of the world mortgage market. Derivatives, tranches, credit swaps, short selling were explained in ways most people could understand.

The show went viral as a podcast, and NPR described the public response to the program as the most positive it had ever seen. The success of the program grew out of the unique way Blumberg and Davidson chose to tell a complicated story on the radio. They constructed the report with a cast of characters who described their own involvement in the crisis, making the complex subject understandable because it was put into human, personal terms—the characters were real, not journalistic templates or caricatures. As Jay Rosen, a journalism professor at New York University and author of the blog PressThink, said, "coming out of the program, I understood the complete scam: what happened, why it happened, and why I should care. I had a good sense of the motivations and situations of players all down the line on many fronts and different levels." Civic mastery was mined over a complex, unfolding story, dense with technical terms. That came about because the producers had thought hard about how to tell a complex story in a new way.

The Moment in Context

Over a period of forty years, John Kifner developed a reputation as one of the best "parachute" journalists in the business—someone who at a moment's notice could be sent to "jump" into a breaking story almost anywhere in the world. When in need of a reporter to cover the riots in the 1960s to revolutions in the Middle East or the Balkans in the 1990s, editors at the *New York Times* reflexively called him.

Kifner has always had an eye for exquisite texture and detail. After the police cut down the leader of the Black Panthers movement in his Chicago apartment, Kifner was the reporter who counted the bullet holes in the room and disproved the police account of how the shooting occurred. When National Guard troops said they were responding to a sniper when they opened fire and killed protesting students at Kent State University, it was Kifner who marshaled the detail that challenged that claim.

But what makes Kifner's work truly special is his passion for finding context and meaning, even in stories he was sent to cover on the spur of the moment. "Nothing makes sense, real sense, if you can't report it in a

context larger than the moment. It's that context that I was always looking for," he said.

In 1973, he found it in Pine Ridge Oglala Sioux Reservation when he
covered the armed confrontation between federal officials and members
of the American Indian Movement (AIM) who had occupied the town of
Wounded Knee. The conflict, at the scene of an earlier massacre of Indians by federal forces, attracted worldwide attention.

As he filed daily accounts, Kifner kept asking, "Why are they doing
this? What's this all about?" What he learned, as he continued searching for deeper meaning, informed a long article he produced called "At
Wounded Knee: Two Worlds Collide."

"Beneath it all," Kifner concluded "was a story of frustration pent up
under an imposed democratic authority that required everyone make
choices imposed on top of a older tribal authority that avoided choices.
Tribal authority was based on consensus. Authority was divided among a
group of specialized chiefs to preserve consensus . . . Wounded Knee was
not just a story of a face-off between U.S. Marshals and AIM Indians but
a story about the demoralization of the ruling people of the tribe. The
story couldn't communicate anything of value without that context."[12]

To find context and underlying themes in unfolding events—often
those he was not yet covering—Kifner developed a method for being
prepared. He read widely through daily papers, books, and news magazines, collecting information on running stories. He built a personal library of books on the history and current events of volatile regions, like
the Middle East, where he might at any moment be sent. He was prepared because he had been asking questions in his own mind ahead of
time. When he boarded a plane on the spur of the moment to fly off to an
assignment in Iran, for instance, he did so with a history of the area in
hand and a few more books in his rucksack. By the time he landed,
Kifner was prepared to seek out local experts and authorities who could
help place current events into a cultural and historic context.

Readers can sense this in Kifner's work. Consider this story, filed over
the weekend of February 26, 2006, trying to make sense of a one-day
curfew imposed in Iraq the day before.

> Iraq teetered on the brink of civil war last week. Then, Friday, it
> seemed, for the moment anyway, to have taken a step back [with
> the one-day curfew, which ended 48 hours of violence] . . .

The sequence of events evoked past crises involving conflict between entrenched ethnic or religious groups—the fodder for civil war. They have a rhythm of their own. Often tensions seem to build to an unbearable level, then suddenly ease.

Sometimes something so awful happens that it is a turning point. That was the case during the Serbian siege of Sarajevo. At the beginning of February 1994, a mortar fell on an outdoor market where Bosnians bought used goods from one another. It exploded on a table full of secondhand hardware, turning bolts, hammers and screwdrivers into shrapnel, creating a bloody tableau in which 68 people died and a severed head rested among old shoes.

International attention was suddenly focused on the struggles in the former Yugoslavia. A take-charge British general, Sir Michael Rose, was sent to lead the lackluster United Nations force. Despite hundreds of years of warlike mountain traditions intensified by religion and nationalism, he hammered out a cease-fire that eventually led to peace accords.

But at other times, it seems, tension builds, ebbs, then builds again, each time starting at a higher point. Events—bombings, gunfights, even massacres—that once were almost unthinkable become mundane. This was the case during the 15-year Lebanese civil war.

Even in these few paragraphs, the reader can see something unmistakable in the conversational yet authoritative tone of Kifner's assessment of the curfew. The detail of the bomb that hit the table full of old tools, the image of the severed head, the credit given to the now-forgotten U.N. general, the simple description of what makes up the fodder of civil war—all these are elements only a perceptive and experienced hand would have seen. One can not only feel wisdom in these paragraphs but can also sense that Kifner was doing more. He was looking for patterns, reading history, looking for lessons. It doesn't read like conventional journalism. It reads like something deeper.

The approaches we have listed here are only a handful of methods developed by journalists whose work we consider remarkable. Many good reporters talk about other methods in their own work. Though you may not detect it in a single story, you can sense method and a renewed sense of mission in many new media experiments at places like GlobalPost, GroundReport, and Globalvision. These sites and others are pioneering how to match the potential of new technology with the values of trusted news. And precisely because they are new, they often are more conscious of what they are doing, more interested in method, and more transparent than legacy media. Over time the best have become more careful about verification.

The point here is not that there are a certain number of fixed models for producing significant coverage of a topic, or that we should look for the sociological approach or the storytelling technique to deem a story "important." Rather, important work tends to bear evidence that it has been produced by people who have developed a method, a conscious angle of approach, that gives the work an unusual depth or weight. It may be subtle. You may not see the method itself. But, like the subtle timbre of a virtuoso musician or that something special in the dishes of a gifted chef, there is something recognizable in special work. That signature, that sign of method, is a good indication of a journalist whose work is worth following as you navigate your way as a news consumer.

The constant we see in such work is that these reporters bring us a world, not merely a collection of stories. There is always a larger context. And these stories tend to be alive with detail that seems particularly real, carefully observed, and poignantly authentic—never clichéd or forced. Important coverage is full of echoes, resonance, and implication. And that resonance is built from observation and information in sufficient detail that it has become evidence and then has been vetted to assure that it means what it suggests. This can exist even in fast-breaking stories, if the reporter is careful. We simply need to know how to look for it.

How to Fulfill Our Larger Responsibilities as News Consumers

Searching for journalists who consistently produce valuable work is one trick for making sure we use our time as news consumers efficiently. But it does not answer the larger question of how to know if we are really getting the full diet of news we need to live life well, to be informed, to be engaged. How do we make use of the news in the way that people say they want to—news as a social activity, a civic activity, as something that can improve our lives?

Here too there is no formula. There are, however, various techniques for trying to answer whether we are getting what we need. We have distilled these from listening to critics of the press, journalists from various media, smart news consumers, and advocates of new media. Readers may decide for themselves which are useful. Or they may refine these into some technique of their own. The point of the following lists and bits of tradecraft is not that everyone should follow them precisely. Rather, they are offered to help people become more conscious of their news consumption, in the same way that we have become more conscious of our food consumption. The first step is simply asking the question: Am I getting what I need from the news? What follows is a variety of ways to answer that question.

Could I Explain This Subject to Someone?

One technique is take a subject in the news, any subject, and ask yourself three questions about it:

- Could I explain this subject to someone—my child, my parent, a friend—who isn't paying attention to it?
- If not, what information would I need to know to do that—or in other words, what is it I don't understand?
- Where could I find that information?

Try it. Take a news subject and then spend twenty minutes online finding answers to any questions you may have about it. Then remember the Web sites where you found the best answers. After researching a few subjects, you will begin to see patterns of where you found the most useful and responsible information.

The device is a variation of one journalists use to write stories more simply and clearly. Nearly every young journalist has heard this advice from an editor at some point: "If I were explaining this to my mother in a letter, what would I tell her?" Those who learn how to explain it become better writers.

Make a List of What Matters

The technique above can help you understand what you need to know about a given subject. But which subjects should you even be exploring? What news is important to know about?

One bit of tradecraft for answering this is to make a list of the ten issues or topics that matter to you most.

Making the list may force you to stretch. Ten is a lot. Ordering them is hard. Then think: How often do you consume information about them?

This exercise will force you to think about what subjects are in the news. They may be ongoing stories, such as those covering the Israeli-Palestinian conflict, or one's favorite sports team. Or they may cover a more general topic, like computer technology.

One virtue of this exercise is that making one such list can have a lasting impact on your thinking about the news. Take ten minutes to make the list. It may help you for years.

Questions to Test Whether You're Getting the News You Need

Another technique focuses on how you are spending your time with the news. Think back over the news you encountered today and ask yourself these questions.

- What news did I get about what topics? Where did I get it? Is it important? Did I miss other news I wish I had spent time learning?
- Did the news advance my knowledge about a subject in a significant way or did it just record tentative or incremental changes that seem likely not to be meaningful? Was the reporting stenographic, merely taking notes and passing them along, or did it reveal important details?
- Did the news tell me something important, fundamentally new, something that gave me a new understanding, or did it merely give details that reinforced what I already understood?
- Did I learn something about one of the things that I am most worried about or consider important?

If the information we encounter is fundamentally new, more than incremental and more than stenographic, that goes a long way toward telling us we are getting value. If we learned something, even one fundamentally new thing, about a subject we think is vital, that is telling as well. Our answers go back to identifying, again, what kind of news we encounter. Is it a straight news account providing new facts? Is it sensemaking news, and if so, is it asserting something or actually establishing it, like Tofani's fully documented series on Chinese imports? Inevitably we need a mix. But if everything we consume is incremental, that is a likely sign that we are not getting information that helps us understand important events and issues. If everything we encounter is analytical, and we agree with all of it, that should be a sign that we are not straying far enough from our zone of comfort. If nothing we encounter seems revelatory, or changes our view somehow, then we should venture further.

This technique is derived from a smart news consumer we knew, a U.S. senator, who told us he used a similar exercise to review his workday to see if he had done everything he could in each encounter that day. It was, he thought, a key to his successful career.

Stories You Remember

Finally, there is another device we have used in our work as press critics to identify exceptional reporters doing exceptional work. Think back over the past couple of years. Are there stories you encountered in the media that you still remember? Where did you encounter them? Who did them? What made them special?

In our experience, there are stories that linger in memory; we have listed a number of them in this book. Recalling what you liked about them can help tell you what it is you like in the news, what you consider valuable.

We don't expect anyone to follow all these techniques, or necessarily any of them. They are designed, rather, to make us be more conscious of how we consume the news, in the same way we try to be conscious about exercising or eating well. In the twenty-first century, we are becoming new citizens, responsible for ourselves in new ways. We have access to more information, from more sources, with a greater ability to triangulate what we see and become better informed. Those of us who take advantage of this will be energized by the stimulation of learning and growing. Those of us who do not will be further left behind. In the early days of the Internet, social critics often worried about an information gap based on which populations had access to computers and broadband. Some of those concerns are being mitigated by the advent of mobile smart technology, which has much higher penetration. The real information gap, which cannot be bridged by social policy or new technology, is between smart consumers of news and those who are more inclined to disengage, or engorge themselves on diversion and amusement.

This brings us to the checklist we introduced in Chapter 3, for becoming a more conscious and careful consumer of news about the world. Those steps involve answering six basic questions.

1. *What kind of content am I encountering?*
2. *Is the information complete; and if not, what is missing?*
3. *Who or what are the sources, and why should I believe them?*
4. *What evidence is presented, and how was it tested or vetted?*
5. *What might be an alternative explanation or understanding?*
6. *Am I learning what I need to?*

As you look at this list, having moved through the chapters that explain it, you need to try to be objective about yourself as well. The age of aggregation gives all of us the power to ask our own questions and to seek our own answers. As we do so, we should ask ourselves if we are *really* asking questions. Are we really trying to expand our knowledge? Are we willing to entertain the possibility that we might have something to learn, that we might even change our minds, or at least our understanding? Are we willing to accept facts that don't reinforce our preconceptions? Or are our questions really rhetorical ones designed to reassure ourselves that what we believe is true? Do we gravitate mainly to assertions that fit our sense of morality? Do we look to the news as evidence of how things are? Or do we mainly look for proof of how we wish they would be?

In other words, how open are we to the possibility that we don't know? Where do we sit on the spectrum of knowledge that takes us all the way back to the questions posed by the French and Spanish cave drawings—what's fact and what's belief?

We will get less from the news if we fall too close to the side of the closed mind. We will learn less if we spend too much time listening to the journalism that is there only to affirm or amuse us. If we always arrive exactly where we began, we will not have traveled at all.

All this raises yet one more question. If we succeed in becoming more capable consumers of news, how in turn should we expect journalists to change? That is the next matter to consider.

CHAPTER 9

What We Need from the "Next Journalism"

Probably the most ambitious and idealized description of how journalists saw their role in the twentieth century came from Walter Lippmann, the newspaper columnist and author.

It was 1920 and Lippmann, a cofounder of the magazine *New Republic* and a former aide to Woodrow Wilson, feared for the prospects of democracy. The world seemed to be splitting apart. In Russia, he had just witnessed the rise of Bolshevism, a philosophy that was the sworn enemy of capitalism and predicted the collapse of democratic republics. In the Great War, he had seen the birth of modern propaganda, the use of media for political persuasion. In the scientific work of Freud and others, Lippmann began to recognize new ideas about subjectivity, the subconscious, bias, and relativity in perception that raised doubts about the ability of journalists to recognize facts. If democracy were to survive, he thought, journalism needed to find a clearer sense of its role and elevate itself to perform that role.

He retreated to the woods to produce a small book, *Liberty and the News*, outlining how his profession might accomplish this. "The news of the day as it reaches the newspaper office is an incredible medley of fact, propaganda, rumor, suspicion, clues, hopes and fears," Lippmann wrote. "And the task of selecting and ordering that news is one of the truly sacred and priestly offices in a democracy. For the newspaper is in all literalness the bible of democracy, the book out of which a people determines its conduct."

The passage captures the idea of the press as "gatekeeper" on behalf of the public. Journalists select and order the medley of fact, propaganda, rumor, and suspicion and transform them into news that is true and reliable. This gatekeeper notion governed newsrooms for most of the twentieth century and instilled the sense of civic responsibility in the journalist. After all, who else could stand sentinel at the gate of public knowledge? The newsroom was the sole intermediary between the citizen and newsmaker. Anyone who wanted to reach the public with information needed to go through the "working press." It is an idealistic notion certainly, and even Lippmann would soon have his doubts about whether the press was up to the task and whether the public was intellectually competent to comprehend the news.[1] Despite those doubts, Lippmann continued to dedicate himself to the proposition of the press, remaining a journalist for the rest of this life, and his optimistic vision helped define the press's aspirations.

Now, however, the metaphor of the solitary gatekeeper mediating facts on behalf of the public is increasingly problematic—or even obsolete. There are many conduits between newsmakers and the public. The press is merely one of them. In the 2008 presidential race, videos produced by the Obama campaign staff were viewed more than one billion times on the candidate's own YouTube channel, without any press involvement. A third of Americans now get news recommended to them from non-journalists they follow on social networks. Almost half of all Americans have watched or read news that was sent to them by friends in e-mails. Six in ten of those online get news assembled for them by aggregators. A third of those online read blogs, and six in ten watch videos on sites like YouTube. And the same technology that makes it easier for citizens to produce their own content also makes it easier for government or corporations or any other entity to communicate directly. With all this, journalists stand sentinel at a gate with no fence surrounding it.

What role, then, should journalists play? If we citizens are our own editors, at times even our own reporters, what do we need from the press? What should the gathering and dissemination of news look like, who will produce it, and how will it be consumed? What, in other words, do we need from what might be called the "next journalism"?

This chapter will lay out our vision of what that is, what journalism—old and new—needs to provide to civil society in the digital age and how the press will need to change to provide it.

Observers have offered various responses. Many have suggested that journalism must become a dialogue, not a lecture. Others have gone so far as to argue that we no longer need journalists at all because we live in a world where we are all journalists and truth can be more effectively found in a thousand voices than a few—in this view, the news is a kind of real-time ever-changing Wikipedia account of the day's events. Still others have contended that we should abandon the outworn, failed notions of objectivity, in which journalists delude themselves into thinking they are not creatures of their own biases. Just admit it.

We believe the answer is a combination of old journalism and new: The gatekeeping function of the press does not disappear entirely, but it is now a smaller dimension of what the press must provide and by itself is inadequate to explain the press's role. The press must perform a more complex set of functions than gatekeeping, and it also must must adopt new forms of storytelling and dissemination and embrace public participation in the news. The press is still a mediator, but that mediating role will become more varied and more complex, and fulfilling it in a world of unlimited channels of communication will be more difficult. In the twentieth century, journalism used to be whatever journalists decided it was. Today, consumers have a greater role in the decision, and the next incarnation of journalism must embrace and serve that more-active citizen. In that regard, journalism is no longer a lecture. It is more of a dialogue—and potentially richer than ever before.

As the press changes, however, we believe certain standards and values of the traditional vision of journalism remain. If anything, indeed, they become more urgent, since those values are the primary way that consumers can distinguish reliable information from the other kinds of media vying for their time. In *The Elements of Journalism*, we outline the norms to which professional journalism aspires.[2] Those values include independence, verification, a primary allegiance to citizens rather than political faction or corporate interests, and a dedication to consideration of events, rather than a commitment to forcing a specific outcome or policy solution. We also argue there that objectivity does not suggest neutrality. Its true meaning is that the press should employ an objective and transparent method of gathering and verifying the news, a definition of "objectivity" much closer to that in science. We do not think today that those values and ideas should disappear. After all, they were not derived in the last century for the economic convenience of the press. Nor were they handed down from philosophers or journalistic ethicists working at some academic remove. Instead, these norms evolved by trial and error based on what citizens needed from the news. While its history is a messy one, and many bad publishers have thrived along with good ones, journalism and its norms came from the street, from what worked over the long haul, from what citizens gravitated to over time. Today, as consumers are more empowered and more discriminating, those elements are no less relevant. Technology may change the delivery and form and may create different economic incentives for people and companies that aspire to deliver news. But it will not change human nature and the imperatives of what people need to know. The more pressing issue is how journalism changes to maintain those values for a new age.

Beyond Gatekeepers: The New Metaphor

The first step is to understand the new ways in which we now acquire our news. We have already begun to rely on some new authorities to alert us to what might be important. We get e-mails from friends; we get news from non-news sources we follow on social networks; we read blogs, sort through aggregators, and more. These new behaviors are only one part of a larger change. Very few of us rely on a primary news source, a single institution, for most of our information. Instead, we have become "news grazers," who acquire information from multiple platforms at different times. Only 7 percent of Americans rely on one medium—say television or the Internet—for most of their news, let alone a single news organization.[3] Half of all Americans get news from four or five different platforms every day.[4] And we get news now throughout the day, in bits and pieces, not all at once at prescribed times, the way we did a generation ago. These two changes, the reliance on multiple sources and continuous news consumption, represent an enormous shift with profound implications about public learning. Instead of getting the news all at once in an ordered way, scanning the newspaper or watching the whole newscast, we increasingly acquire our news one story at a time, subject by subject, at different times and in fragments. News consumption online, for instance, spikes after lunch, after people hear about something during their lunch break and then go back to their office to read about it and other subjects. What this means is that the news has become unbundled from the news organization. We don't turn to our favorite morning newspaper or evening newscast to have them tell us what's happening. Instead, increasingly we check the news to find out more about the stories we are curious about. We seek the news today, in effect, by story rather than by news organization.

As we hunt for news on our own, instead of relying on what a news gatekeeper provides in a single newscast or newspaper, news consumption has become a more proactive experience. Some have even come to call it a "lean forward" experience, in which we look for things we are interested in—for answers to our questions. Getting the news is no longer a "lean back" experience, in which we put our feet up and have an anchorperson tell us what's happening or flip through the newspaper.

This shift away from relying on one news organization to be our primary news provider is the real meaning of the breakdown of the gatekeeper role. People have not abandoned traditional news values or news brands. Online, indeed, traditional news sources dominate the traffic to a degree many did not predict. (Of the top two hundred news Web sites in America as of 2010, roughly 80 percent of them were either "legacy" news sources—with ties to print or television institutions—or aggregators of legacy news sources, and they attracted 83 percent of the traffic.[5]) But people access these sites differently than they once did their siblings in print or television. They move among several of these sources frequently and for short periods of time. And at the top of the list of news destinations online are aggregators (such as Yahoo and AOL) and demi-aggregators (such as CNN and MSNBC) that give consumers more choice.[6] Nor, as some predicted, are people narrowing their vision for news, going mostly to news destinations that focus on their favorite subjects or that tell the news from only a partisan perspective. Niche or specialty news sites are less popular than broad-topic sites, and the average person visits specialty sites half as often and stays half as long per visit.[7] Contrary to many predictions, in other words, a close look at hard data reveals that consumers still want traditional news values and sources. And they still want a wide array of subject matter. They just interact with these sources differently. We are becoming a culture of on-demand news consumers, accessing what we want when we want it.

What those who want to provide the news must understand is that this new lean-forward consumer requires a new kind of journalism.

In the broadest terms, journalism must shift from being a product—one news organization's stories or agenda—to being more of a service that can answer the audience's questions, offer resources, provide tools. To this degree, journalism *must* shift from being simply a lecture—telling the public what it should know—to becoming a public dialogue, with the journalist informing and helping facilitate the discussion. Sometimes it can be news development in concert with members of the public. But it does not imply professionalism in the news is now obsolete, or that storytelling is irrelevant. They are, by themselves, however, insufficient.

The important idea is this: In the future the press will derive its integrity from what kind of content it delivers and the quality of its engagement, not from its exclusive role as a sole information provider or intermediary between newsmakers and the public.

To do this, newspeople must replace the singular idea of the press as a gatekeeper with a more refined and nuanced idea based on what consumers require from the news—particularly reportorial news, rather than commentary and discussion. We see eight essential dimensions or functions that the new news consumer requires from journalism. These eight functions, in effect, define the idea of journalism as service or dialogue. Some of them are not new. They were embedded in, or perhaps obscured by, the gatekeeper idea. And some of these, thanks to new technology, may be performed with the help of citizens or by new-media journalists working outside large media institutions. We hope readers will refine these eight, break them up or add their own. The journalism of the future—both new and old—must be rooted in how people use news and what they require of journalists. Here are eight that we see:

Authenticator: We will require the press to help *authenticate* for us what facts are true and reliable. While we will not look to journalists as our sole information provider, we will need some way of distinguishing what information we can trust, and some basis in evidence for why that is the case. As we have more sources offering us information today, this role may be more important than ever. We need some way of sorting out what is believable and accurate amid the growing array of arguments coming at us from all sides, the talking points and spin, the alternate realities of partisan sources who speak so freely now in the journalism of assertion and affirmation, and from corporate and partisan outlets that are growing in number. Those working in more traditional or more independent, nonideological newsrooms are well positioned to help perform this authenticator service for us. These institutions aspire to derive their authority from their accuracy and verification and dispassionate assessment of information, not from an ideological affinity with audiences or simply their speed and omnipresence. Playing this authenticator role, however, will require a higher level of expertise from newsrooms, particularly on their franchise subject areas. It will also require that journalists provide this information with more documentation and transparency about sources and methods than they may have in the past. We can no longer assume that something is trustworthy because we read it in the paper or heard it from the media. The authenticator role will be a critical one at the heart of any news organization's authority, and a key element of remaining relevant when such organizations no longer have a monopoly over information or our attention.

Sense Maker: Journalism is also well suited to play the role of *sense maker*—to put information into context and to look for connections so that, as consumers, we can decide what the news means to us. We have discussed this role throughout the book, and talked at some length about sense-making stories. Now this role must expand. The reason this role is becoming more important is precisely because information has become more plentiful. The expansion of available information has made creating knowledge more difficult. This idea is critical to understand. When information is in greater supply, knowledge becomes harder to create, because we have to sift through more data to arrive at it. Confusion and uncertainty are more likely. This is why, in part, the journalism of affirmation has become more popular. But reinforcing prejudice, retreating to the familiar, is a false way of making sense, a retreat from learning. To arrive at a more meaningful understanding we need to open our minds to information, not narrow them. Journalists of verification must help us do that. They must look for information that is of value, not just new, and present it in a way so we make sense of it ourselves.

Sense making is not the same thing as interpreting the news. Each one of us can arrive at meaning only for ourselves. But sense making does imply looking for connections among facts to help us answer questions on our own. It implies looking for information that explains why or how things happened. It implies looking at the implications of the news and identifying what questions are left unanswered—the seventh element of the five Ws and one H we discussed in Chapter 3—and helping us know which questions will become important next. The sense-maker role, in other words, is not a commentator role necessarily. It is reportorial. It involves finding facts and information that, as good sense making does, makes the tumblers click.

Investigator: Journalists also must continue to function as public investigators, in what many call the *watchdog role*. Journalism that exposes what is being kept hidden or secret is so central, so essential, to a democratic government that its importance is fundamental to the new journalism as well as the old. And some elements in our media culture are less likely to provide it precisely because it is fundamentally a reportorial function grounded in verification. We do not see much of it in the fast-paced journalism of affirmation or the interpretative and propagandistic partisan-audience-pandering of the journalism of assertion. It is less likely to come from a blogger largely offering opinion. The press stands as an independent prosecutor of sorts, and by the power of its searchlight, it shapes, not simply follows, agendas, whether it is uncovering public malfeasance in an exposé or shifting paradigms.

Witness Bearer: Not every light that the press shines exposes wrongdoing. There is something powerful and essential, if less celebrated, in the press simply showing up and *bearing witness* to events. This is the monitoring function of journalism, which is less prosecutorial than the watchdog or investigator function. There are certain things that occur in any community that should be observed, monitored, and scrutinized. When they are not, government and the people who want to exploit it are more apt to act out of self-interest than public good. Abuse and malfeasance are more likely to occur. This is as certain as the axiom that power is corrupting, or that communities without police will have more crime. The same goes for nongovernmental institutions in our community. The press plays a critical role here simply by showing up, by being there. It provides democracy with a life-ensuring sunshine by its very presence. In this new era, a diminished press cannot be everywhere. So a critical step, at minimum, is to identify those places in the community that must be monitored for basic civic integrity and to show up, and by having a presence, tell those in power they are being watched. If resources do not exist, then the press must also find ways to create and organize networks of new technology and citizen sentinels to ensure that this monitoring occurs. Here lies a potential for the creation of new partnerships with citizens, new bonds that can energize communities. If the press does not help create these, it is possible that more self-interested groups will fill this space to control the information flow about critical points. Thus it is important, when allocating resources, that we not simply get another witness to events already being hotly debated, that the press not simply pile onto a commoditized conversation that people can get anywhere. This is more tempting than it seems. Journalism is apt to do stories people are already talking about rather than those that focus on what is being ignored. It is easier to add to an existing conversation than to create a new one. But to bear witness of us, we need journalism to make a special effort to gather the news others ignore and not just add another voice to the chorus because it is an easy way to bring traffic to a Web site. Here new media are particularly powerful.

Empowerer: The press should also give us tools as citizens to achieve the new way of knowing. A big part of this is viewing the public as part of the process of the news and not just an audience for it. It is mutual *empowerment*. The citizen is empowered by sharing experience and knowledge that informs others—including the journalist. The journalist is empowered by tapping into experience and expertise beyond his or her formal and official sources. This partnership benefits both the citizen and the journalist by breaking the news out of the mold of relying on a limited well of information and ideas to frame and draw conclusions. It expands the dialogue. It makes understanding a process, not a product. And it starts with recognizing that the consumer or citizen is a powerful partner in this process, someone to be listened to and helped, not lectured at. This process of partnership also will make the journalist better by forcing her to think harder about how to put information in a context that is useful, that offers consumers ways to act on it, that tells them how they might do so, and where else they can go for more information, and does so while events are still unfolding, not just after they have occurred. The end result of this is a continuing conversation.

This is the point at which fact and belief, the two ends of the understanding spectrum, begin to merge. You have to believe in the power and use of information. Journalists must believe in it to conduct this kind of journalism. And consumers must believe in it to learn and expand their understanding. The journalist and the consumer also must respect one another. The consumer must accept that the journalist is dedicated to facts and is trying to present them to help the consumer think for herself. And the journalist, whether in an old newsroom or new, must respect the citizen's capacity to understand information and act on it.

Our great friend the late journalism scholar and Columbia University professor Jim Carey once wrote that communication is conversation and that the product of this conversation is the creation of community. The essence and purpose of this book, of determining "how to know what to believe," is to have faith in that proposition.

Smart Aggregator: We also need help harnessing the power of the Web. We need a *smart aggregator* that patrols the Web on our behalf and goes beyond what computer algorithms or generic aggregator Web sites can offer. The news organization of the future should comb the information landscape, monitoring on behalf of its audience what other information might be helpful. The idea of the "walled garden," in which a news organization offers only its own reporting, is over. For a news organization to be really helpful, to serve that lean-forward news consumer, it must also point its audience to other Web sources that it considers valuable. This is how the Web becomes a more powerful tool. We will value the news source that can help us harness the Web for us. This goes far beyond adding a Google toolbar to a Web site. Smart aggregators should share sources they rely on, the stories they find illuminating, the information that informed them. And we use the term "smart aggregator" here for a reason. In the same way that the press is an authenticator and a sense maker, the aggregation it engages in should save people time and steer them to trusted sources. A computer algorithm might give someone infinite choices in a list. The smart aggregation of journalism might offer a half-dozen recommendations that a newsperson, as a knowledge source, considers the most valuable. Individual writers and bloggers do this already. It is a journalistic function. But these writers often cite only stories that contain information they want to talk about or that support some point they want to make. Large news operations can serve audiences well by basing aggregation recommendations more widely, identifying for audiences content that serves the full range of journalistic functions. Newsrooms are combing the Web constantly on subjects to inform their own stories, and they can now pass that along to audiences. Curation is knowledge.

Forum Organizer: Journalists, especially local ones, also should help create conversation and *discourse* for citizens to actively participate. The print press helped create this model when it invented the letter-to-the-editor feature in the nineteenth century, as well as op-ed pages written by outside contributors. The term "op-ed" is short for "opposite the editorials" and refers to those columns written by individuals from the community, as opposed to the voice of the newspaper editorial board, and typically appear on the page opposite the papers' official editorials. We think it would be harmful to civil society, and perhaps financially devastating to news companies, if traditional news institutions were to abandon this role or cede it to others. A community's news institutions, new or old, can serve as public squares where we citizens can monitor voices from all sides, not just those in our own ideological affinity group. As citizens, we all have a stake in having a public square where everyone feels welcome. If newspeople imagine that their goal is to inspire and inform public discourse, then helping organize this discourse is a logical and appropriate function. We all have a primary vested interest, as well, in this public forum being built on a foundation of accuracy. There is little value in arguments based on pseudo-facts and rumors. Reportorial news institutions are well suited to build a public forum on reliable information.

Role Model: The new press, especially those tied to legacy brands, if they survive, will inevitably serve as a *role model* for those citizens who want to bear witness themselves and operate at times as citizen journalists. Inevitably people will look to journalists to see how this work is done, emulating what they see and like and altering what they do not like. Some news organizations have gone so far as to set up classes for citizen journalists and to enlist them in their news gathering. We applaud that. But we also need something more than that. Journalists must understand that their conduct is public, not just their stories. And to a degree that markets and brand consultants do not understand, the public has detected the cynicism and pandering embedded in slogans to "be on your side," to "work for you," and the rest. This decline in public regard is reflected in the depiction of the media in almost any entertainment program or movie, or the declining trust of the press over the past thirty years. In the open world of the digital age, a press that does not live up to its constitutional claims is only more disappointing because the public measures performance against its best hope for journalism, not its worst expectations.

Virtually all of these functions have existed previously. But now they must become more dynamic. If news is to be useful in the changing way we consume it, the people who produce the news professionally must think about the function that each story or piece of content has for citizens. It is not enough for news operations to simply have a story each day on what they consider the most important subjects. They need to understand what purpose each story serves for the audience, what service it provides or questions it answers. If it offers no service, it is a waste of resources and time to a more demanding proactive news consumer. A story of limited or incremental value is a sign that the news operation is not offering much service.

Journalism, in other words, is not becoming obsolete. It is becoming more complex.

A Better Journalism

Implicit in this expanded and more complex vision of journalism as service is that new technology, far from damaging the press, should improve it. Technology has given people who cover and report the news drastically more capacity as well as more responsibility. The Internet is not only creating a new journalism; it is creating a better one that can dig deeper and better engage with the public.

To get a concrete sense of how technology is enriching what we can get from journalism, consider how an older medium might react to news, versus a digital platform.

In a newspaper story, journalists might be able to offer six elements in covering an event:

1. a main narrative or news story
2. a sidebar feature or analysis piece
3. photographs
4. headlines
5. a graphic or background-information box
6. a "pull quote," a dramatic line or quote from the story set in large type to draw readers' attention to what the story says

Coverage of the same event on the Web can draw on a far more diverse array of elements to tell the story. The list keeps growing—our current count, enumerated in the appendix, is fifty. In addition to the main narrative, graphics, and photos, a Web story can utilize original documents, biographies of major newsmakers, backgrounders, archives of related stories, an expanding array of citizen comments, and more. We offer a short list of these elements here, and readers may have others to contribute:

1. customizable graphics that can be manipulated by users
2. photo galleries (staff or citizen produced)

3. links embedded in keywords in the story taking readers to definitions or elaborations
4. links to the newsmakers and organizations mentioned in the story with biographical and other details
5. links supporting key facts in the story, including primary documents or materials
6. complete interview transcripts
7. video and/or audio of interviews
8. a biography of the story's author
9. interactive timelines for key events leading up to the current news moment
10. searchable databases relevant to the story, some on the news organization's Web site, some hosted on other Web sites, including government sites
11. a list of frequently asked questions on issues related to the story
12. links to blogs covering the story or reacting to it
13. an invitation to "crowd-source" material in the story or questions the story raises—when the news organization asks for information from users about elements of the story that are not yet fully reported
14. an opportunity for citizens to tell the news organization what else they would like to know
15. background on what the reader can do about issues raised in the story
16. buttons to "share this story" with social media sites like Digg and Reddit
17. corrections and updates to the story, with crossouts and addenda added directly to the original text

Compared with that in the print environment, the data in the networked-information environment are denser, broader, deeper. The Web offers the potential for richer coverage and therefore better understanding. But producing that coverage is far more challenging. It is unlikely that any one source can produce all those elements, even on the most important story. Nor can audiences often absorb them all. So those who cover the news must be much smarter, and exercise much shrewder judgment, about which elements fit best with which kind of news story.

The great news executive running a newsroom of the twenty-first century might not be the operation's most celebrated correspondent. The most sought-after talent, instead, might be the person who has an intuitive feel for which tools on this expanding list are best suited to which story. And the process of "covering" the news must be transformed to take advantage of these tools. In legacy newsrooms, reporters traditionally were sent out in the morning to "do stories." They came back all vying for a spot in the newscast or on the front page, and then decisions were made about where and how long each story would go. Now that process is different. For a news operation is unceasing, and the editors and producers need to constantly decide whether an interactive graphic, or a database, or biographies, or citizen stories, or other elements make sense.

At one level, the elements of the story are disintermediated into individual components. At another level, the story is given fuller context because of the associations that can be built into it. Among other things, this means the digital, linked format invites browsing and "horizontal" reading, rather than linear "vertical" reading of a story from start to finish. Networked information also invites participation. The Internet is full of applications and opportunities that encourage people to share information, express their reaction to it, and add to it. A marriage of print and other media allows the story to be experienced on multiple platforms.

It is as if journalists used to build houses with only a hammer, saw, screwdriver, and level and now have access to all the power tools available at Home Depot.

The New Newsroom

To fulfill these new and expanded roles, to use this capacity, another change must take place. The newsroom of the future must be organized differently and must operate differently, whether it is a legacy newsroom trying to adapt or a new virtual newsroom just starting out. It must, in short, develop a more rigorous and diverse culture.

How must the newsroom change?

The Level of Proof Must Be Higher

First, if the public is to look to journalists to help them authenticate and make sense of things that they might have originally learned elsewhere, the level of proof the press offers to us must be higher than before. It was once the case that the medical writer who took a week to write about new developments in breast cancer treatment would provide information that might be all new to most readers concerned with the disease, often even some who had it. Today, anyone who has a mother suffering from this disease might have spent the past year online learning about the latest research. The one week the journalist spent on the story wouldn't compare. The journalist must now do something quite different. Providing a new level of proof will explain how that can happen. It means that everything we have discussed in this book—evidence, verification, sourcing, and other items that add to a story's completeness—is even more important, and more challenging.

Journalism Must Be More Transparent

The press must become more transparent about how it verifies the news, so that the public can know why the press should be trusted and can develop their own process of verification. The voice of the omniscient narrator in news, simply assuring the audience, is now insufficient. Since the press is no longer the only source of news, its authority must come from how it gathers and authenticates its facts. How do you know this? Why should I believe it? These are questions audiences now demand, and journalists must answer. The new transparency of citizen engagement begins to change the dynamic. Transparency comes closer to conveying the original meaning of what came to be called objectivity in news.[8]

We have alluded to this idea of transparency throughout this book and even more extensively in *The Elements of Journalism*. Transparency is the best measure of the confidence the organization itself puts in the information it provides. Transparency is the way an organization creates credibility. It demonstrates how much critical thinking has been done before any assertions are made of what is true or untrue, what is real or unreal—about whether the organization values a more meaningful relationship with a better-educated audience.

The basic idea of transparency is simple: Never deceive your audience. Tell them what you know *and* what you don't know. Tell them who your sources are, and if you can't name the sources, tell them how the sources are in a position to know and what biases they may have. In other words, provide your information so that people see how it was developed and can make up their own minds about what to think.

In this complex and tumultuous world, we believe it is important that journalists keep an open mind—not only about what they hear but also about their ability to understand. Journalists should not assume. They should avoid an arrogance about their knowledge and be sure to submit their own assumptions to a process of verification.

The Press Must Develop or Access More Expertise

The new press also must develop more expertise, particularly in the areas in which each news organization decides it is going to define and stake its brand. In the new era of journalism, each press outlet is not going to be equally good at everything. That era of specialization has already begun. In an age when the press is no longer a monopoly it must earn its authority by providing knowledge.

The networking that new technology permits has dramatically increased our ability to find more experts, more viewpoints, more data, and more stories in the search for and the sharing of factual and reliable information.

One such effort, called Public Insight Journalism, has helped Minnesota Public Radio put together an e-mail network of thousands of listeners and contributors. The network is made up of people who agree to provide somewhat detailed background and personal information. They are organized by profession, location, age, religion, ethnicity, and interests. The news operation sends out queries on stories, scans the responses, and chooses responses with unusual perspective or special insight into the story's subject matter.

This database is activated for specific stories by an analyst and reporter teams, who select from the network those who would likely be of most help. The reporter then works with those chosen to produce the report. This use of "crowd sourcing" often produces gripping personal stories as well as a broader array of expert opinion, which often results in unexpected new story possibilities.

When gasoline prices began to rise in 2008, the news media across the country focused on what impact this was having on weekend trips and vacation plans. Minnesota's Public Insight Journalism network alerted reporters to the fact that the rising gas prices were keeping rural health care providers from getting to their patients, thus breaking a more important public health story that other news organizations had to chase.[9] Others are following suit. The *Guardian* in England has employed the public in its news gathering in so many different ways it has coined its whole approach to news it calls "mutualization." This is the future.

The Newsroom Must Be Reorganized and New Skill Sets Added

A look at most of the new tools available to journalists reveals, among other things, that journalism now must be more than storytelling. Information must come in more forms—statistical, graphic, audio, visual. Technology that allows interaction between the consumer and the journalist, jointly analyzing a proposed budget, for example, must become a much bigger part of journalism. To employ these tools journalists must reorganize their newsroom.

Newsrooms typically have been very simple organizations, especially print and radio newsrooms. There are storytellers and former storytellers who supervise them. These newsrooms also accommodate photographers and some graphic artists and, more recently, a handful of information technology staffers. The cultures of these print and radio newsrooms, however, are dominated by narrative storytellers. It is a rare event when a photographer or a graphic artist rises to a position of real power over their narrative cohort. Television newsrooms have always been more complex, given the power and central role of pictures. These newsrooms are organized in teams, and, at the elite levels of network TV, producers who neither appear on camera nor operate cameras can be very influential. Ultimately power resides in show producers and the network executives above them. Yet even this culture is relatively simple, and traditionally the anchors and correspondents and show producers rule.

The modern newsroom in all these media must become far more complex and accommodating, honoring many more skill sets than it does now. Those with skill sets that need to be honored include programmers, database managers, information managers (formerly called librarians), and information gatherers who do not write. The modern newsroom might even need to have a staff methodologist, someone who can look at data and help reporters know what kinds of statistics make sense and which don't, which kind of data analysis is logical and which is flawed. A modern newsroom might want to have access in some special way to local historians who could be involved in story meetings or planning of news coverage. CBS News briefly experimented with making its morning story meetings public online. At the *Sacramento Bee*, our good friend and then–executive editor Gregory Favre began a program in which a citizen sat in on news meetings to decide what would appear on the front page of each section. Each citizen would participate in the give-and-take for a week. They were usually quiet the first day, becoming fully engaged as the week went on. "My thought always was, if we are afraid to talk with our readers and hear what they are saying, regardless of the delivery platform, then we are being shortsighted and arrogant. If we are afraid of our audience, we will not succeed," Favre said.

The former definition of newsroom skills is too limited, and it has helped create cultures that are too restricted. But the technological advances in the past decade are destroying that culture and its business model.

One of the things that held legacy media back, and may indeed prove its mortal weakness, is that it did not understand the essential power of the Web as an aggregating force. This understanding was embedded in the mentality of those who wrote computer code, who programmed, who imagined harnessing the power of the Web itself rather than simply using it as a platform for distributing a limited amount of original content. Legacy media companies had the opportunity to create (and later, in some cases, to buy) the sites that came to destroy their economic foundation, including eBay, Craigslist, Google, Realtor.com, and Monster .com. They let these opportunities slip by because they did not fundamentally understand the value that these technologies might play. They didn't add to the immediate business that generated revenue for old media. They seemed to be different businesses, and they are. But what news companies failed to recognize is that they are not essentially different functions. The news organization of the future needs to rethink and reidentify its essential purpose.

Journalism is far more than storytelling. It is far more than producing narratives. And it is far more than delivering advertising alongside those narratives. Civic knowledge is broader than that. And if the news operations continue to define themselves in their traditional, limited way—as a description of the product they produce rather than the function they serve in people's lives—the chances that journalism and the values it represents will survive become much more limited.

The legacy press has always claimed to cover public debate. In reality, it was much better at covering official debate, that which took place in public office buildings and among established experts. It was much more limited, however, at covering the debate among people around kitchen tables. The emerging new media is far better at this broader public discussion. It has made the public more real and more robust. This is the bridge in many ways between new media and old.

The Editor Will Become More Important, Not Less

While this may seem counterintuitive to some, as journalism becomes more complicated, the role of the editor will become more important. To begin with, editors must do more than simply edit narratives. They must understand which of the new tools on an expanding list should be used to communicate. But perhaps most critical, they must curate the expanding dialogue with audiences as well as the material available throughout the Web. The pioneers of the new media understood this. New York University's Jay Rosen, in creating one of the first open-source-reporting experiments, NewAssignment.Net, explained it this way: "What's open to the wisdom of the crowd is vulnerable to the actions of the mob. Wanting to be helpful, the volunteer may slant reports without realizing it. Through the portals marked 'citizen,' the paid operative can also go."[10] Preventing that from happening, Rosen suggested, has many elements, from self-policing users, making verification an easy and accessible part of the Web site, and making verification a critical part of the editors' job. In the old model, editors largely relied on reporters to get the facts right. In the new age, with the audience helping to create the news as part of the reporting process or to refine it postpublication, verification becomes a bigger part of the editors' job, not a smaller part of it. "We are in an age of volume," journalist Gary Kamiya wrote at Slate.com. "Editing is about refinement . . . In the chaotic new online universe, the old-fashioned, elitist, non-democratic system of sorting information will become increasingly important, if only because it enforces a salutary reduction of the sheer mind-swamping number of options available."[11]

The Definition of News Must Change

Finally, implicit in this expanded new role of the press is that the news is more complex than people have generally considered it. We have discussed this throughout this book, in the different types of news and models of news gathering, from a story breaking new facts to the prosecutorial brief of a watchdog exposé. But the press must be far more conscious of what function each story or piece of content that is produced plays. The press must ask, How are people going to use this content? How will it help them? What is its value? What else could be done instead?

The news organizations that survive will be the ones that can answer those questions. Those that cannot will perish.

The News Organization as Knowledge Creator and Disseminator

Everything we have discussed so far in this chapter involves the idea that for journalism to survive in some recognizable form, news organizations, new or old, must understand and define the function they actually play in people's lives. We want to spend another minute on this question of the essential purpose of journalism. If the fatal mistake that buggy companies and railway companies made was not understanding that they were in the transportation business, what is the analogy for news organizations?

Strip away platform. Strip away technique. Strip away culture. What function does a newsroom serve in its community? What is its essential purpose, apart from generating revenue.[12]

Telling stories is not the answer. Neither is delivering the news, or even monitoring government. All those have been part of it historically. But we think the essential function is something broader and more conceptual, and the future of journalism depends in part on embracing this broader notion.

A news gathering organization is a place that accumulates and synthesizes knowledge about a community, either a geopolitical community or a community of subjects and interests, and then makes that knowledge available and interactive in a variety of ways.

Traditional advertising is one form of that knowledge—ads for what goods and services are for sale, especially new ones. Listings and bulletin boards are another form. So are names of community experts and authorities. In a sense, each reporter's Rolodex or list of sources is a kind of knowledge accumulated in the newsroom, one that the individual reporter has filtered and controlled but still indirectly makes available to the audience at the reporter's discretion.

Then there are more abstract kinds of knowledge that the newsroom accumulates and makes available. It answers questions like How does the mayor's office really work? Who can you believe and not believe in town? Who is a trustworthy person to listen to about the local economy? Who are the clowns in town, who make fools of themselves without knowing it? Which persons in town deserve our pity because they have been victims of bad luck? Who deserves our admiration? Where is the best place to get pizza? All of these are examples of knowledge that newsrooms have accumulated, the kind of institutional knowledge that resides in collected memory. Much more knowledge resides in these newsrooms than is ever written down. The newsroom, as an abstraction, disseminates knowledge in one highly restricted form—the individual story.

The problem is that news companies have never fully had to understand this role in such a conceptual way. They were thriving financially. They had only to produce the same kind of product they had always produced, improving it marginally, finding new ways of telling stories or new topics to cover. As a result, much of the knowledge that's been created in newsrooms has never found its way to the public. It sits in files, or in the minds of the reporters and editors. News companies generally did not think about new product lines or new ways of disseminating knowledge. And the narrowness of the way creating civic knowledge has been defined is one reason the industry missed new business opportunities, whether it was failing to move into search and aggregation or standing by while others built superior online classifieds.

In understanding this broader definition—the function the newsroom plays in the community, the role it serves, rather than the product people are engaged in producing—we think news operations can find some of the answers they will need moving forward. This includes discovering new businesses that they can monetize.

What are the some of the kinds of knowledge that newsrooms have accumulated and not yet exploited? What other kinds of knowledge could they begin to accumulate? What are some possible markets for that knowledge? What are some of the ways to disseminate it? And how might those be monetized? This is how a Silicon Valley start-up company in an emerging market examines its potential. The challenge for newsroom organizations is that they are both a declining business in one platform and an emerging business in another. But they largely think like an old business. They operate like Wall Street in that way, and work along the short time horizons of those old industries, and are staffed by people who flourished in those cultures. The list of new business models is only emerging: virtual community retail malls and earning transaction fees; data sets offered to targeted paid audiences; pay services to research and answer questions; specialty sites for professional audiences; audience research and consulting; real-time advertising based on immediate location; and much more.

Only in understanding the function that news plays in people's lives can the news industry navigate a future. This is the difference between a railroad executive thinking of himself as being in the business of moving things on rails and being in the transportation business.

Others will improve on the definition we have offered here. And certainly we hope others will figure out other ways for news organizations to create civic knowledge and monetize it. But the future of journalism lies in the function that news plays in people's lives, not in the techniques and practices of the twentieth-century newsroom.

The New Atomic Unit of News

If what matters is the value news has in our lives, but not necessarily the form or format that news has taken in the past, it follows that we need to think in fresh ways about how news is presented. Storytelling and words, while no longer the only elements of news, are still at the center of it. But that does not mean that we should hold tight to the traditional forms of storytelling.

In many ways, the daily story is an artifact of the nineteenth century, when news was delivered on paper and an entirely new version was produced every day.

In the age of the Internet, the idea of a perishable story, or that news starts fresh each day, is obsolete. The story can be a living thing, growing each day. In thinking along these lines, we have heard one idea that strikes us as particularly potent, though doubtless there are others. This idea builds on one from a Silicon Valley executive, Marissa Mayer of Google, not from a newsroom. It does not shift news away from narrative storytelling. But in addition to the daily story, it would create a new "atomic unit" of news. This atomic unit could be something much closer to a Wikipedia page than a daily story. Call it a "knowledge page." The knowledge page would have a running account of everything a news organization knows on a subject, and it would be built on rather than replaced, along the lines of a living encyclopedia entry, something richer and more dynamic even than a Wikipedia entry, something more complete than today's newest story. It would include all the material that the news organization had accumulated, organized in a way that makes it easy to find and scan. And the spine would have a running central summary or narrative on the topic. This would be a powerful new way of "telling" the news and accumulating and organizing civic knowledge. To learn about something, the citizen consumer would no longer need to hunt through the archive of past stories, or "clips," nor assemble a larger narrative by reading between the lines of each discrete account or story. A knowledge page could include a What's New section with the latest story. But it would have much more. And a central synopsis, along with a table of contents, could direct people to the resources and tools that the news organization had gathered. From a commercial standpoint, there is another advantage. Rather than driving people to a different URL or Web page for each new incremental event, the news organization would have a central page with one URL that would generate far more traffic and thus could be amortized or monetized in potentially far more potent ways.

In late 2009, Google partnered with the *Washington Post* and the *New York Times* to experiment with a version of this idea, called "The Living Story." Built by Google in collaboration with journalists from the two papers, it was designed to use new technology to offer a standing or living page that told the story of a few major running events, such as health care reform or the politics of global warming. The experiment lasted from December 2009 to February 2010. It had many virtues, but also problems. One problem was that it resided at Google. It was not fundamentally built into the way either the *Post* or the *Times* was trying to tell these running stories on their Web sites. Another was it focused heavily on using graphics and technology to illustrate elements of the story. It was not, as we saw from a distance, a way to fundamentally rethink how to write stories so that they would not be perishable daily events but rather would build into single running accounts of the news that were more coherent, more complete, and more useful. The experiment foundered, but the idea behind it, we believe, is important. It should be taken up again in a form where it will be owned by a news operation and viewed as an attempt to write the news in a new way, not create an experiment in design and graphics.

Should We Care About the Old News Institutions?

Finally, one question that lingers is the degree to which we should care whether the institutions that have provided us with the news in the past survive.

Perhaps we shouldn't. Hot type came and went. So did the typewriter. Many great newspapers have passed into history. The era of big-city newspaper competition largely vanished, and it was accompanied, as the surviving monopoly papers got bigger, by more professionalism and ethical responsibility, though also perhaps by rising questions about bias. There is no reason to cling out of fear or nostalgia to what is familiar, simply because it has certain virtues.

History repeatedly offers evidence that innovation is more likely to spawn in small places than large, in garages (Apple and Hewlett-Packard) and grad school carrels (Google), in a founder's unlikely vision rather than a Fortune 500 corporation's task force.

All these are reasons to watch and root for outsiders.

But we do think that society and citizens have a stake in whether some of the core journalistic values that reside in the old institutions survive. If a new journalism is to be created, we think civic life has an interest in these values transferring to the new media and the new newsrooms. These values are the envy of journalists worldwide who come to America to study them and learn.

The question is whether, and to what extent, these values of independent and reliable journalism will transfer to new institutions. It is important, in considering this subject, to not be nostalgic. It is also important to understand history. Not all news organizations observed these values equally well. Many of these values became more refined in the last half of the twentieth century. But the fact that some of them were late in coming, or were observed more in the breach in some places than others, does not diminish the fact that the best newsrooms aspired to them most strongly. A careful look at media history suggests there is no guarantee that all new newsrooms will adopt these values—even those with ties to legacy media or those started by people who came from legacy press. Television news in America began with traditional values of radio and gradually, over a generation, cast many of them aside. Cable news began (at CNN) by emulating traditional broadcast evening newscasts and in a similar time frame changed as well.

Tactically, perhaps, the best chance for the fundamental values we admire to survive is for the institutions that guard them to survive, but that is hardly guaranteed. Our focus is on these fundamental principles and in articulating them so that they can be understood and manifested in new technology, in new platforms, and by new means.

On balance the companies that have lived up to these values have won the journalism wars over time, while the companies that have strayed from them have vanished. With the creative destruction brought by the digital age, the values alone are not enough. For reportorial journalism and the values that have propelled them to survive, news organizations need to find new sources of revenue beyond twentieth-century-style display advertising simply moved to the Web. That may involve creating new kinds of advertising with targeted coding to match advertisers, content, and readers. It may involve creating new "knowledge products" that can be sold or monetized—aimed at niche rather than general audiences. It may involve public policy solutions, perhaps bundling news with Internet access, or partnering aggregators and news producers. We believe it will involve reinventing the newsroom and expanding the definition of news. Who will do this, and whether it is likely to include some of the major news companies of today, is less important than whether those who do this hold those values. Our guess, though it is only a guess, is that this reinvention will come from new places, younger people who understand the technology but adhere to the old values if not the old ways.

That may be less our prediction than a profound hope.

As we said at the outset of this book, we have seen disruptive change before in media. The changes we suggest here are no greater in their way than the change that led to the appearance of an independent press beginning in the nineteenth century. Those changes were sparked by the invention of the telegraph, the rapid decline in the cost of paper after the Civil War, the rise of the reform movement, and more. The changes we propose here are suggested to modernize journalism while at the same time preserving the values of the twentieth-century press that are worth preserving.

Those values are grounded in empiricism and a reality-based understanding of public life. They collide, inevitably, with the values of spin and propaganda. And while they can be companion to the contemplation of events of opinion journalism, they will always be in tension with the journalism of affirmation that strays away from fact into propaganda and partisanship in an effort to effect outcomes rather than to evoke public consideration of issues.

Some things about the future of journalism are all but certain. Electronic audiences will continue to fragment. Individual citizens will create their own news diet and even their own content. More important, in this new atmosphere, public-interest journalism will have to compete with more self-interested information from these sources:

- government institutions capable of inserting information into the public stream to create a "conditioned" response to government actions and proposals—information that has been shaped by the deepest and most sophisticated computerized profiles of intimate details about our behavior to be presented in its most appealing form
- social institutions that become more politicized as they use their communicating power to create new realities based not on communities of tolerance but on encouraging conflict between belief and independent pursuit of knowledge
- entertainment interests that rival all others in creating a popular culture of a passive public, not the informed public democracy requires
- media that want to use political affinity to gather an audience

In this new competition, it is critical that we use the promise offered by emerging communications technologies to create a journalism that joins journalists and citizens in a journey of mutual discovery.

The next journalism, we propose here, recognizes that to assure the principles of traditional journalism do not disappear, journalists must adjust to those things that are irrevocably changed by technology in the distribution and organization of news. The new distribution will be determined by the portability of technology and by the end user; the organization of the material will be adjusted to serve those differing audiences; and the interactivity will be used to create new relationships with the public to bring them into the process in ways that help create communities of interest.

But one thing has not changed. Democracy stakes everything on a continuing dialogue of informed citizens. And that dialogue rises or falls on whether the discussion is based on propaganda and deceit or on facts and verification pursued with a mind willing to learn.

The New Way of Knowing

Are people really up to the task of being partners in developing their own news? Is the press capable of creating a "next journalism"?

The answers are hardly a matter of philosophy or academic curiosity. If the public and the press are not up to the task, then the whole question of whether democracy works falls into doubt.

The English philosopher John Stuart Mill argued a fundamental case about the connection between truth and freedom. In the marketplace between truth and falsity, Mill wrote, truth will prevail. If Mill is now wrong, and truth can no longer win, because it is no longer a fair fight, then he would have also had to admit that liberty will not prevail. Or is the fight more fair than ever, as the new-technology optimists argue?

Walter Lippmann argued the key to democracy was an aggressive reportorial press. "Where all the news comes at second-hand, men cease to respond to truths, and respond simply to opinions," he wrote in 1920. "The environment in which they act is not the realities themselves, but the pseudo-environment of reports, rumors and guesses. The whole reference of thought comes to be what somebody asserts, not what actually is." Radio and television news pioneer Edward R. Murrow worried that accurate reporting was often at a disadvantage because it took time: "A lie can go around the world while the truth is still getting his pants on."

This perception about technology and human nature, however, didn't persuade Murrow that working for truth was futile. Rather it deepened his conviction to apply moral human values to its pursuit.

One notion that has become popular lately is that perhaps it doesn't matter if most people can't distinguish between reliable and unreliable information. Elites can. That might be enough. Elites have always had access to information. The first professional journalists, as Jay Rosen has noted, were people hired to write rich merchants private letters about market conditions in other city states. The corporations that buy Bloomberg news content—and for that matter Bloomberg's news operation—are doing just fine. Now those elites making the fullest use of the new communication technologies will be even more informed. And citizens who, empowered with the same tools, choose to tune out the news in favor of other channels of media, or engorge themselves on diverting matters of celebrity rather than civic life, have opted out. Nothing can be done about it. The technology has radically accelerated stratification. No amount of hand-wringing will change the nature of people.

This, however, is not how civic life really works. Regardless of the level of engagement or the quality of media, those who are less interested and even those who are almost entirely disengaged are never irrelevant. They remain a decisive factor in civic life, helping set the parameters of public policy through voting (and research shows voters and nonvoters continue to mirror one another in attitudes) and through the growing body of polling data from a broad representative sample of all Americans taken on all issues in virtually real time. Richard Nixon dubbed this forgotten broad public the "silent majority" during his presidency. Franklin Roosevelt tended to this broad group through his radio broadcasts, bringing Americans slowly to his sense of the inevitable need for internationalism to save democracy worldwide. Corporations, rich interest groups, viral marketers, governments, and powerful forces will always try to influence and sway that group of citizens who may be less engaged on some issue, precisely because it is an effective way of altering the landscape. The point of democracy is not perfect government. It is self-government. Thus journalism and the news are inevitably intertwined with engagement. A press that can engage more people more fully will not be a dumber press by being more populist. It will be a more capable one, with more resources, more people to gather the news, and more skills. A press that aims only at elites, because it is easier, is one that is not only abdicating its constitutional claims and its broadest responsibilities. It is also taking the easy way out. It is giving up on imagining a better journalism.

In our earlier writings, we have argued that the notion of elites itself is something of a myth. The notion that some people are simply ignorant in all things, while others are knowledgeable and interested in everything, does not reflect real life. There is, we think, a more realistic description of how people interact with news. We see the public instead as a shifting mix of different groups in which a member of the elite on one subject is among the non-elite in another. Some people are more informed and more interested in certain subjects, while different people are interested in other topics. We all have areas of expertise, regardless of station, education, or other factors. The immigrant child care worker may be an expert on certain aspects of U.S. government. The laborer with a high school education may be an avid fisherman who knows a great deal about local rivers and lakes, their health, habitat, and wildlife. The Ivy League–educated judge may be ignorant on these subjects yet be an avid gardener. We have suggested that there is something we call the "interlocking public," in which, for the sake of argument, we have described three broad categories of public engagement, interest, and knowledge. On any given subject, we might be a member of the *involved public*, with a direct personal stake in an issue and a strong understanding; a member of the *interested public*, with no direct role but a recognition that we are affected and we pay some occasional attention; and an *uninterested public*, which pays little attention. These three groups, and their subtle gradations, form a public that is richly pluralistic, fluid, and ever-interacting, with its members influencing one another. And any community is actually wiser when these three different groups blend, offering varying levels of knowledge and interest. No policy is best left to only the most interested—or the least. Pluralism implies not only the balancing of different factions and agendas in our public policy. It also involves balancing the concerns of the most interested and engaged and the least.

How does this notion of a changing, dynamic, differing interlocking public affect the idea of a new kind of citizenship demanded by new technology and requiring a new journalism? What we imagine is a process that is more synergistic and more public than the one we have known. Social networking and professional journalistic inquiry will go hand in hand, often in a structured way. Imagine the way one reads the newspaper on the weekend with family, reading a story, often out loud, stopping at different points to comment and discuss with the clan over the breakfast table. The news story is the spine of that discussion, the starting point. But the processing of the information—and the critique of the journalistic presentation and inquiry—is more dynamic. That process has now become public. The breakfast table is the Web. And journalists must endure in front of everyone what was once a purely private dissection of their work by citizens, sometimes laudatory and sometimes suspicious.

The future of press and democracy, the new public square, is found when these multiple dynamic conversations are robust, and also when they converge at key moments on a single subject—an election, health care, war, our national and global hopes. Only a robust press interested in engagement, not exclusion, will thrive.

If learning about public life is becoming more of a group discussion and less of a lecture, what we have to come to grips with is that this new discussion both adds and subtracts something. New elements, more depth, and more diversity are added. So is more prejudice, more falsehood, more manipulation. Like any public discussion, some is enlightening and some is not. But it is, and will be, the new way of learning. And the dialectic between the two ways of learning about the world, the tension between the empiricism of facts and the belief-oriented influence of how we assign those facts annotative meaning, will be even more intense, particularly in the near term, as the sorting out of new authorities is unfinished and uncertain.

The real information gap in the twenty-first century is not who has access to the Internet and who does not. It is the gap between people who have the skills to create knowledge and those who are simply in a process of affirming preconceptions without ever growing and learning. It is the new gap between reason and superstition.

For citizens, this means new responsibilities and risks as they are drawn into the process of determining "what out there can I believe?" For those who participate in trying to gather and present the news, the new or next journalism means a new role of being something of a Socratic teacher, in which the presentation of the news is accompanied by material, perhaps even tutorials, to help develop the skills needed to turn that material into knowledge.

We also think the outcome of the dislocation and disruption we see today is not inevitable. Things could move in various directions. We are only at the outset of the current disruption. The history of learning is the story of human ingenuity reacting to technology, and it occurs differently depending on how cultures respond, just as it evolved differently in some parts of the world than others, and even vanished for periods of time. As we said at the outset of this book, it is a story of push and pull, of old structures fighting to find a way to the new, of two steps forward and one step back, and of walking at times off the trail.

If much of the journey now depends on the skills of citizens themselves, one critical step, which people have already identified, is the need to reintroduce civic literacy—and news literacy—into middle and high school curricula. Civic literacy, in our minds, is a curriculum that would teach what we need to know to function as citizens of a community. It is something beyond civics, something more engaged, more Socratic and more personal. News literacy is a subset of it. And by "news literacy," we mean something different from "media literacy," a curriculum developed mostly from a left-leaning perspective that teaches how the media in all its forms manipulates us on behalf of commercial and establishment interests. By "news literacy," we mean the skills of how to "read" the news—the discipline of skeptical knowing. We hope the ideas outlined in this book help inform such an effort. But we won't pretend that we have created a curriculum here, and that is not our intent. Instead, we have tried to outline that there are skills that can be called news literacy. We hope we have helped identify the core ideas that are embedded in that. And we hope we have identified some examples of how that is done by professionals at a high level and how it might be translated generally.

A century ago, the journalist Walter Lippmann and the philosopher John Dewey engaged in a public argument about whether people were capable of being free. Lippmann proved the more persuasive in shaping the nature of commercial media in the twentieth century. He argued that the public was ill-equipped to function as informed citizens. But he thought the press was hardly more able than its audience, and he called on elites to refine the information for both. In a sense, the press in the last half of the twentieth century tried to take on that role for itself, becoming more interpretative and analytical. Dewey did not differ with Lippmann's critique of the public or the press, but he thought Lippmann's prescription for elitism missed the point. The only justifiable role for the press, Dewey said, was to help educate the public, to make them more capable of participating in democratic society. The press had no other claim to exist. Nor, incidentally, did education. Democracy could not be saved by losing faith in it.

A century later, technology has caught up to Dewey's vision. The time for education has arrived.

Appendix

Tools for Covering a News Event Online

1. main narrative
2. headline
3. graphics produced by the news organization's staff
4. customizable graphics that can be manipulated by users
5. photos, often staff-produced and citizen-produced photo galleries
6. pull quotes
7. sidebars
8. links to backgrounder material both on the Web site and beyond
9. links to previous relevant stories
10. links embedded in keywords in the story taking readers to definitions or elaborations
11. links to the newsmakers and organizations mentioned in the story with biographical and other details
12. links to the stock prices of businesses mentioned in the story
13. links to key facts in the story, including primary documents or materials
14. complete interview transcripts
15. video and/or audio of the story itself
16. video and/or audio of key interviews
17. video of the reporter at work on the story
18. a biography of the story's writer
19. information about who else worked on the story and similar background material

20. a clickable button to send the writer or editor an e-mail

21. interactive timelines for key events leading up to the current news moment

22. searchable databases relevant to the story, some on the news organization's Web site, some hosted on other Web sites, including government sites

23. a list of frequently asked questions on issues related to the story

24. a "sociograph" or "map" of related stories tied to the story through keywords or a tag cloud

25. clickable maps of places relevant to story

26. comments and information "tags" from reporters and citizens related to the maps and photos

27. links to bloggers covering the story or reacting to it

28. links to other stories by the author

29. the opportunity for readers to comment on the story

30. an invitation to "crowd-source" material in the story or questions the story raises—when the news organization asks for information from users about elements of the story that are not yet fully reported

31. the opportunity to offer the news organization guidance on future stories

32. the opportunity for readers to say what else they would like to know

33. the opportunity for observers to post video

34. the opportunity for observers to post pictures

35. a moderated discussion on the story (and an unmoderated discussion)

36. an RSS (really simple syndication) feed of the story so that it is pushed to consumers rather than available exclusively on a news organization's Web site

37. other tools to allow the information to be exported to and embedded in other Web sites

38. the ability to sign up for e-mail alerts about other stories on a subject

39. background on what the reader can do about issues raised in the story

40. a 3-D video tour of the site of the story

41. online follow-up chat opportunities with the reporter and editor who covered the story

42. buttons to "share this story" with social media sites like Digg and Reddit

43. corrections and updates to the story, added directly to the original text

44. an invitation to e-mail the story to a friend

45. the ranking of a story in a list of the "most read" and "most e-mailed" stories of the day

46. the ranking of a story's photos and videos in a list of the "most viewed" and "most played"

47. a listing of the story in a customized page of "MyTimes" or an RSS aggregator page

48. an opportunity to customize e-mail alerts and text messages about the subject of the story

49. a clickable graphic of related topics and tags, with an accompanying "tag cloud"

50. links to quizzes or polls related to the story

Acknowledgments

We have many to thank. We owe a special debt to Josh Appelbaum, who served as researcher, tracking things down, debating ideas, and generally elevating our conversation. We also owe more than we can say to our colleagues at the Project for Excellence in Journalism, past and present, whose work each day has informed our thinking for nearly fifteen years. Our ideas about how news and news consumption are changing have been enriched in particular by the annual *State of the News Media* report, whose many contributors have included, among others, Tom Avila, Dante Chinni, Erica Felder, Emily Guskin, Jesse Holcomb, Jon Morgan, Kenny Olmstead, Dana Page, Atiba Pertilla, David Vaina, and Niki Woodard. We have learned much, too, from the never-ending conversation that takes place with other friends and colleagues, and while that list is also too long to include in full, we would be remiss not to mention Clark Aldrich, Rick Edmonds, Michael Dimock, Wally Dean, Carroll Dougherty, Paul Hitlin, Hong Ji, Mahvish Kahn, Scott Keeter, Dean Mills, Mike Oreskes, Nora Paul, Lee Rainie, Charles Stamm, Tricia Sartor, Paul Taylor, and Esther Thorson. John Gomperts, Jon Haber, and Mark Jurkowitz are constant sounding boards. We thank John Carroll, Jack Fuller, Don Kimelman, and Jack Rosenthal for reading the manuscript. Our continuing gratitude to Rebecca Rimel and the Pew Charitable Trusts for allowing us to contemplate this revolution by day so we could put these thoughts on paper by night. Thanks to Annik LaFarge for believing in this book and to Kathy Belden for improving the manuscript. Our thanks, too, to David Black, the man in our corner.

Two other people deserve particular mention: Virtually all the ideas in this book bear the stamp of Amy Mitchell, an extraordinary colleague.

And we can never repay our debt to Andy Kohut, a friend and a mentor.

And no amount of thanks is enough to Rima and the girls, who suffered through too many nights and weekends with a husband and father not entirely present as he hunched over his work.

Finally, we want to thank those who work as journalists and those who aspire to do so, in new media and old. It is fashionable to deride people who try to report and verify news on behalf of the rest of us. We know them to be heroes.

Notes

1. How to Know What to Believe Anymore

1 Recorded on the Center for History and New Media, George Mason University Web site, http://echo.gmu.edu/tmi.

2 Ibid.

3 Ibid.

4 Peter Goldman et al., "In the Shadow of the Tower," *Newsweek*, April 9, 1979, p. 29.

5 Arlie Schardt et al. "Covering Three Mile Island," *Newsweek*, April 16, 1979, p. 93.

6 Walter Truett Anderson, *All Connected Now: Life in the First Global Civilization*. Westview Press, Boulder, 2001.

2. We Have Been Here Before

1 Philip B. Meggs, *A History of Graphic Design*. John Wiley & Sons, 1998, pp. 58–69.

2 Lester Faigley, "Print and Cultural Change," www.cwrl.utexas.edu/-faigley/work/material_literacy/print.html.

3 Morris Bishop, *The Middle Ages*. Houghton Mifflin, Boston, 1996, p. 252.

4 Some scholars credit a politician, rather than a journalist, with its creation. In an effort to announce the death of Abraham Lincoln in a way that would be more credible and have a calming authority over a panicked nation, Secretary of War Edwin Stanton dictated the telegram that would run in newspapers across the world. His announcement, written as a notice to another government official, had a powerfully matter-of-fact structure and tone, starting with Lincoln's death, followed by the supporting evidence and subsequent

details about what would occur next. David T. Z. Mindich, *Just the Facts.* New York University Press, 1998, p. 73.

5 *See It Now* was the CBS program created by Edward R. Murrow and Fred W. Friendly.

6 Chris Anderson, "The Long Tail," http://www.adtechblog.com/blog/detail/the-long-tail-has-destroyed-mass-media.

7 Project for Excellence in Journalism, *State of the News Media,* 2009, www.journalism.org.

8 Matthew Hindman makes the same point in the *Myth of Digital Democracy,* Princeton University Press, 2008.

3. The Way of Skeptical Knowing: The Tradecraft of Verification

1 William Prochnau, "The Wary Chronicler who Inspired a Rebellion," http://www.aliciapatterson.org/APF1201/Prochnau/prochnau.rtf.

2 Interview with the authors, April 29, 2007.

3 Homer Bigart, *Forward Positions: The War Correspondence of Homer Bigart.* University of Arkansas Press, 1991, pp. 192–195. The original story, headlined "U.S. Copters Help in Vietnam Raid," appeared in the *New York Times,* March 9, 1962.

4 Interview with the authors, April 29, 2007.

5 This definition of truth comes from Howie Schneider's work on news literacy at the State University of New York at Stony Brook.

6 C. John Sommmerville, *The News Revolution in England.* Oxford University Press, New York, 1996, p. 14.

7 John Lloyd, *What the Media Are Doing to Our Politics.* Constable & Robinson, London, 2004, p. 144.

8 Bill Kovach and Tom Rosenstiel, *The Elements of Journalism: What Newspeople Should Know and the Public Should Expect.* Three Rivers Press, New York, 2007, pp. 38–39.

9 Ibid., p. 36.

10 Reese Schonfeld, *Me and Ted Against the World: The Unauthorized Story of the Founding of CNN.* HarperCollins, New York, 2001, p. 5.

11 Interview with Tom Rosenstiel, 1990.

12 The Project for Excellence in Journalism first established this finding and its implications in its annual report *State of the News Media,* 2005, www.journalism.org.

13 *Meet the Press*, August 16, 2009.

14 The answer, unearthed later by PBS ombudsman Michael Getler, was that Armey was wrong. Medicare is a voluntary program, and one can even withdraw from it without penalty under some conditions. But Armey was right that under other conditions, withdrawal might cause one to forfeit receiving monthly Social Security checks.

15 Clark Hoyt, "The Public Editor: Reporting in Real Time," *New York Times*, February 8, 2009, p. 10.

16 Deborah Tannen, *The Argument Culture: Moving from Debate to Dialogue*. Random House, New York, 1998, pp. 7, 20.

17 Katy Bachman, "Radio's Head Rush," *Mediaweek*, August 11, 2003. http://www.mediaweek.com/mw/esearch/article_display.jsp?vnu_content_id=1953833.

18 Felix Gillette, "Hard Fall: What Happened to NBC?" *New York Observer*, September 9, 2008.

19 Committee of Concerned Journalists and the Pew Research Center for the People and the Press, "Striking the Balance: Audience Interests, Business Pressures and Journalists' Values," March 1999, p. 79. www.journalism.org and http://people-press.org.

4. Completeness: What Is Here and What Is Missing?

1 John Crewdson, "Code Blue: Survival in the Sky," *Chicago Tribune* special report, June 30, 1996.

2 Debbie Wilgoren and Hamil R. Harris, "Burst Pipe Floods Homes in District: Water Main Break in Adams Morgan Disrupts Traffic," *Washington Post*, May 7, 2009, p. B1.

3 Those details were in an article about the event that appeared on the front page of the same day's newspaper.

4 Amy Harmon, "Genetic Testing + Abortion=???" *New York Times*, May 13, 2007.

5 http://www.propublica.org/feature/economic-guesswork-drives-stimulus -job-targets-090203; http://www.propublica.org/ion/stimulus/item/sorting -those-job-creation-numbers-0916; http://www.propublica.org/ion/stimulus/ item/tracking-highway-stimulus-jobs-is-no-easy-job-724.

6 In *The Elements of Journalism*, we note that there are four categories of exposé reporting: original investigations, interpretive investigations, reporting on investigations, and faux exposés. Original reporting involves reporters doing their own investigative work with original sources. Interpretive reporting uncovers information that involves more complex issues and that

requires careful additional analysis and context to provide deeper understanding. Reporting on investigations involves stories about investigations
already under way by others, often government. Faux exposés look like true
exposés but instead cover commonly known problems or phenomena, such
as dirty hotel sheets or cheap carpet cleaning come-ons. A faux exposé is
designed to build an audience but have marginal value in adding to civic
knowledge; it turns the watchdog role into a form of amusement.

5. Sources: Where Did This Come From?

1 Sourcing stories from war zones is among the most difficult jobs in journalism, and both the journalist and the consumer have to take great care not
to be misled. Control of the field of battle by the military has kept journalists
away from most combat situations, including reporters Carlotta Gall and
Taimoor Shah, who wrote their story from Afghanistan. Reporters have tried
to overcome these restrictions by building up a network of people in the country's towns and villages on whom they can call to tell them what they knew
or saw. Accurate recounting of detail in the chaos of war is difficult enough
for eyewitnesses. Subtle coloring can creep in, and detail can be dropped as it
passes from one person to another. This should stand as a reminder to journalists and consumers alike when determining the character and level of
sourcing we will accept. For both journalist and consumer, transparency is a
most important tool. Transparency in the nature and knowledge of sources
and about what information is unclear or unknown are the natural allies for
furthering trust and understanding.

2 Krist. v. Eli Lilly and Co., 897 F.2d 293 (7th Cr. 1990) lists the findings of
various psychological studies on eyewitness memory.

3 Ibid.

4 *60 Minutes*, "Eyewitness: How Accurate Is Visual Memory?" CBS, March
8, 2009.

5 Bill Kovach and Tom Rosenstiel, *Warp Speed: America in the Age of
Mixed Media*. Century Press, New York, 1999, p. 29.

6 Interview with John Broder, one of the reporters involved, in 1998.

6. Evidence and the Journalism of Verification

1 Conversations with the authors in 1981.

2 Though painstaking, Hersh's method is not foolproof. Hersh had relied on
documents that were later proved to be forged to write allegations about John
F. Kennedy's sexual affairs in articles later collected into a book called *The*

Dark Side of Camelot. The fraudulent nature of the documents was discovered before publication, and the information was excluded from the book. But the incident scarred Hersh and at the time hurt his reputation. "Sometimes I'm wrong," Hersh said, "but I'm quick to correct the mistakes."

3 Interview with the authors, July 29, 2009.

4 Gabriel García Márquez, *One Hundred Years of Solitude.* HarperCollins, New York, 1970.

5 J. Davittt McAteer and Associates, *The Sago Mine Disaster: A Preliminary Report to Governor Joe Manchin III*, July 2006.

6 Pew Research Center for the People and the Press, September 13, 2009. "Press Accuracy Rating Hits Two Decade Low: Public Evaluations of the News Media, 1985–2009." http://people-press.org/report/543/.

7. Assertion, Affirmation: Where's the Evidence?

1 Fully 45 percent of the time on cable news is made up of live interviews—and more during the daytime hours, when there is more broadcasting time to fill. Fully 53 percent of the time on the *NewsHour* on PBS is devoted to live interviews. On morning network programming, even in the more hard-news-oriented first thirty minutes of each show, 30 percent is devoted to live interviews. Pew Project for Excellence in Journalism, *State of the News Media*, 2008, "Cable News, Content Analysis," http://www.stateofthemedia.org/2005/narrative_cabletv_contentanalysis.asp?cat=2&media=5.

2 Tom Rosenstiel, "Yakety-Yak: The Lost Art of Interviewing," *Columbia Journalism Review*, January–February 1995.

3 Sig Mickelson, *The Electric Mirror: Politics in an Age of Television.* Dodd, Mead & Company, New York, 1972, pp. 16–44.

4 Rosenstiel, "Yakety-Yak."

5 Ibid.

6 *The Ed Show*, MSNBC, September 24, 2009.

7 Douglas Walton, *Ad Hominem Arguments.* University of Alabama Press, 1998, p. xii.

8 *The Ed Show*, MSNBC, July 17, 2009.

9 Les Gelb, "Bill Safire," Forbes.com, September 27, 2009, http://www.forbes.com/2009/09/27/william-safire-conservative-new-york-times-obituary-opinions-contributors-leslie-h-gelb.html.

8. How to Find What Really Matters

1 In 2010, 28 percent of those online create custom news pages. Project for Excellence in Journalism and the Pew Internet and American Life Project, "Understanding the Participatory News Consumer," March 1, 2010, http://www.journalism.org/analysis_report/how_people_use_news_and_feel_about_news.

2 As we navigate for ourselves, what we choose to learn about has enormous significance for whether we will continue to have a central, if virtual, public square in our communities—and a common body of knowledge. This is one of the things, as we note in our book *The Elements of Journalism*, that the news has traditionally provided to societies. It has helped create a common vocabulary, a common set of concerns, and a common understanding of basic facts. This common understanding is vital for resolving problems, finding compromise, identifying points of consensus—for the functioning of democratic society. A critical issue for society in the twenty-first century, as technology makes it possible to more easily define community by interests rather than geography, is how we will make these choices.

3 Project for Excellence in Journalism and the Pew Internet and American Life Project, "Understanding the Participatory News Consumer."

4 Pew Research Center for the People and the Press, "Press Accuracy Rating Hits Two Decade Low: Public Evaluations of the News Media, 1985–2009," September 12, 2009.

5 In 2009, the Knight Commission on the Information Needs of Communities in a Democracy tackled the question for more than a year through public meetings and consultations with experts of what people need to know to be citizens. Its conclusions, inevitably, tended toward the abstract and were not designed to help citizens decide which information matters. People need information that is "relevant and credible," it noted. They need the "capacity" to engage with the information. And individuals need to be able to engage with the information, which implies both the opportunity and motivation for involvement.

6 Cole offered a summary of this at the Future of News symposium hosted by Minnesota Public Radio in Minneapolis on November 16, 2009.

7 Interview with the authors, July 2008 and October 2009.

8 Diana K. Sugg, "Turn the Beat Around," Poynter Online, October 5, 2001, www.poynter.org/content/content_view.asp?id=85367.

9 Sugg, "Angels and Ghosts, Anatomy of a Story," Poynter Online, July 15, 2005, www.poynter.org/content/content_print.asp?id=85199.

10 Sugg, "Turn the Beat Around."

11 Address to Nieman Foundation fellows, 1996. Transcript from Harvard Nieman Foundation archives.

12 Interview with the authors, October 2009.

9. What We Need from the "Next Journalism"

1 In his 1922 book *Public Opinion*, Lippmann proposed that government panels of objective experts select the news; the press would then communicate their selections.

2 The principles of professional journalism:

1. Journalism's first obligation is to the truth.
2. Its first loyalty is to citizens.
3. Its essence is a discipline of verification.
4. Its practitioners must maintain an independence from those they cover.
5. It must serve as an independent monitor of power.
6. It must provide a forum for public criticism and compromise.
7. It must strive to make the significant interesting and relevant.
8. It must keep the news comprehensive and in proportion.
9. Its practitioners have an obligation to exercise their personal conscience.
10. Citizens, too, have rights and responsibilities when it comes to the news.

3 Project for Excellence in Journalism and the Pew Internet and American Life Project, "Understanding the Participatory News Consumer," March 1, 2010, http://www.journalism.org/analysis_report/understanding_participatory _news_consumer.

4 We can see the same pattern when we ask how many different news sites people routinely visit. Most people (almost two thirds) do not have a "favorite" news Web site. But they graze only a few trusted places. Most routinely visit fewer than six news Web sites, and only 3 percent regularly visit more than ten.

5 Project for Excellence in Journalism, *State of the News Media*, 2010, "Nielsen Analysis," March 15, 2010, http://www.stateofthemedia.org/2010/specialreports _nielsen.php.

6 Ibid. The average visit to these sites is just two minutes long.

7 Ibid.

8 For a fuller discussion of transparency, see the second edition of *The Elements of Journalism*.

9 Interview by the authors with Michael Skoler, July 23, 2009.

10 Jay Rosen, "Citizen Journalism Expert Jay Rosen Answers Your Questions," October, 3, 2006, http://interviews.slashdot.org/article.pl?sid=06/10/03/1427254.

11 Gary Kamiya, "Let Us Now Praise Editors," July 24, 2007, Salon.com, www.salon.com/print/html?URL=/opinion/kamiya/2007/07/24.

12 This question of what does a newsroom do is different from the question we asked in *The Elements of Journalism* about the purpose of journalism. There we defined journalism's purpose as providing people with information they need to be free and self-governing.

—

Index

A Note on the Authors

In his fifty-year career, Bill Kovach has been chief of the *New York Times* Washington bureau, served as editor of the *Atlanta Journal-Constitution*, and directed the Nieman Fellowship program at Harvard University. He is founding chairman of the Committee of Concerned Journalists and senior counselor for the Project for Excellence in Journalism.

A journalist for more than thirty years, Tom Rosenstiel has worked as chief congressional correspondent for *Newsweek* and as a media critic for the *Los Angeles Times* and MSNBC's *The News with Brian Williams*. His books include *Strange Bedfellows* and *We Interrupt This Newscast*. Rosenstiel is vice chairman of the Committee of Concerned Journalists and director of the Project for Excellence in Journalism.

Together, Kovach and Rosenstiel have authored two other books: *The Elements of Journalism*, winner of the 2002 Goldsmith Prize from Harvard University, and *Warp Speed*.